A BEGINNER'S GUIDE TO SNOWSHOEING
IN THE CANADIAN ROCKIES

A PERFECT DAY ON CAMERON LAKE.

A BEGINNER'S GUIDE TO SNOWSHOEING IN THE CANADIAN ROCKIES

2ND EDITION

ANDREW NUGARA

RMB

RMB | Rocky Mountain Books Ltd.
rmbooks.com
@rmbooks
facebook.com/rmbooks

Cataloguing data available from Library and Archives Canada
ISBN 978-1-77160-184-9 (paperback)
ISBN 978-1-77160-185-6 (electronic)

All photographs are by Andrew Nugara unless otherwise noted.

Front cover photo: The Nugara family start on the wonderful journey across Bow Lake, with the Wapta Icefield in the background.
Back cover photo: Stunning Wapta Falls. (photo by Shawn Benbow)

Printed and bound in Canada by Friesens

Distributed in Canada by Heritage Group Distribution and in the U.S. by Publishers Group West

For information on purchasing bulk quantities of this book, or to obtain media excerpts or invite the author to speak at an event, please visit rmbooks.com and select the "Contact Us" tab.

RMB | Rocky Mountain Books is dedicated to the environment and committed to reducing the destruction of old-growth forests. Our books are produced with respect for the future and consideration for the past.

We acknowledge the financial support of the Government of Canada through the Canada Book Fund and the Canada Council for the Arts, and of the province of British Columbia through the British Columbia Arts Council and the Book Publishing Tax Credit.

Disclaimer

The actions described in this book may be considered inherently dangerous activities. Individuals undertake these activities at their own risk. The information put forth in this guide has been collected from a variety of sources and is not guaranteed to be completely accurate or reliable. Many conditions and some information may change owing to weather and numerous other factors beyond the control of the authors and publishers. Individuals or groups must determine the risks, use their own judgment, and take full responsibility for their actions. Do not depend on any information found in this book for your own personal safety. Your safety depends on your own good judgment based on your skills, education, and experience.

It is up to the users of this guidebook to acquire the necessary skills for safe experiences and to exercise caution in potentially hazardous areas. The authors and publishers of this guide accept no responsibility for your actions or the results that occur from another's actions, choices, or judgments. If you have any doubt as to your safety or your ability to attempt anything described in this guidebook, do not attempt it.

To Skye, Kian and Rogan.

Contents

STUNNING WAPTA FALLS. (SHAWN BENBOW)

Preface to the Second Edition

There are 44 new trips in this edition. They are all listed in Appendix E. New areas covered include Crowsnest Pass, The Highwood and Highway 93 South.

A group of the new trips in this edition are geared toward introducing the beginner snowshoer to elements of higher-level snowshoeing, such as steeper terrain, route-finding and longer trips. This does not include travel in avalanche terrain, and all trips in this book still require no avalanche training or equipment. Yet again, however, it is strongly suggested that even the beginner snowshoer familiarize him/herself with the section on avalanches. These trips are listed in Appendix D.

In the introductory information, there are new sections covering Technology and Other Types of Traction Devices, as well as updates on the specific brands and models of snowshoes typically being used.

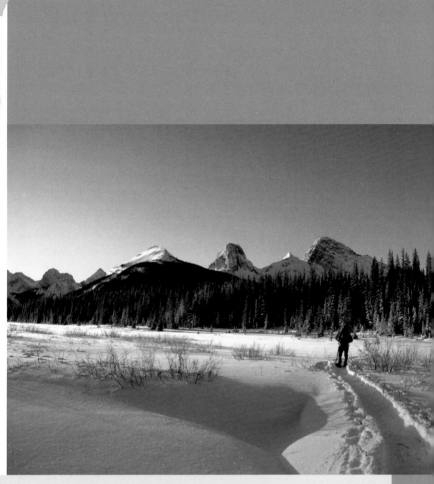

SMUTS CREEK PROVIDES ACRES OF OPEN SPACE
AND SPLENDID VIEWS IN ALL DIRECTIONS.

Acknowledgements

Once again, this book would have not have been possible without the tireless efforts of Gillean and Tony Daffern. A good number of the routes described are based on Gillean's work in Kananaskis Country. Following in their footsteps, I discovered innumerable routes that I would not have even considered to be accessible on snowshoes. To my sheer delight, those routes invariably turned out to be fantastic snowshoe trips. Also, my thanks go to Gillean and Tony for providing me with some invaluable photos.

Thanks to Bob Spirko and Dinah Kruze, whose interesting and well-written trip reports always inspire one to get out and explore the unknown or less frequented areas of the Rockies, and also for the photos they are always happy to share with me. Thanks as well to the Rock Mountain Ramblers and all who post snowshoeing trip reports on the Internet. Always excellent resources.

Dave McMurray's website for trips in southern Alberta was the impetus for adding a Crowsnest Pass section to this edition. A huge thank you to Dave for inspiration and many terrific photos.

For this edition I was delighted to have Nicole Lisafeld join me for many of the trips. A big thank you to her for her outstanding company and wise counsel.

Also for fantastic photos, thanks to Matthew Clay, Jack Tannett, Tanya Koob, Nicole Lisafeld, Scott McLean, Vern Dewit, Andra MacKnight, Rob Ashpole, Peter Hopkins and So Nakagawa (SOISTHEMAN). Also to everyone who supplied images for the first edition.

The RMB staff are fantastic to work with and they have brought so many wonderful books to our shelves. Thanks to Don Gorman for running the show and to Chyla Cardinal for her outstanding design work.

Lastly, and as always, for their continual support and encouragement I sincerely thank my growing family – Mum, Larry, John, Mark, Keri, Rogan, Kian, Skye, Dad and Lori.

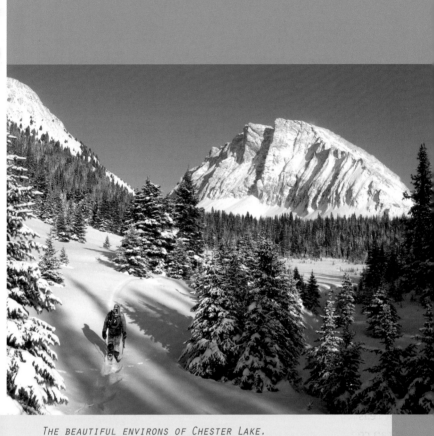

THE BEAUTIFUL ENVIRONS OF CHESTER LAKE.

INTRODUCTION

The Canadian Rockies in winter are nothing short of spectacular. Endless kilometres of untouched pristine terrain, strikingly beautiful mountains everywhere the eye can see, and snow and ice scenery that is guaranteed to render you breathless. Regardless of how many visits to the mountains you have made in the summer, you really haven't experienced the Rockies until you have seen them up close during the snow season. There is absolutely no place I'd rather be on a crisp, cold and clear January day than in the Rockies, surrounded by mountains and snow, a deep blue sky above and the sun illuminating the landscape in unequalled brilliance.

Getting around the mountains in winter has unique challenges. Many choose to negotiate the landscape on cross-country or AT (alpine touring) skis, others simply go on foot, while a few more take the motorized approach on a snowmobile. Then there are snowshoes.

Snowshoeing is fun, great exercise and allows you to travel into places of surreal beauty that would otherwise be inaccessible during the winter and spring. The activity is growing in popularity at a phenomenal rate in western Canada.

This book was written for people who are just getting into snowshoeing and want to start with easy trips. All the routes in the book steer clear of avalanche terrain and most require only a reasonable level of physical fitness. As well, young children can complete many of the trips in this book. Most of the official snowshoe trails are included in this guidebook.

Before a beginning snowshoer "aims for the skies," a healthy dose of easy and hazard-free trips are compulsory. Hopefully this guidebook offers just that. When all is said and done, many snowshoers will decide that the easy trips in this book and similar trips are all the adventure they require, and that is just fine!

THE PRELIMINARIES

Before setting out to enjoy some of the most wondrous scenery on this planet, it is important to be properly informed about snowshoes, snowshoeing and the environment you will be entering. Ignorance is not bliss here – it can be deadly! Please read all the preliminary information presented in the next section before setting out.

THE CHANGING FACE OF SNOWSHOEING

The world of snowshoeing seems to be undergoing rapid changes and shifts in focus. Historically, snowshoeing was a primarily utilitarian activity – that is, snowshoes provided an efficient means to get from A to B when the terrain between A and B was covered in deep snow. The invention of backcountry skis and significant design improvements over the past 35 years, however, have dramatically decreased a person's need, and often his or her desire, to use snowshoes for practical travel in the backcountry. Thus, snowshoeing has started to become more recreational in nature.

Although snowshoeing as a recreational activity can be traced back to the late 19th century, it is in the mid- to late 20th century that we have seen a significant increase in this pastime. Fifty or so years ago, the recreational aspect of snowshoeing may have been limited to following summer trails or exploring open areas of low-angled terrain – basically, easy hiking in the winter. However, with the recent and tremendous increase in the number of people taking to snowshoes, and significant technological advances in snowshoe design, snowshoers can now set their sights on far loftier objectives that formerly were the domain of mountaineers and ski mountaineers.

Do Snowshoes Really Work?

I'll let the following photos by Dave McMurray and Nicole Lisafeld answer that question!

ABOVE: THE AUTHOR UNSUCCESSFULLY TESTS OUT LIFE WITHOUT SNOWSHOES. LINDSAY ROUSSEAU CLEARLY KNOWS BETTER! (NICOLE LISAFELD) LEFT: JEFF LANG COURAGEOUSLY PERSEVERES THROUGH SOME EXTREME POSTHOLING ON MOUNT BACKUS. NOTE THE DEPTH OF THE SNOWSHOE TRACKS IN FRONT. (DAVE MCMURRAY)

Of course this is not always the case. Postholing while wearing snowshoes is not completely uncommon, especially early in the season. However, as a general rule, snowshoes will dramatically improve your flotation, eliminating most nightmares. Also, snowshoes prevent the brutal shin-bashing ordeals that many encounter when they break through a hard layer of snow (much like the crust of bread) only to have their shins bash into that layer. It can be quite painful!

THE BENEFITS AND ADVANTAGES OF SNOWSHOEING

Snowshoeing is great for your health and easy on your wallet, and practically anyone can do it. In addition, snowshoes can take you to places inaccessible to you when you are on skis or foot. Provided you approach the activity sensibly, you have everything to gain by exploring the mountain environment on snowshoes.

HEALTH

The health benefits of snowshoeing are undeniable and profound. Snowshoeing is as good a physical workout as you can get in the winter. Calgary's Fit Frog Adventures (www.fitfrog.ca) considers snowshoeing to be a safe, cross-training, conditioning sport that provides simultaneously a low-impact, aerobic, strength-training and muscle-endurance workout. As an aerobic workout, snowshoeing will help you improve or maintain cardiovascular fitness. As well, because snowshoeing uses every major muscle group at relatively high intensity for extended periods of time, it requires high caloric expenditure (400–1000 calories per hour).

Further, choosing snowshoeing as your primary winter-training activity has many benefits. Fit Frog notes that if you are a runner, substituting snowshoeing for running during the winter may improve your running fitness more than simply running through the winter. The muscles snowshoers use are the same ones used in walking and hiking hilly terrain. However, snowshoers' hip flexors may receive more of a workout and their quadriceps may get more exercise than walkers' or hikers' would; this is because of the lifting motion of each snowshoeing step. As well, snowshoeing on slopes works not only the hip flexors but also the extensors, which are important muscles for cyclists. Finally, if you choose to use poles while snowshoeing, your shoulders, arms and back muscles will also get a workout!

Expense

Snowshoeing is also a very inexpensive form of winter recreation. Assuming you already have the appropriate footwear (hiking boots), the only equipment needed is a pair of snowshoes ($100–$300) and a set of ski or hiking poles ($50–$150). That's quite a deal compared to the average $1200–$2000 price tag for a decent AT setup (skis, bindings, skins, boots and poles). Renting snowshoes is also incredibly inexpensive – as low as $10 a day. For those who are new to snowshoeing and unsure if they will take to the pastime on a regular basis, renting is a great idea.

Who Can Snowshoe?

Anyone can snowshoe! Although a cliché, the saying "if you can walk, you can snowshoe" is fairly accurate. Those of us who have been walking for many years already have a huge head start in gleaning snowshoeing skills compared to those learning how to backcountry ski! Unlike backcountry skiing, the learning curve for snowshoeing slopes gently. While for some it may take a trip or two to become completely comfortable on snowshoes, many will learn the art within hours of stepping out into the snow. Essentially, snowshoes just make your feet bigger – quite a bit bigger – so, if you can walk with really big feet, you can snowshoe.

Of course, the "anyone can snowshoe" rule does not apply to the extreme end of snowshoeing – snowshoe mountaineering. The technical demands of that activity require formal training and are outside the scope of this book.

"To Boldly Go Where No One Has Gone Before"

The only significant advantage snowshoeing has over backcountry skiing is superior manoeuvrability in tight spaces. This applies specifically to treed terrain. Weaving in and out of closely spaced trees on skis can be a nightmare – not so on snowshoes. There are some areas and peaks that are accessible in the winter only on snowshoes.

A secondary advantage to snowshoeing over skiing is the footwear required. Anyone who has scrambled or climbed wearing ski mountaineering boots knows how awkward they can be. Snowshoes allow you to choose footwear appropriate to the terrain you may encounter. Hiking boots are sufficient footwear for all trips in this book.

Another small advantage snowshoes have over skis is that they are less susceptible to damage when on rocky terrain. Naturally, it is strongly recommended that you remove your snowshoes when snow has given way to rock or if there are unavoidable rocks protruding from the snow. However, if these rocky sections are short-lived, the effort of taking your snowshoes off and then putting them back on minutes later may not be worth it. Stepping carefully should be enough to avoid any damage to your shoes.

Types of Snowshoeing

Since there are three types of snowshoes, most sources divide snowshoeing into three categories – racing, recreational and mountaineering. The focus of this book is the most basic form of recreational snowshoeing: snowshoeing that doesn't take you into avalanche terrain and requires no formal training in the fundamentals of mountaineering.

TYPES OF SNOWSHOES AND BUYING EQUIPMENT

Snowshoes have evolved considerably since the early days of wooden frames bound together with animal-hide webbing. Today's snowshoes are lightweight, extremely durable and easy to put on and take off. They have superior traction and can be used to ascend steep slopes that would have been impossible with older-style snowshoes. The types of snowshoes available are categorized according to the types of snowshoeing described above. For example, racing snowshoes are small and light. They are designed to allow you to run in your natural stride. Racing snowshoes are not appropriate for trips in this book.

As snowshoe design has advanced, in recent years the differences between recreational snowshoes and mountaineering snowshoes have become less and less distinct. Your average pair of recreational snowshoes now has good crampons for better traction, heel lifts for steep slopes, and advanced binding systems to keep the shoes firmly attached to your feet. I have one pair of mountaineering snowshoes and two pairs of recreational snowshoes. I routinely take the recreational ones on more serious terrain and have never found them lacking.

Having said that, most companies are still (and for good reason) producing snowshoes for three different uses:

- Trail-walking snowshoes are designed for flat or gently rolling terrain. Usually these models do not have heel lifts and have toe and heel crampons only. If you intend to go only on well-used trails with little to no steep terrain, these snowshoes will serve you well. As of 2016, specific models include

THE LIGHTWEIGHT ATLAS RENDEZVOUS.

THE TUBBS FLEX TRK. THE TRACTION RAILS, JUST VISIBLE AT THE LEFT, ARE AN EXCELLENT FEATURE OF THIS SNOWSHOE.

THE TUBBS FLEX VRT OFFER SUPERB EASE OF USE AND SUPERIOR PERFORMANCE.

Tubbs Flex ESC, Roam and Meridian; Atlas Rendezvous; and MSR Evo and Revo Trail.

- Hiking snowshoes are designed for steeper terrain and off-trail travel. Most models have heel lifts and aggressive crampons. These snowshoes can provide a good compromise between the other two categories and will be more than enough snowshoe for all the trips in this book. If you are interested in leaving the beaten path and tackling steeper terrain, these are the recommended type to use. Specific models include Tubbs Flex TRK, RDG, Elevate and Xpedition; Atlas Access and Treeline; and MSR Revo Explore and Lightning Explore.
- Mountaineering snowshoes are designed for serious backcountry travel involving very steep terrain. This is more snowshoe than you will need for any trip in this book, but there are only minor differences between mountaineering and hiking snowshoes. If at some point you intend to transition to intermediate and advanced snowshoeing, you will eventually want to use mountaineering snowshoes. Specific models include Tubbs Flex Alp, VRT, Mountaineer and Xpedition; Atlas 12 Series and Aspect; and MSR Revo Ascent and Lightning Ascent.

I presently have three pairs of snowshoes that all see their fair share of use: the Atlas 11 Series, the Tubbs Flex TRK and MSR Lightning Ascent. My MSR Lightning Ascent snowshoes come out for serious mountaineering ascents. The entire frame of the Lightning acts as a crampon, and it gives unparalleled traction on steep terrain.

For easier trips and terrain I use the Atlas 11 Series. They offer excellent flotation and traction and a solid binding system that effectively distributes pressure over a maximum area of the foot (Wrapp Plus bindings). This snowshoe is built with an aluminum

V frame that also has a durable stainless steel toe crampon and flexible decking. The heel strap adjusts easily.

For more serious trips where I may encounter steeper and potentially icy terrain, I go with the Tubbs Flex TRK. The traction rails on these snowshoes are fantastic, offering amazing grip and stability on hard-packed and icy surfaces. In addition, this snowshoe has the Flex tail and torsion deck, which also aids in stability. Wearing these shoes, I've ascended 30° icy slopes with ease. The simple but effective binding system is also excellent.

My newest and most aggressive pair of snowshoes is the Tubbs Flex VRT and they are fantastic! The DynamicFit binding, featuring the Boa Closure System, produces evenly distributed tension around your boot and the Viper 2.0 toe crampons dig deep in any conditions. These shoes are super easy to put on and take off, and of course the traction rails give superb grip on the iciest and steepest slopes. For any trip that I consider "serious" the Flex VRT are on my feet!

If you plan to undertake trips in this book, I recommend that you look into a hiking snowshoe model. As stated, they are well suited to most types of terrain and give you the option to be a little adventurous if the spirit moves you. After all, life does often take you into places where you never thought you would go (just don't venture into avalanche terrain).

SNOWSHOE SIZES

After you have determined what type of snowshoe you are going to use, getting an appropriate size becomes the issue. Adult snowshoes now come in a wide variety of sizes, ranging from 21 to 36 inches. The width of most modern snowshoes varies from 8 to 10 inches.

The balance a good snowshoe must strike between flotation, weight and manoeuvrability can be a delicate one. Larger

WEARING MY BAFFIN BOOTS WITH SNOWSHOES ON A VERY COLD DAY IN JANUARY.

snowshoes have better flotation, but they are heavier and less manoeuvrable in tight places. Smaller shoes offer good manoeuvrability but less flotation. On long trips with extensive sections of trail-breaking, the reduced weight of smaller-sized snowshoes will be negated by the increased difficulty of breaking trail. Renting various sizes of snowshoes and trying them out can be a good strategy for determining what size works best for you, before committing to the purchase of a specific size.

For more objective guidelines, the specific size you choose is determined primarily by your weight and what type of terrain you plan on tackling. For your weight, as a general guideline we can designate 22 inches as being small, 25 inches as medium, 30 inches as large and 36 inches as extra-large. Use the following very basic parameters as weight guidelines. The weights include your clothes, boots, backpack and additional equipment.

• Under 32 kilograms – Kids
• 32 to 59 kilograms – 22 inches
• 59 to 77 kilograms – 25 inches
• 77 to 100 kilograms – 30 inches
• Over 100 kilograms – 36 inches

In regards to terrain, if you intend to snowshoe only on well-packed trails and rarely engage in deep trail-breaking, you can also afford to get a smaller-sized snowshoe, since flotation will not be of great concern. Those snowshoers who want to get out into the deep stuff will want to choose a larger size.

When choosing a pair of snowshoes, going to a reputable snowshoe dealer and asking for advice is always a good idea.

Footwear

Buying appropriate footwear for snowshoes is an easier activity than buying snowshoes because snowshoers most frequently use regular hiking boots. Be sure to treat your boots with a water-resistant barrier before heading out. Since the average air temperature you'll experience on most snowshoeing trips is considerably lower than it would be on the same trip during summer, keeping your feet warm is paramount. Buying hiking boots that are a half-size or even a full size too big is often an effective strategy for dealing with cooler temperatures. The extra space in the boots allows you to wear two or even three pairs of socks if necessary. For temperatures ranging from −5°C to −20°C, I will often wear a thin pair of liner socks and one or sometimes two pairs of thick wool socks. This combination always keeps my feet warm, and I have never developed blisters or suffered other foot irritations. Make sure your socks aren't too tight. Tight socks constrict blood flow to your feet and soon lead to cold feet.

When the temperature drops below –20°C, hiking boots may not be enough to keep your feet warm. In this case, footwear designed specifically for colder temperatures may be necessary. Baffin makes boots that are rated to –50°C. Should the temperature ever plummet to those kinds of levels, personally I have no intention of stepping out of the house, let alone traipsing around the mountains. However, it is comforting to know that if you do, your feet will be well protected. The weakness of these boots is that they are often too big to take crampons. As such, you may be limited to trips of a less serious nature.

ADDITIONAL EQUIPMENT

The intermediate to advanced snowshoer may need to pack crampons, an ice axe, climbing gear and other paraphernalia to complete a trip (and make your pack really heavy). Fortunately, for the beginner snowshoer there is no need to worry about such things. The only piece of additional equipment needed is a set of poles.

POLES

Ski poles or trekking (hiking) poles with baskets are essential for all snowshoers. Even on "very easy" flat terrain, poles have their purpose. Primarily, poles are used for stability, balance and support: they turn a biped into a quadruped. As such, poles can reduce strain and stress on your knees, ankles and feet. In the same way that fallen skiers use their poles for leverage to regain a standing position, so too can snowshoers use a similar technique, though it is not as difficult.

As a general rule your arms should form a 90° angle when holding the poles in front of you. The length of your poles will need to be different when going up- or downhill – shorter for up-hill and longer for downhill.

Although having poles is essential, it's your choice whether to use them or not, much the same way as one can choose to wear snowshoes or go on foot. On beginner trails that don't involve trail-breaking and/or steep sections, poles may be of little use. Having said that, I would never leave them in my car. On easy trails, I attach my trekking poles to my backpack and take them out when needed. Ascending steeper terrain without poles is usually not too difficult. Descending that same terrain can often be much easier with poles. They can be used for balance and also enable you to lean forward a little when descending, thus helping you to keep your weight over your feet. Another reason to bring your poles and have them handy is to clean off snow, which can ball up on the bottom of your snowshoes.

All of this said, poles are not essential for young children, whose low centre of gravity can make poles more of a hindrance than a help.

For adults, however, a collapsible set of poles is strongly rec-ommended, for their ease of use, adjustability and for carrying them on your pack.

Clothing

Clothing doesn't really qualify as additional equipment, unless of course you usually go out naked, but this is a good place to talk about the specific kinds of clothing you will need when snowshoeing.

Dressing in layers is the key to being comfortable outside in the winter months. Wool and synthetic materials, such as poly-propylene, work best. Most people wear a base layer, a mid- or insulation layer and a waterproof yet breathable outer layer.

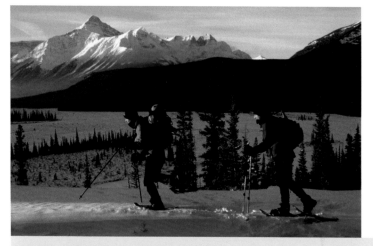

ABOVE: WITH MOUNT OUTRAM IN THE BACKGROUND, MARK AND DAN DEMONSTRATE THEIR FLAWLESS TECHNIQUE!
BELOW: POLES USED FOR BALANCE AND STABILITY ON STEEPER TERRAIN.

When travelling outdoors in the cold months, you can never take too much extra clothing with you. Though impractical to take a spare of everything, your backpack should at least have one or two pairs of extra socks, an extra top layer and extra gloves. A balaclava or equivalent is also essential. When preparing for a trip, I often ask myself: will the contents of my pack allow me to survive should I be forced to bivy overnight?

When considering clothing, it is also important to remember that even if the forecast calls for a warm, windless day, conditions can deteriorate very quickly and without warning. You must be prepared for anything. The clothing contents of my backpack are usually the same whether the forecast low is −5°C or −30°C.

Also note that high and low temperatures in weather forecasts are for the valley bottoms. Expect the temperature on a summit to be significantly colder than what has been predicted for the valley. A windy summit can exacerbate already low temperatures to an alarming degree.

When travelling in cold temperatures, it is important to minimize sweating or completely avoid it if possible. Ironically, sweat caused by generating body heat can lead to hypothermia when you slow down or stop. The sweat cools very rapidly and can cause your body temperature to do the same. Stopping and taking the time to remove or add layers of clothing when necessary is one of the keys to safe winter travel.

Sunscreen and Sunglasses

Finally, don't forget to pack a tube of sunscreen with a high SPF (I use a 60) and a good pair of sunglasses that have 100 per cent UV protection. The sun's rays reflecting off snow can be intense. Getting a serious sunburn or burning the corneas of your eyes happens more easily than you might think.

Other Winter Traction Devices

A good pair of snowshoes will provide excellent traction on any snow and/or ice surface. However, if the terrain is more a combination of ice and bare ground or ice throughout, then a different form of traction is in order. Having another form of traction has almost become a necessity these days, especially for front range trips, where snow conditions can vary wildly from week to week. Tony Daffern has written a terrific article on the other types of winter traction devices, on his and Gillean's kananaskisblog.com. Personally (and Tony agrees), I have found Kahtoola Microspikes to be best suited to the types of terrain you may encounter in the Canadian Rockies. Microspikes are very well designed and rugged and provide excellent traction, digging into ice or hard-packed snow with ease. They are a little heavier than other traction devices, but that extra weight is necessary for good performance and durability. You will find Microspikes referenced multiple times throughout this book. If I suspect at all that I may need them at any time during a trip, Microspikes are in my backpack.

The Snowshoeing Season

Snowshoeing season in the Canadian Rockies usually starts in December and ends in mid-May. The earliest snow of the season, in October and November, is often not consolidated enough to make snowshoeing worthwhile. Of course, unconsolidated snow can persist during any month of the season; it all depends on the prevailing weather. Objectives in the Front Ranges, where the snow may not be as deep, can provide decent day trips during these months. However, they may not be snowshoe trips. Be prepared to carry your snowshoes on your backpack for long stretches.

That said, the Rockies' snowpack in December and into January is typically a tough one to snowshoe on. Powdery,

KAHTOOLA MICROSPIKES. GREAT TRACTION AND THEY
FIT ANY BOOTS OR RUNNERS. AWESOME PURCHASE!

YOU NEED TO BE PREPARED. AN HOUR BEFORE MY ICICLE EYEBROWS FORMED, THE SKY WAS CLEAR AND THE TEMPERATURE QUITE MILD.

unconsolidated snow offers little to no support, even for snowshoes. This may cause you to experience the unpleasant phenomenon known as postholing, where you sink through much, if not all, of the snowpack. As such, expect trail-breaking during this time to be physically taxing. Again, the Front Ranges may be your best bet. Also, objectives along Highway 742 will start to see some traffic at this time of the year, and you may even find a fully broken trail!

Late January and February often see the snowpack gain strength as the melt–freeze cycle runs its course. By late February, hopefully, you will experience a significant decrease in the postholing ordeals that are so common in December and January. Reduced hours of daylight will limit you to shorter routes, but that should not pose a problem for trips in this book. Also note that these, along with March, are the best months to snowshoe on lakes. The ice and snow surface on most lakes is very strong during these months.

March and April are generally the best snowshoeing months. The snowpack at this time is usually strong and supportive, daylight hours are a little longer, temperatures are milder (although above treeline you can still expect to encounter brutally cold conditions), and trails have already been broken and reinforced. Plan to try some longer trips in these months. By April you will probably be looking at objectives farther west, as warm spring weather will often put an abrupt stop to snowshoeing in the Front Ranges. The warmer temperatures associated with daytime heating also mean you have to be more aware of afternoon avalanches.

Important Note: Many of the routes described in this book that involve snowshoeing on or around lakes will become less feasible by mid-April. Realistically, many lakes may still have another solid month of strong ice, but personally I always start to err on the side of caution around mid-April when thinking about lake trips. Refer to the section "Frozen Lakes" on page 51 for more information.

May can also be an excellent month for snowshoeing, but forget about going on lakes. All lake routes in this book will be off limits unless you plan to snowshoe around them, not on them. Areas near the Continental Divide are often still under a substantial layer of snow. Head up the Icefields Parkway and visit Bow Lake (but stay off the lake) and the Peyto Lake Viewpoint. Isothermal snow could be your greatest nemesis on May trips. This condition occurs after repeated melt–freeze cycles, which cause the temperature of the whole snowpack to be consistent (0°c), thereby making the snow weak and unsupportive. As well, snow that is supportive in the morning can be soft and slushy in the afternoon. At this time of year, even if your snowshoes end up on your backpack instead of your feet, it's still a good idea to take them along and hope for decent snow.

You are really pushing the season if you pack your snowshoes when you head out to the Rockies in June. Still, it is possible in certain years and certain areas to find snowshoeing conditions in late spring. Expect your snowshoes to spend most of the trip affixed to your backpack. Areas farther west, such as Lake Louise and Yoho, may be your best bets. Clearly, unless you want to use your snowshoes as flippers for swimming, don't go anywhere near a lake in June.

Snowshoes or No Shoes?

The question whether to wear snowshoes or go on foot arises often in snowshoeing. This is especially true in low-snow years, when chinook winds have melted the snowpack, very early or very late in the season, or for trips to the Front Ranges. As a very general rule, I would recommend that you should wear snowshoes if the snow is of any depth greater than 5 centimetres. Snowshoes help your balance and allow you to take big, aggressive, confident strides without the fear of stepping into a snow-covered hole and breaking your ankle. Wearing my snowshoes I have run down snow-covered slopes that I would not have dared to run down on foot, in fear of falling or tripping and breaking some body part!

The added traction that snowshoes offer, even when the snow is not deep, is a tremendous benefit. This is especially noticeable on hard-packed snow and icy terrain. Many people will choose to carry their snowshoes when they find themselves on trails, such as Chester Lake, that have been fully packed down. I would say that this is actually one of the best times to put your snowshoes on. Heavy traffic on any trail will eventually cause icy and slippery sections to develop. Your snowshoes will help you to negotiate this kind of terrain with ease. Although I can recall, with some degree of embarrassment, several face-plants into the snow, when my snowshoeing technique became careless, I cannot remember a single incident of slipping with snowshoes on. I have slipped many times on snow and ice when wearing hiking boots.

If the snowpack is shallow it may be easier to ascend on foot and then descend wearing snowshoes. This strategy gives you more freedom to move fast and can be very effective on uneven terrain. For this reason, if my snowshoes are not on my feet, they are attached to my backpack. On countless ascents, I've trudged up a mountain on foot and then enjoyed a speedy descent on snowshoes. You may regret leaving your snowshoes behind, but rarely will you regret carrying them, even if they stay on your pack throughout. At an average weight of 1.9 kilograms, snowshoes are a relatively light addition to your backpack.

All of this said, however, travelling on foot to the detriment of an established trail is always bad form. Postholing creates holes that may be dangerous to other snowshoers and skiers. You should wear your snowshoes if there is a chance you might damage the trail.

The aesthetic experience of gliding and fluid movement is one of the joys of backcountry skiing. While snowshoeing has no such equivalent, over the years I have come to appreciate the beauty and freedom of movement with snowshoes. While not as pronounced as carving perfect turns with skis, plunge-stepping rapidly down a steep snowy slope on snowshoes can be very exhilarating and the rhythm of moving through deep snow is its own aesthetic. Just another reason to place the snowshoes where they belong (for the most part) – on your feet!

When all is said and done, the decision to use snowshoes or

go on foot is an individual one. I would say as a final personal note that if you intend to go snowshoeing, SNOWSHOE!

SNOWSHOEING WITH THE FAMILY

For those looking for an outdoor winter activity for the whole family, snowshoeing can't be beat. As stated, snowshoeing is easy and inexpensive, certainly a cheaper alternative to a day at a ski resort.

Children as young as three are usually capable of strapping on a pair of kids' snowshoes and making strides through the snow. Most snowshoe companies make models specifically for the different weight categories of children. The smallest size of snowshoes are designed for children three to five years old and up to 19 kilograms. These snowshoes weigh only 0.7 kilograms.

If you have young children with you, very short trips on well-packed trails are recommended. Remember that children may

KIDS, SNOW AND SNOWSHOES — A RECIPE FOR FUN AND GOOD TIMES. (ANITA HOFER)

ABOVE: The Chariot Carrier, with the CTS Cross-country
Ski Kit. BELOW: The Chariot in action on Cameron Lake.

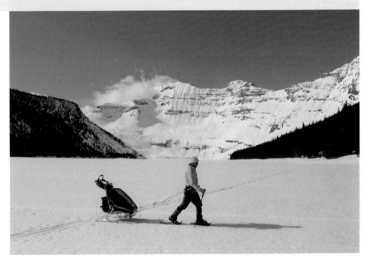

have to take two or even three steps to your one. Obviously, the older the child, the longer the route you can take on. Children 10 and up are usually ready to tackle some fairly long trips and as an added bonus are also ready to break trail for you!

Although they may not be able to snowshoe, children younger

MARK, ROGAN AND THE MEC HAPPYTRAILS CHILD CARRIER.

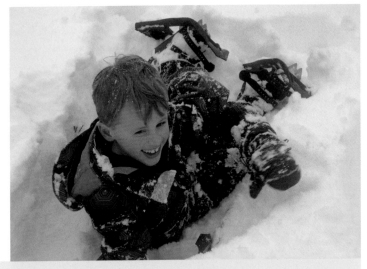

ABOVE: MICHAEL ENJOYS THE SNOW IN THE BEST WAY
POSSIBLE! (KEN SCHMALTZ) BELOW: THE NUGARA CLAN AT
CRANDELL LAKE. SIXTEEN-MONTH-OLD ROGAN TOOK THE CHARIOT
THERE BUT INSISTED ON EXPLORING THE LAKE ON FOOT.

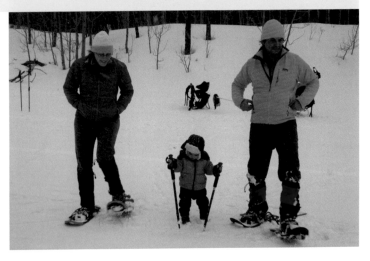

than three can still accompany you on a day out in the Rockies. Regardless of the manner in which you bring young ones along – listed below – I strongly recommend that you stick to easy, relatively flat and well-travelled routes. The sometimes uncertain nature of trail-breaking may put a child in danger should you fall or step into a tree well, creek or other hazard.

- Pull toddlers along in a Chariot Carrier with the CTS Cross-Country Ski Kit. The Chariot offers more protection than a baby carrier and will not affect your balance as much. As well, the Chariot is very comfortable for the child, allowing for longer trips. The child may even take a nap! The Chariot works best on the easier routes described in this book, such as Cameron Lake. It glides easily across the snow and performs well on routes with very gently graded terrain. More challenging and steeper terrain like Crandell Lake can be done with a Chariot, but such routes will prove to be more challenging for you because of the push and pull of the Chariot. (A second person walking behind the Chariot to help guide it does help on routes like Crandell Lake.) I do not recommend using the Chariot on routes with tight curves because of its large turning radius. Please note that you must use the five-point harness in the Chariot to ensure the safety of your child.

- Carry children aged three and under in baby carriers specifically designed for the outdoors. Baby carriers are just like backpacks and allow you to tackle steeper terrain and narrower trails without compromising manoeuvrability. Be sure to research specific models and choose a high-quality carrier. That does not necessarily equate to a high price. Mountain Equipment Co-op (MEC) makes a very inexpensive carrier (the Happytrails Child Carrier backpack) that does its job wonderfully.

- Pull toddlers along in a toboggan or sled. This method is very inexpensive, but toboggans are also often cumbersome and difficult to manoeuvre. If you choose to use a sled, pick very short, easy trips that cover flat terrain.

One note about taking the kids out: don't expect them to stay clean or dry. Kids will be kids, and they may have more fun trying to swim in the snow than snowshoe across its surface. Pack some dry clothes for them to change into when you get back to your vehicle.

Refer to Appendix C on page 499 to reference a list of snowshoe trips recommended for families with very young children.

TRIP RATINGS

The trip ratings in this book are not equivalent to those found in *Snowshoeing in the Canadian Rockies*. Even though there are beginner routes in that guidebook, it is geared toward intermediate and advanced snowshoers, who are used to multiple hours of strenuous trail-breaking, steep terrain up to 35°, avalanche assessment and the basics of mountaineering. Since all routes and areas in this guidebook stay away from avalanche terrain and require no formal training in mountaineering techniques, the three rating levels correspond primarily to trip length, trail-breaking challenges, general steepness and the amount of elevation gain required.

Descriptors for each rating are as follows:

- **Easy** – A trip on flat or very gently graded terrain. Completion times from 0.5–3 hours and elevation gains less than 100 metres. Strenuous trail-breaking is unlikely, though there may be some trail-breaking after a snowfall.
- **Intermediate** – Sections of steeper terrain, but still manageable. Completion times from 2–4 hours and elevation

gains from 100–300 metres. Possibility of some strenuous trailbreaking.

- **Advanced** – Short sections of steep terrain up to 25°. Completion times of 3–6 hours and elevation gains of 300+ metres. Strenuous trail-breaking is likely. Snowshoes with good crampons are recommended.

These are just general guidelines, of course, and some trips don't fit all the criteria of each rating. For example, Chester Lake requires only 310 metres of elevation gain but is rated Advanced because of several short, but steep, sections. Similarly, the Ink Pots earn an Intermediate rating (even though the trip breaks the mark of 300 metres of elevation gain) because the terrain is moderately graded.

Avalanches

With a few minor exceptions, there are no routes in this guidebook that go into avalanche terrain. As such, it is not necessary for users to carry avalanche equipment or know how to use it. However, even a beginner snowshoer may want to leave the beaten path and go exploring, simply for the enjoyment and reward of the activity itself. Therefore, the following section on recognizing avalanche terrain is included in this book. If you do venture away from the described routes, being able to identify potential avalanche terrain will give you the ability to stop and go back immediately. Unless you have taken an avalanche safety training course (AST 1 and/or AST 2), and are carrying avalanche equipment and know how to use it, do not tempt fate by continuing. Every year backcountry users are injured or killed by avalanches. Statistically, most avalanche incidents involving humans turn out to be fatal.

Regardless of whether you intend to go into avalanche terrain or avoid it completely, it is a good idea to become acquainted with the avalanche bulletins at www.avalanche.ca. These bulletins give an up-to-date and comprehensive analysis of present avalanche conditions.

The excerpt below is taken from *Snowshoeing in the Canadian Rockies* and is intended for snowshoe mountaineers; however, it is every bit as applicable to those who seek only to avoid avalanche terrain.

RECOGNIZING AVALANCHE TERRAIN

Gaining the ability to recognize avalanche terrain is the first step in the complex process everyone must go through to ensure safe travel in winter. With proper training, lots of reading and a diligent effort in the backcountry, the following skills can be learned and developed quickly.

Slope Angle

The most important factor in determining if terrain has the potential to produce an avalanche is slope angle: angles between 25° and 60° have that potential. Generally, angles of 35° to 40° produce the largest number of slab avalanches. Slopes of these angles deserve the most scrutiny and should be carefully studied and tested before traversing or ascending them.

Measuring the angle of a particular slope is best accomplished using an inclinometer. Use of this tool is especially important when you are first developing avalanche-recognition skills. Putting a specific number to your own observations will dramatically increase your ability to accurately determine a slope angle without an inclinometer.

Always be aware that in regards to "eyeing" the angle of a particular slope, human perception has limitations. Often what appears to be low-angled can be far steeper than estimated and vice versa; this is something to think about when heading to that 20° slope that is actually 38°.

Slope Orientation

The leeward slope is the side of the mountain that is opposite to the direction from which the wind is blowing. As such it is usually wind-loaded and very unstable. In the Canadian Rockies, the primary wind direction is from west to east and southwest to northeast. Therefore, slopes facing east or northeast are far more likely to be avalanche-prone than those facing west and southwest. Remember that this is just a generalization and by no means infers that all west- and southwest-facing slopes are safe. Serious destructive avalanches occur on all slopes.

Slope Shape

Three terms describe slope shape: convex, concave and planar (see diagram below). Avalanches can occur on all three types; however, convex slopes present the most serious risk for a slide. The shape of a convex slope puts a great deal of stress on the snow just below the bulge. Always be on the lookout for convex slopes and be ready to assess possible consequences if they release.

Concave slopes, because of their bowl-like shape, are capable of supporting the weight of the snow above them to a greater degree than convex or planar slopes. This rule only applies to a certain extent, however. When that weight becomes excessive, concave slopes will release, just like convex ones do. The location from which an avalanche may start on a concave slope is difficult to determine.

The consistent angle of planar slopes means they can avalanche anywhere.

CONCAVE   CONVEX   PLANAR

MOUNT JOFFRE DISPLAYS THE THREE TYPES OF
SLOPES. C=CONCAVE, V=CONVEX, P=PLANAR.

Anchors

As the word implies, anchors help keep snow attached to the slope it's on, thus rendering the slope more stable than one without anchors. Anchors include trees, vegetation and rocks. Unfortunately, like many other aspects of avalanche physics, anchoring is a double-edged sword. The snowpack around anchors is obviously thinner and therefore weaker and prone to instability. In other words, avalanches can start around anchors.

Forested terrain on a slope is typically a good indicator that the slope is relatively safe. When a slope is abundantly covered in full-grown trees, you know there has usually been little to no avalanche activity on that slope for a number of years. Ascending through heavily treed terrain is always preferable to being out on open steep slopes.

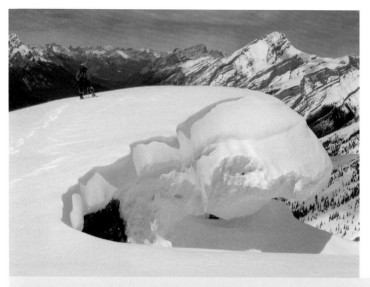

ABOVE: A CORNICE ON RED RIDGE. BELOW: A LARGE
OVERHANGING CORNICE ON KENT RIDGE NORTH.

Elevation

The categories of terrain and their corresponding ratings on the avalanche bulletin provide pretty clear evidence that the higher you go the more avalanche risk there is. On rare occasions the ratings maybe the same in each zone, but the overwhelming majority of days will see a more severe rating for terrain in the alpine than below it. Increased elevation means more snow and more wind to blow that snow around. As a general rule, as soon as you move above treeline and into the alpine, expect the avalanche risk to rise.

In conclusion, hopefully the preceding text will at least introduce you to the very basics of recognizing avalanche terrain. I would encourage all winter mountain users to take an avalanche safety course regardless of your goals. You simply can't be over-informed about the subject. If you can recognize avalanche terrain, you can stay away from it.

OTHER HAZARDS AND CONSIDERATIONS

While of primary concern, avalanches are certainly not the only elements of nature to be cognizant of when out on snowshoes. Cornices, glaciers and bad weather can be just as deadly.

CORNICES

Cornices are one of my favourite aspects of winter travel. These shapely and unique formations can add tremendously to the scenery and views on any trip. However, they can also be a source of great danger. Having a cornice collapse beneath you will probably have deadly consequences. As it may be difficult to ascertain whether there is solid rock beneath the snow you are travelling on, it is always best to play it safe by staying very far away from the edge when snowshoeing or hiking along a ridge. Cornices can grow to enormous sizes and may overhang the edge of a ridge by a significant distance.

Cornices can be dangerous not only when you are near them. When cornices collapse onto steep slopes they can trigger massive avalanches. The cornices hanging off the summit ridge of Mount Ogden are classic examples (see Sherbrooke Lake, page 441).

Although cornice danger is fairly limited in the routes described in this guidebook, it is certainly something to be aware of.

BAD WEATHER

Inclement weather can be troublesome at any time of the year, but the trouble it causes is especially pronounced in the winter months. Getting caught in a snowstorm with whiteout conditions can be very serious. A storm will quickly cover up the tracks you made, making it difficult to retrace your steps. This is not likely to be too big of a concern with beginner routes, but if you do choose to go out when the weather is suspect, pick the shortest and easiest routes where route-finding is very straightforward. Better yet, refer to the section entitled Picking Good Weather Days (below), and try to avoid nasty weather completely.

LIMITED DAYLIGHT

On December 21 of each year, the mountain parks receive a little less than 8 hours of daylight. That's not a large number when compared to the 16.5 hours we get on June 21. Plan your day accordingly and always have a headlamp with extra batteries in your backpack. A forced bivouac in winter is not only unsavoury because of the cold temperatures but also because you may have as much as 16 hours of darkness to get through.

Standard time (November–March) also means that early starts are almost imperative. Thankfully, the daylight situation dramatically improves after the second Saturday in March,

ABOVE: The deep-blue sky that often accompanies a high-pressure system. Of course the sun must be in the right position. Taken from Commonwealth Ridge, with Chester Lake just visible near the lower right. BELOW: A shapely cornice and low-lying clouds on an ascent of Kent Ridge Outlier.

when clocks in Alberta move ahead an hour for daylight saving time. This doesn't impact the amount of daylight hours available but at least puts the sunset an hour later, allowing for longer trips or later starts.

ON AN ASCENT OF WHIRLPOOL RIDGE, LOW-LYING CLOUDS BLANKET THE VALLEY BELOW.

PICKING GOOD WEATHER DAYS

Snowshoeing is very much a good-weather activity. Lacking the exhilarating run down that skiers are accustomed to, or the speed of a snowmobile, the primary thrill of snowshoeing comes from experiencing beautiful surroundings. Clear skies enhance that experience to an infinite degree.

Predicting the weather in the Canadian Rockies is often a crapshoot at best. Many meteorological factors contribute to the uncertainty of weather forecasting in this area, factors that render even the most experienced and knowledgeable forecasters incapable of accurate prediction of the weather. In short, be prepared for any type of weather and be understanding when the weather is not as glorious as one of the local forecasters predicted. Of course, many times I've gone to the mountains, a bad weather forecast in hand, only to enjoy beautifully clear skies.

Following are some procedures to go through and some tips for maximizing the amount of time you spend under clear skies and minimizing that spent under clouds.

Check the weather forecasts online. Environment Canada, Accuweather and The Weather Network are presently the most popular online sources for weather in Canada. Monitor the forecasts several days before your trip, but expect them to change frequently. Always check again the night before your trip and, if possible, the morning of the trip.

Look at a current satellite image just before the trip. Sometimes the satellite image very much contradicts the forecast. In

THE BEAUTIFUL AND VARIED TERRAIN OF SPRAY LAKE. MOUNT SHARK IS TO THE LEFT AND MOUNT TURNER THE RIGHT.

general, I trust a satellite image far more than a computer-generated forecast. Knowing how to read and analyze weather patterns from satellite images can be a very useful skill and may save you from spending a frustrating day in bad weather.

High-pressure systems are your best friend. When the forecaster on the local news mentions "a ridge of high pressure," start salivating and do your best to get out to the mountains. High-pressure systems are generally predictable, stable and result in the best possible weather.

Be flexible about changing your plans at the last minute. Bad weather in one area of the Rockies does not mean bad weather throughout. In general, the farther west and the farther north you go, the worse the weather. The Front Ranges may be basking in full sunshine while mountains of the Continental Divide are consumed by clouds.

All of the above doesn't mean you should stay at home on cloudy days. Sometimes cloud cover can lead to very atmospheric lighting and views. Also, on very rare occasions, the clouds may be lying very low in the valley, and you can ascend above them, which is always an amazing experience.

FROZEN LAKES

Snowshoeing routes on or around frozen lakes, streams or rivers make up almost 40 per cent of the trips in this book. Therefore it's very important to know some facts about them, especially the lakes. The best time to go out onto a frozen lake is between mid-December and April. However, an unseasonably warm autumn or spring might encroach on that time span, and discretion and caution should be used. In 2002, for example, a late-December sojourn out onto Emerald Lake ended abruptly when the ice started cracking beneath me and a friend. Thankfully we were very near the shore at the time and got off the ice before I became Leonardo DiCaprio (Jack Dawson) slowly sinking into the unfathomable depths. January, February and March are almost guaranteed to be safe for lake traverses.

A lake's elevation is an important factor in determining how soon into the season it freezes. At a low elevation of approximately 1400 metres, Barrier Lake (not described in this book) may not be safe for travel until January or even later. In contrast, Spray Lake (see page 283), sitting at an elevation above 1800 metres, can be frozen to a depth of over a metre by mid-December. Keep this in mind if you are planning to take an early-season excursion onto a frozen lake.

If you are wondering about how much weight the ice on a frozen lake can handle, on a March attempt of Mount Nestor, my brother and I witnessed a full-sized truck drive the entire length

LOOKING DOWN ON BOW LAKE. THE MAJOR PEAK
BEHIND THE LAKE IS MOUNT THOMPSON.

of Spray Lake, right down the middle. Admittedly, we instantly felt a little foolish about the apprehension we experienced when crossing the lake with snowshoes, several hours earlier. Needless to say, this example cannot be applied to all frozen lakes. Spray Lake does have a notable reputation for thick ice. However, I wouldn't be risking my brand-new truck on Barrier Lake during any month – good thing I drive a Honda CR-V!

An actual determination of the strength of the ice you will be travelling on in the Canadian Rockies is almost always an impractical proposition, simply because the ice will most likely be covered in deep snow. Excavating the snow to get a look at the ice is hardly worth the time and energy. Also, if you have to dig through a significant amount of snow to get to the ice, this usually indicates the ice will be quite strong. The best way to be confident of ice strength is to simply go to the mountains in January, February and early March.

Nevertheless, there are several points you should be aware of:

- Ice at an inlet or outlet to a lake can be very weak, even if the ice on the lake is very strong.
- The strongest ice is blue to clear in colour; the weakest will be light grey to black.
- A slushy ice surface is a warning that the ice is weak and/or deteriorating below.
- Ice thickness of 10 centimetres and greater is suitable for snowshoeing.

The south end of Spray Lake is my favourite of the lake trips, boasting terrific views of the surrounding mountains and interesting ice, which you can see when it is blown clear of snow. The great thing about Spray Lake is that you are afforded completely different views and perspectives from either end or from the middle of the lake. Other lakes that you simply must visit (preferably on clear days) are Emerald Lake (page 445), Sherbrooke Lake (page 441), Bow Lake (page 462) and Waterfowl Lakes (page 472).

SNOWSHOEING TECHNIQUE

You would think that snowshoeing requires little, if any, technique. After all, it's simply walking with bigger feet. Certainly snowshoeing does not require all the skill and technique that accomplished backcountry skiers possess, but there are some techniques that make snowshoeing an efficient, safe and enjoyable experience. Most of the techniques described in the subsections Getting Up, Getting Down, and Side-sloping (below) are for more advanced snowshoers, but even beginners should be aware of them, just in case they find themselves on difficult terrain.

FLAT TERRAIN

There are really no great revelations to be made relative to snowshoeing on flat terrain. You simply walk with as normal a stride as the width of your snowshoes will permit. The narrow design

LEFT: GOING STRAIGHT UP A RELATIVELY GENTLE SLOPE. RIGHT: USING A HERRINGBONE TECHNIQUE ON THE SAME SLOPE HIGHER UP.

of most modern snowshoes makes this very easy. Although you may have to widen your gait slightly, you will very quickly adapt to it. Soon, you won't even be aware you are taking a wider-than-normal step.

Getting Up

Following are some different techniques you may wish to employ on steeper terrain, as well as some useful tips to keep in mind.

1. If your snowshoes have heel lifts, put them up to reduce strain on your calf muscles and Achilles tendon.
2. Snowshoe in switchback patterns so you are not going directly up a steep slope.
3. If the snow on steeper slopes is soft, kick-step into it with your snowshoes, then flatten the snow by stepping down into it.
4. If the snow is hard, use snowshoes with aggressive crampons. The best styles are advanced models that allow the frame of the snowshoe to act as a crampon. When using this type of snowshoe, maximize the amount of the frame making contact with the hard snow surface. Frame crampon snowshoes can tackle slopes up to a very steep 35°.
5. For steeper slopes of soft snow, a similar technique to the skiing herringbone (feet angled out) may work better than switchbacking (see photos).

Getting Down

Like ascending, descending gentle slopes on snowshoes is very easy. Plunge-stepping and even running downhill can be fun and will get you down in no time at all. Steeper slopes require more attention to technique. When going downhill, keep the following tips in mind:

ABOVE: DESCENDING A STEEP SLOPE BY FACING IN AND
KICK-STEPPING. BELOW: RUNNING DOWNHILL ON SNOWSHOES
CAN BE FAST AND FUN. MICHELLE AND NICOLE RACE DOWN
A SMALL HILL ON THE WAY BACK FROM BURSTALL FLATS.

1. Bend your knees slightly and keep your weight over your feet. Avoid the temptation to lean too far forward. Use poles for balance and support.
2. For steeper slopes, it may be necessary to face into the slope and descend using a kick-stepping technique. Your poles can be used for balance and also in a self-belay technique, similar to that used with an ice axe.

SIDE-SLOPING

When side-sloping (traversing) go slightly uphill as you go across.

1. In soft snow, kick-step into the slope with the inside edge of your snowshoe.
2. In hard snow, use the snowshoes' crampons. Traversing very steep slopes may require you to face into the slope and move

TRAVERSING A STEEP SLOPE OF HARD SNOW — HEEL LIFTS TURNED UP, SNOWSHOES POINTING FORWARD.

sideways, keeping your snowshoes pointed uphill. This technique allows for the most effective use of the snowshoes' crampons.

Running

If you do decide to run wearing recreational snowshoes, remember to lift your knees higher when running through powder – the deeper the snow, the higher the lift. You don't need a pair of racing snowshoes to run, but recreational snowshoes will be more difficult and clumsy to run in. Go slowly at first and get used to the feel of moving fast. Also note that running is best done without poles.

For those looking for some rigorous cardiovascular and muscular exercise, running in snowshoes provides an intense workout.

Balling

Balling is the accumulation of large and often heavy clumps of snow on the bottom of your snowshoes. This occurs when warm temperatures have softened the snow. Balling makes travel very difficult, and you have to stop often to clear away the snow from the snowshoes. Unfortunately, very little can be done to prevent it, although

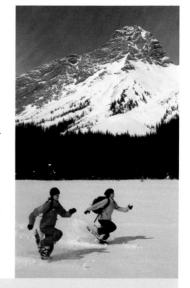

KEEP THOSE KNEES HIGH. MICHELLE AND NICOLE RUN THROUGH FAIRLY DEEP POWDER.

I have heard that spraying your snowshoes' crampons with non-stick cooking oil can help. Having a set of ski or trekking poles to knock away the snow is the best way to deal with balled-up snow. Sometimes just banging the side of your snowshoe with a pole will release the snow; other times you have to dig it away.

Another method that sometimes works quite effectively is to flick your heel violently as you step. This causes your snowshoe to bang up against your heel, knocking away unwanted snow.

Snowshoes with large crampons are more prone to balling.

TRAIL-BREAKING

Breaking new trail on snowshoes can be all things: fun, tiring, exhilarating, challenging or a physical brutality of Biblical

A GROUP OF 17 BREAKS TRAIL THROUGH DEEP SNOW IN KANANASKIS, OFF HIGHWAY 742. (BERNIE NEMETH)

proportions! You may experience one, two or all of the above when wading through new snow. Here are a few things to keep in mind:

1. Try to keep a consistent stride and make your stride shorter for deeper snow.
2. Lift your knees high.
3. Pace yourself. You don't want to expend all your energy and then give up (or not have enough energy to return).
4. Go in a group (a large one if possible) and take turns breaking trail.
5. Put the person with the biggest snowshoes at the front of the line (sucks to be big!).
6. Walk in single file to pack down a solid trail that will be easy to return on.

Try to keep a positive attitude when trail-breaking becomes arduous. Remember that you are forging a path that will then be infinitely easier to return on. This is especially true when you are going uphill. I vividly recall a solid 90 minutes of brutally strenuous, uphill trail-breaking going up to Smuts Pass in December of 2009. I recall with even greater clarity the exhilarating 18 minutes of plunge-stepping to get down that same slope on return.

When all else fails, I try to stick in my head the old proverb "The journey of a thousand miles begins with the first step." Even if you are moving farther away from your vehicle, every step you take is one step closer to it. That rationale has helped me get through some pretty long and exhausting days in the mountains.

SNOWSHOEING ETIQUETTE

As more and more people make their way into the mountains on snowshoes, the importance of good etiquette becomes increasingly important. There really isn't much to snowshoeing etiquette, but in following and respecting a few basic guidelines we can ensure a good relationship with all mountain users, such as skiers, hikers and snowmobilers.

SKI TRACKS AND TRAIL-BREAKING

The most important guideline for snowshoers is to avoid snowshoeing on ski tracks whenever possible. Many winter trails are wide enough to support separate tracks for skiers and snowshoers. If a ski trail has already been established on the route you are on, make a new trail for snowshoers as far away as from the ski trail as possible. This may seem like a great deal of effort when an established trail is right there, but trail-breaking is the

THERE IS PLENTY OF ROOM FOR SEPARATE TRACKS ON THE WAY TO THE BURSTALL LAKES.

price of travel for all winter users. At some point, everyone must take on the burden of breaking new trail. If all travellers share that responsibility then it is possible that you may only have to break new trail a few times each season. Everyone who follows on the new trail will appreciate your efforts, and skiers will also be thankful you have stayed off an established ski trail.

For trails with no visible signs of snowshoe tracks, try to stay to the far right on the way in and the same side on the way back out. The right side is an arbitrary choice; however, it is probable that skiers will use the right side on the way in, when they are moving at the slower speed, and the left on the way out, when they are moving much faster. Using one side for both directions of snowshoe travel may help to eliminate collisions. If snowshoers get into the habit of using the right side going in, a rule of etiquette may develop over time. This will invariably make life easier for all winter travellers and minimize conflict. Note that snowshoers should always use the same track going in and out, whereas skiers may choose to make a separate trail for their return trip to avoid skiing into one another.

Regarding trail-breaking on any trail, a point of contention may arise after a heavy snowfall has sufficiently covered an established trail. In this situation the responsibility of trail-breaking falls upon the first party to start along the trail. If at all possible, snowshoers should try to avoid breaking trail over what might have been a ski track before the new snow arrived. Again, staying well over to the right side may be the best solution.

Simple common courtesy and decency, however, should be enough to avert any conflict between the different types of winter travellers. Remember we all share a common goal – to enjoy the beauty of the mountains.

Official Ski Trails

Groomed trails specifically for cross-country skiers are a little different from unofficial ski trails, such as the one to Burstall Pass. Snowshoers should try to avoid groomed trails completely. Damage to these trails, especially early in the season, can be dangerous to skiers who might ski into a hole made by snowshoers or hikers. Serious injury can result from such a ski accidents. Later in the season, these trails are usually well packed down and less susceptible to serious damage, but snowshoers should still stay away from them.

There are exceptions to this general rule. Some groomed trails provide the only access into certain areas. If this is the case, it may be necessary for snowshoers to use the trails, but they should always minimize the amount of time spent on them. Fortunately, for the most part, these trails are very wide, and getting in the way of skiers shouldn't be an issue. The trails leading out from the Mount Shark parking lot are good examples.

Avoid the following areas if possible:

1. Elk Pass (except the official snowshoe trail)
2. Pocaterra
3. Shark (except to see the south end of Spray Lake and Watridge Lake)

There are plenty of places to snowshoe in the Rockies without resorting to groomed trails. Be considerate and stay away from them.

Official Snowshoe Trails

Since the first edition of this book, Alberta Parks and Parks Canada have done an excellent job in creating more official snowshoe trails in the Canadian Rockies. This is especially true in Kananaskis. Official trails are a great place to start for beginners. They are usually relatively flat and short and have few to no objective hazards. Several of the official maps associated with these trails are included in this edition.

Right of Way

This point of etiquette is a simple one to practise and far less potentially contentious than the trail-breaking issue. Very simply, parties that travel faster have the right of way. For example, skiers are faster than snowshoers. Even on level or uphill terrain, skiers move at a slightly faster speed. Always be aware of this and move over to the right side of the trail to let skiers pass if required. Hopefully you'll be on different trails so moving over won't be necessary.

Obviously, the difference in speed between skiers and snowshoers is far more pronounced when going downhill. Try to stay to the correct side of the trail and make yourself visible to skiers when going down through treed terrain. Wearing brightly coloured clothing is always a good idea. When in treed terrain, moving completely off the trail to let skiers pass is the best course of action.

Snowmobilers and Snowmobile Trails

The etiquette of right of way applies doubly when you encounter snowmobilers. Not only should you move over for them but you should also get completely off the trail when they approach and pass. If this happens to put you in a metre and a half of snow, so be it! Snowmobilers can move at terrific speeds. Being struck by a fast-moving, 80-kilogram skier would be very unpleasant; being struck by that same 80-kilogram person atop a 260-kilogram snowmobile, both moving at 60 km/h, would ruin your day in a big way! Snowmobiles are very noisy and so you will be afforded plenty of warning that one is coming your way. Try to make yourself visible to snowmobilers, even when you are well off the trail.

Snowmobiling is not permitted in Banff and Jasper National Parks, nor is it allowed in most areas of the Kananaskis region. For routes in this book, you are only likely to encounter snowmobilers in the Bragg Creek area.

Note that snowshoeing on snowmobile tracks is an accepted practice, unlike snowshoeing on ski tracks.

Technology

The days of navigating mountain terrain with a map, compass, and a healthy dose of fear that you may get lost and never see humanity again, are fading rapidly, if not completely gone. From an idealistic standpoint, everyone would know how to get around using these "old-school" (but also "good-school") methods. In reality, however, advances in technology have rendered them not obsolete or undesirable but simply impractical. In addition to a map and a compass, my gear now routinely includes three additional forms of navigational technologies: a handheld GPS, a SPOT device and my cellphone.

GPS

Global Positioning System has revolutionized the way we move around this planet. GPS uses satellites orbiting the earth to triangulate your exact position, down to the nearest metre. It is remarkably accurate and reliable these days. Some form of built-in GPS is now the standard on many cars, cellphones and even cameras.

Most mountain enthusiasts now carry a handheld GPS unit. While older units were limited to giving location coordinates (GR numbers or latitude and longitude coordinates), with some route-mapping features, the newer models will pretty much do everything, except make your breakfast! Most GPS units now show your exact location and elevation on a topographical map, allow you to download routes and waypoints into the unit, and allow you to access geocaching information.

SPOT

SPOT stands for Satellite PersOnal Tracker and has widely become the weapon of choice for location tracking and for calling for help if necessary. The device uses a GPS signal to communicate with satellites and so a phone signal is not required. You can also use SPOT to notify friends and family of your GPS position and status, mark waypoints, or track your progress on Google Maps. The device is extremely light and easy to use and the yearly fee is a very small price to pay for the peace of mind and access to help that SPOT gives you.

Up to late 2016, I have yet to use my SPOT for an emergency, but I will never go into the mountains without it anymore. SPOT can save your life – period!

CELLPHONES

I obstinately denied myself a cellphone ("mobile phone" for all my dashing relatives in England) until 2010, but now that I have the little gizmo, it's hard to imagine life without one. I likewise denied myself the use of that phone in the mountains until late 2013, but now that I do use it,... you get the picture!

Very simply, the cellphone has singlehandedly replaced the need for maps, a compass and for some even a separate GPS unit. Utilizing satellite signals, not cellphone signals, the Topographic Maps Canada app on my phone shows a topographical map and pinpoints my exact location on that map, all far out of the range that any cellphone signal can reach. Newer versions of this app include trail and mountain routes and greater map detail.

SOME SERIOUS AVALANCHE TERRAIN BEHIND ME ON SMUTWOOD PEAK. WE DIDN'T GO ANY FARTHER THAT DAY.

As well, cellphone signals are now reaching areas that were previously unreachable. I've been shocked and pleasantly surprised on many occasions to find myself FaceTiming my nephews and niece, atop some fairly remote mountains.

The major limitation of cellphones in the mountains, and especially in regards to this book, is cold weather. The lithium-ion battery that most cellphones use for power drain much faster in cold weather. In fact, even with a full charge, your cellphone can lose power within minutes in very cold temperatures – a compelling argument for never relying solely on a phone in the mountains. Carry your phone as close to your body as possible to keep it warm.

At present, other inadequacies of cellphones in the mountains include the inability to call for help and lack of versatility when compared to GPS. However, it is certainly within the realm of possibility that in the near future a single cellphone will have the capabilities of all the above devices and it will become the only unit that a person carries.

Apps

In addition to the Topographic Maps Canada app, here are a few other apps you may find useful:

1. ViewRanger – similar to the Maps Canada app but also allows you to upload and download routes onto your phone.
2. SunCalc – great app that displays sunrise, sunset and the path of the sun on a topo map, for any day of the year. Very useful in helping to decide what time of day and what time of year to do routes, in order to get the best sun.
3. Accuweather – weather forecasts for all mountain areas pertinent to this book.
4. Avalanche.ca – not especially important for this book, but always worth having.

But Don't Forget the Classics

As wonderful as the technological world can be, "overwhelming" is also often an appropriate adjective to describe it. Embracing technology is a good thing, but relying on it completely may not be. Self-reliance in the mountains is paramount, and that includes the ability to navigate the terrain without the latest gizmo or app.

Personally, I love all the new technologies, but with all the new tools available to me, a paper map and compass have been, presently are and probably always will be in my backpack on every trip I take into the mountains. As stated, "old school but good school"!

BEYOND BEGINNER SNOWSHOEING

Where do you go from here? If you have exhausted all the beginner routes around the Rockies and are looking to "step it up" into the world of intermediate and advanced snowshoeing, there are several steps to take.

First and foremost is to take an Avalanche Safety Training (AST) 1 course. This course will teach you the basics of avalanche assessment, avoiding avalanches and using beacons, probes and shovels. After honing your skills with AST 1, AST 2 is strongly

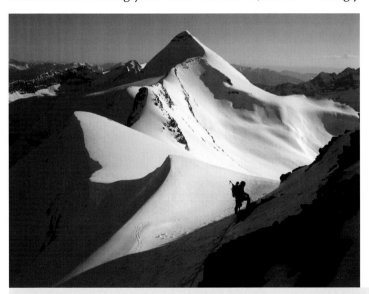

BLACKFOOT MOUNTAIN IN GLACIER NATIONAL PARK, MONTANA. THE PAYOFF FOR SNOWSHOE MOUNTAINEERING CAN OFTEN BE SCENERY LIKE THIS.

recommended. You may eventually decide that you are happy to keep things simple by steering clear of all avalanche terrain. At least, having taken an AST 1 course, you will have the knowledge you need to make informed decisions about terrain. Thus, you will have the option to leave the beaten path and explore a little without putting yourself and others in harm's way.

Once you have an avalanche course under your belt, it's time to enroll in a mountaineering course. The Snow and Ice Long Weekend, offered by several companies, is highly recommended. In this course you will learn the fundamentals of glacier travel and rescue, using crampons and an ice axe, self-arrest and other valuable skills. Note that this and AST courses are general in scope and not geared specifically toward snowshoers. Check out the websites for Yamnuska Mountain Adventures (http://yamnuska.com), University of Calgary Outdoor Centre (https://

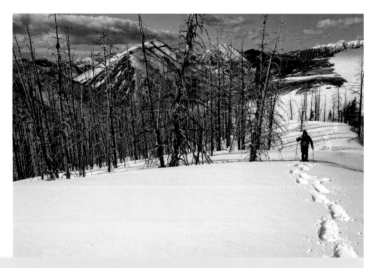

JEFF LANG COMES UP THE RIDGE ON "POKER PEAK." (DAVE MCMURRAY)

www.ucalgary.ca/ActiveLiving/registration/Browse/All/Avalanche?filters=Outdoor-Centre) and Try That (www.trythat.ca/experiences/Alberta/Land/mountaineering) for more details on the Snow and Ice Long Weekend.

The third type of course you'll want to look into is an introduction to rock climbing. Rope-work, belayed climbing, using anchors, rappelling and the basics of rock-climbing technique are the primary focus of this course. An average snowshoe trip will not likely require you to employ any of the skills learned in a rock-climbing course (certainly they will not be necessary for trips in this guidebook), but the acquired skills and knowledge will be invaluable to those looking to widen their experience in the mountains and reach new levels of achievement.

With AST, mountaineering and climbing courses under your belt you are granted almost unlimited potential in your mountain adventures.

CONCLUSION

Hopefully the preceding text has not only been informative but also served to pique your interest in the exciting activity of snowshoeing. Snowshoeing can be as simple or as complex as you want it to be. However, regardless of the level of trip you are undertaking, it is extremely important to be informed about the dangers of the environment, etiquette in that environment, and choosing appropriate objectives for the conditions and your skill level. The Canadian Rockies is an inherently dangerous environment, but snowshoeing in the Rockies does not have to be a dangerous activity. Be informed, be sensible and have fun! Enjoy the trips to follow.

THE TRIPS

The routes in this book cover many areas of the southern Canadian Rockies, from majestic Waterton in the far south to the amazing environs around Bow Lake, about 500 kilometres farther northwest. The lack of routes in some areas does not mean they are not snowshoe friendly – it simply means I have yet to explore those areas fully. The Kananaskis area is heavily favoured, simply because snowshoe routes in Kananaskis are easy to get to, and there are plenty of them. The snow, especially in the southwest section of Kananaskis, comes early and stays late. Kananaskis also has the greatest concentration of official snowshoe trails.

Each area detailed below offers opportunities for the easy snowshoe trips outlined in this guidebook and the serious snowshoe-mountaineering trips described in *Snowshoeing in the Canadian Rockies, 2nd Edition*. Needless to say, the scenery and views throughout the Rockies are fantastic, regardless of the area you choose. Personally, my favourite destinations for beginner snowshoeing routes are Highway 742 in Kananaskis, and Yoho. However, each area has several awesome trips that are worthy of multiple visits.

Two final reminders before you set out: read the introductory information for each trip carefully so that you are aware of the level and demands of the trip; and check the weather forecast before you set out.

You are now ready to explore one of the most magical environments this planet has to offer – enjoy!

WATERTON

Opportunities for easy snowshoeing trips in Waterton are fairly few due to the lack of official snowshoe trails and limited road access. Waterton essentially closes down from the end of November to May and therefore services are minimal. This may change in the future. Several vendors have recently opened their stores on a limited basis throughout the winter months. Nevertheless, if you are in the area or simply love the southern Rockies as much as I do, several trips are more than worthwhile.

The length of the snowshoeing season can vary dramatically in Waterton. Warm chinook winds sometimes melt huge amounts of snow in short order. However, Waterton does see the greatest yearly precipitation of any place in Alberta. The late and heavy snowfalls of 2011 left many of the residences in the townsite with drifts up to the top of their front doors late into the spring. Typically, February, March and early April are the best months to get a good snowshoeing trip in.

A word of warning about Waterton: it's windy down there. Not your average inconvenient gusts that are an annoyance at worst, but full-force gale-strength winds that can knock you off your feet. Gusts of 150 km/h have been recorded in the Waterton townsite. When checking the weather for this area, make it a point to note the predicted wind speeds and any wind warnings. Any wind speed exceeding 70 km/h may ruin your day. After close to 100 visits to Waterton Park over the past 11 years, I was treated to my first and unbelievably rare sight of a mountain reflection in the Upper Lake on April 8, 2012. It took that long for me to be there on a day when the wind wasn't disturbing the lake's surface! I should have rushed to the nearest store and bought a lottery ticket.

ROUTES

A VERY RARE REFLECTION OF VIMY PEAK IN THE UPPER AND MIDDLE WATERTON LAKES. NOT EXACTLY A WINTERY SCENE, BUT I DID COMPLETE CRANDELL AND CAMERON LAKES ON THE SAME APRIL DAY, AND THEY WERE COMPLETELY SNOWBOUND (SEE PAGES 81 AND 86 RESPECTIVELY FOR PHOTOS FROM THOSE TRIPS).

1 BEAR'S HUMP

(MAP 1, PAGE 479)

RATING INTERMEDIATE
MOUNTAIN HEIGHT 1542 M
ELEVATION GAIN 215 M
ROUND-TRIP DISTANCE 2.8 KM
ROUND-TRIP TIME 0.75–1.5 HOURS
MAPS 82 H/4 WATERTON LAKES, GEM TREK
WATERTON LAKES NATIONAL PARK

TYPICAL TERRAIN ON THE EASIER SECTIONS OF BEAR'S HUMP.
THERE IS NO WAY MARK COULD HAVE MADE IT TO THE TOP WITH
40-LB ROGAN ON HIS BACK HAD HE NOT BEEN USING SNOWSHOES.

NO NEED FOR SHOES ON THE WIND-SCOURED SUMMIT.
MARK AND ROGAN RETREAT FROM THE EDGE.

The hike up Bear's Hump is easily the "most bang for your buck" of all the trips in Waterton. It's very short and takes you to a fine viewpoint of the Waterton townsite, Waterton Lakes and surrounding mountains. While the Hump sees most of its ascents during the summer months, winter ascents can be very rewarding. The trail can become very icy due to heavy traffic and so snowshoes with good crampons or another traction device will make the ascent safer and far more enjoyable. I've witnessed many people experiencing great difficulty because they had hiking boots only. Even though the trip is very short, it earns an intermediate rating because of several steep sections. Lastly, the trip generally favours ascents late in the season and early in the day or vice versa (early in the season and late in the day) when the sun is in a better position to illuminate the terrific view to the south.

LOOKING UP THE ROUTE TO THE START OF THE CRANDELL SCRAMBLE. YOU CAN SAFELY ASCEND TO THE VERY PROMINENT ROCKBAND AT TREELINE.

DIRECTIONS

Park at the Visitor's Centre and find the trailhead. A detailed route description is not required as the switchbacking trail is obvious and usually well packed down. There are some steep sections and quite a few steps to negotiate but your snowshoes will make easy work of it. At a decent pace you can reach the summit in less than 30 minutes.

You will probably have to take your snowshoes off just before you reach the top. The summit is often snow-free. Walk up to the high point to take in the fabulous view. Return the same way. With snowshoes and good snow conditions you can bomb down many sections of the trail with great ease: 9 minutes from summit to car is my fastest descent time wearing snowshoes. Occasionally you may have to practise your side-stepping technique to negotiate some of the wooden steps placed there by the park. Microspikes or crampons will also make the return trip much easier.

For the scrambler in you, note that the summit of Bear's Hump is the jumping off point to Alan Kane's excellent and difficult scramble route up Mount Crandell, as described in all editions of Kane's *Scrambles in the Canadian Rockies*. Don't attempt it in winter though!

Those comfortable with some scrambling on steeper terrain can continue the trip to the base of the Crandell scramble. However, extreme care is often required for this ascent as the snow can hide deep, narrow crevices between large rocks. Snowshoes will get you a short ways up, but you'll probably have to ditch the shoes in order to negotiate the scramble sections. You may be able to safely make it up to the base of a huge rockband, around GR867384, 1783 m. Here, there is a pretty decent view of Mount Blakiston, with Ruby Ridge in front of it, as well as back down toward the lakes. Return the same way.

2 CRANDELL LAKE

(MAP 2, PAGE 479)

DIFFICULTY INTERMEDIATE

ELEVATION GAIN 150 M

ROUND-TRIP DISTANCE 2.4 KM

ROUND-TRIP TIME 1–2 HOURS

MAPS 82 H/04 WATERTON LAKES,
GEM TREK WATERTON LAKES NATIONAL PARK

Crandell Lake is a good introduction to the Waterton area and great for a snowshoe trip. The route is short in horizontal distance but has a decent amount of elevation gain, thus providing a good workout. Views of Mount Galwey are excellent, so wait for a clear day.

DIRECTIONS

Drive toward the Waterton townsite and turn right onto Cameron Lake Road (Akamina Parkway). Drive approximately 4.2 km along the road and park at Crandell Trailhead, on the north side of the road.

The trail starts at the west end of the pullout and is very easy to follow, precluding the need for a detailed description. Follow the well-defined trail in a northeasterly direction, along the lower slopes of Ruby Ridge. About 600 m up, the trail forks. The right fork goes southeast on the lower slopes of Mount Crandell. The left fork is the one you want. It heads northwest, going up for a short section and then taking a narrow ramp down toward the lake. Turn right at the sign sitting at the bottom of the hill and make your way easily down to the south end of the lake.

At the lake there is a terrific view north to Mount Galwey (a

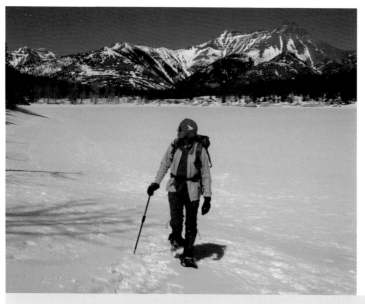

A COLOURFUL CALGARY STAMPEDER FAN AT CRANDELL
LAKE. MOUNT GALWEY TO THE RIGHT.

very enjoyable summer scramble) and several outliers west and
north of Galwey. Hopefully you still have some time and energy,
as a snowshoe around the perimeter of the lake is almost a must.
Strike out in either direction, but make sure you see all four sides.
From the east shore you get to see the snowy east side of Ruby
Ridge. The west shore permits a great view of the western outlier
of Mount Crandell (a terrific scramble, described by Alan Kane in
his guidebook *Scrambles in the Canadian Rockies*), and the north
shore grants views of the east end of Buchanan Ridge.

The north side of the lake is also home to several huge trees
that can be quite photogenic. A shelter nearby may provide a cozy
place to have lunch, but expect it to be snow-filled. Continuing

the trip north toward Crandell Campground on the Red Rock Canyon Road is not recommended, because of a significant elevation loss and possible route-finding challenges. Instead, relax at the north side of the lake and then return the way you came.

RETURNING UP THE RAMP THAT IS USED AS A DESCENT TO THE LAKE. AN OUTLIER OF MOUNT CRANDELL PROVIDES THE BACKGROUND.

3 AKAMINA PASS

(MAP 2, PAGE 479)

DIFFICULTY INTERMEDIATE
ELEVATION GAIN 100 M
ROUND-TRIP DISTANCE 3.2 KM
ROUND-TRIP TIME 1.5–2.5 HOURS
MAPS 82 G/01 SAGE CREEK,
GEM TREK WATERTON LAKES NATIONAL PARK

When compared with the other routes in Waterton described in this book, Akamina Pass may be somewhat disappointing and anticlimactic. The pass is used as a starting point for several amazing trips in the area, but all are advanced trips that venture into avalanche terrain. Unfortunately the pass is also heavily treed and views are very limited. Having said that, the ascent is a great workout, the scenery is pleasant (if not mind-blowing) and the speedy descent can be exhilarating.

DIRECTIONS

Drive approximately 13.5 km to the road closure on Cameron Lake Road (Akamina Parkway).

Snowshoe south along the road for approximately 1.5 km to the signed Akamina Pass trailhead. Please remember to stay off ski tracks. Turn right (west) onto the obvious trail and away you go! The trail is easy to follow and never excessively steep. It twists and turns several times and then hits some straight terrain. The pass is well marked and is also the end of line for beginner snowshoers. You can start snowshoeing down the other side for about 2 km without putting yourself in danger, but there is no objective and it may seem pointless. Take a break and then enjoy a speedy descent the same way you came in.

4 CAMERON LAKE

(MAP 2, PAGE 479)

DIFFICULTY EASY	
ELEVATION GAIN 30 M	
ROUND-TRIP DISTANCE 5 KM	
ROUND-TRIP TIME 1.5–2.5 HOURS	
MAPS 82 G/01 SAGE CREEK, GEM TREK WATERTON LAKES NATIONAL PARK	

Cameron Lake is beautiful year round. Although you can drive all the way to the lake in the summer, the winter road closure forces those who want to see the frozen lake and its environs to work a little for their reward. Nevertheless, snowshoeing along the road is easy and there's tons of room for everyone. This is an excellent beginner snowshoe route with an amazing view of Glacier National Park's Mount Custer once you get to the lake. Yet again, clear skies are almost mandatory here.

DIRECTIONS

Drive toward the Waterton townsite and turn right onto Cameron Lake Road (Akamina Parkway). Drive to the road closure, approximately 13.5 km along, and turn left into the parking area. There are limited parking spots here, and you may have to park along the south side of the parkway.

The route is as obvious as obvious gets! Snowshoe south for about 2.5 km to the lake. Although the road will more than likely be hard-packed, snowshoeing is definitely preferable to hiking. If you do choose to hike, carry your snowshoes for when you reach the lake.

You start off with distant views of Forum Ridge and Forum

Peak (an advanced snowshoe-mountaineering trip), followed by glimpses of Mount Custer's incredible north side. When you arrive at the lake you'll see what I mean by "incredible!" On a clear day, the view of snow-plastered Custer from the north shore of Cameron Lake is one of the premier views in the Rockies – and all for a mere 2.5 km of easy snowshoeing. What a deal!

There are hiking trails on both sides of the lake if you desire to explore a little farther south. The trail on the east side only goes for a short distance, but the west-side trail makes it about halfway down the lake. However, provided the lake is sufficiently frozen and snow-covered, a pleasant stroll down either side is the way to go; directly down the middle works too.

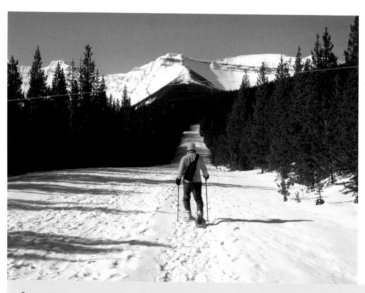

SNOWSHOEING DOESN'T GET ANY EASIER AND MORE OBVIOUS THAN THIS. FORUM RIDGE AND PEAK IN THE BACKGROUND – BOTH ARE ADVANCED SNOWSHOE-MOUNTAINEERING TRIPS, DESCRIBED IN SNOWSHOEING IN THE CANADIAN ROCKIES.

ABOVE: THE MAGNIFICENT NORTH FACE OF MOUNT CUSTER.
BELOW: MARK NUGARA GETS SOME AIR AT CAMERON LAKE.

The views don't change a great deal from either side or the middle of the lake, but the closer you get to Mount Custer, the more awe-inspiring this mountain becomes. Regardless of which side of the lake you choose to travel along, *do not* stray more than 1.5 km south of the north end of the lake. Anything beyond that mark puts you in serious avalanche risk from above. As well, if you happen to be the unluckiest guy or girl in the world, you could be arrested for an illegal border crossing if you go too far south! The south end of the lake sits in Montana, USA. Enjoy the views of America from the Canadian side, and then return the same way.

5 HORSESHOE BASIN TRAIL AND LAKEVIEW RIDGE

(MAP 1, PAGE 479)

DIFFICULTY ADVANCED

ELEVATION GAIN APPROXIMATELY 200 M

ROUND-TRIP DISTANCE 7 KM

ROUND-TRIP TIME 4.5–7 HOURS

MAPS 82 H/04 WATERTON LAKES,
GEM TREK WATERTON LAKES NATIONAL PARK

Horseshoe Basin Trail leads you into a beautiful valley that is surrounded by Bellevue Hill, Mount Galwey, "Rogan Peak" and Lakeview Ridge. Like other Front Range areas, snow levels can vary from none to a full metre. Early or late in the season, this trip may not require snowshoes. Since snow cover may make route-finding a challenge, this rates as an advanced trip.

DIRECTIONS

From the Waterton Park turnoff, drive north for several kilometres, turn left (west) into the Bison Paddock and drive to the end of the road. Do not turn left into the paddock loop. Instead, keep going straight along the north border of the paddock and park on the side of the road just before the gate. Do not park right in front of the gate.

Hop over the gate and snowshoe or hike west, alongside a barbed-wire fence and on the north side of a small tarn. The tarn may be completely dry. At the end of the fence you'll see the

Horseshoe Basin Trail sign to your right. Go to the sign and turn west onto the trail. The trail is generally easy to follow, through open areas and then through trees. It takes a few turns that seem to be taking you in the wrong direction, but eventually it turns to resume a direction up into the Horseshoe Basin valley.

You soon reach a high point where much of the route ahead becomes visible (see photo). The trail turns west here, losing a little elevation as it wends its way through small stands of trees and then out into the open again. Even when the trail is totally snow-covered or impossible to follow, the route is obvious initially. The tempting south face / ridge of Lakeview Ridge is present throughout, but it rates as a scramble or advanced snowshoe trip that may require avalanche gear and certainly avalanche knowledge.

AT THE HIGH POINT, LOOKING WEST INTO THE HORSESHOE BASIN VALLEY. THE SNOWY PEAK AT THE LEFT IS UNOFFICIALLY CALLED "ROGAN PEAK," AND THE SNOWLESS HILL IN THE CENTRE IS PART OF LAKEVIEW RIDGE.

Enjoy excellent views of "Rogan Peak," Lakeview Ridge and Mount Galwey, as you progress farther west into the valley. The end of the line for beginners comes when the trail crosses a creek (probably dried up at this time of year). If snow conditions are benign, the adventurous may decide to continue following the trail as it gains a hill and then goes north. This is an advanced extension, and only those comfortable with assessing avalanche conditions should consider continuing. Most will choose to turn around and return the same way they came in.

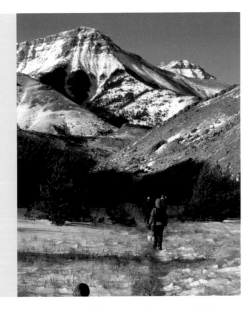

A SURPRISING LACK OF SNOW FOR JANUARY. SNOWSHOES WERE UNNECESSARY FOR HELEN, RAFF, NINA AND KENZIE (NINA'S LITTLE WESTIE). THE PEAK TO THE DISTANT RIGHT OF "ROGAN" IS MOUNT DUNGARVAN – THE MOST DIFFICULT SUMMER SCRAMBLE IN WATERTON.

HIGHWAY 774 (CASTLE CROWN)

The Castle Crown area, north of Waterton Lakes National Park, is home to the Castle Mountain Ski Resort. Not surprisingly, the area receives a large amount of snow, though often a few weeks later than parts of the Rockies farther north. Like Waterton, snowshoeing opportunities are minimal, though the adventurous snowshoer with avalanche training can find somewhere interesting to explore in almost any area. For the beginner, only two routes are described in this book.

ROUTE

THE EXCITING SOUTH RIDGE OF CARBONDALE HILL.

6 MOUNT BACKUS

(MAP 3, PAGE 480)

RATING	ADVANCED
MOUNTAIN HEIGHT	1810 M
TOTAL ELEVATION GAIN	495 M
ROUND-TRIP DISTANCE	5 KM
ROUND-TRIP TIME	3–5 HOURS
MAPS	82 G/8 BEAVER MINES

An ascent of Mount Backus is a great exercise in route-finding and trail-less travel. As such, it is a more challenging trip than nearby Carbondale Hill. The summit view is awesome on a clear day. Yet again, good timing is important to make an attempt. Sufficient snow coverage will make the trip far more rewarding. Bring trail-breaking friends if you make an early season attempt.

DIRECTIONS

From the Pincher Creek roundabout, turn west onto Highway 507 and drive to its end. Turn left onto Highway 774 and follow it for 10.1 km to a pullout on the south side of the road (1.5 km past the "Castle Special Management Area" sign). There is a gravel road going south from the pullout. Be careful not to block the entrance to it.

Cross the road, put on your snowshoes and snowshoe up to the barbed-wire fence and gate. Hop the barbed-wire fence to the left of the gate and follow alongside it in a northeasterly direction for about 30 m, paralleling another barbed-wire fence. Cut left before reaching the aspens and work your way to an open area, then continue north. Eventually you will arrive at the same fence you were paralleling for the 30 m. When this fence curves left, hop over it and continue northward.

ABOVE: THE START OF THE ROUTE. BELOW: FROM AN
OPEN AREA JUST BELOW THE HIGH POINT, THE REMAINDER
OF THE ROUTE IS VISIBLE. THERE ARE MANY OPTIONS
FROM HERE. AIM FOR OPEN AREAS. S=SUMMIT.

The goal now is to gain the high point in front of you, lose about 60 m of elevation and then ascend varied terrain to the summit. As stated, your route-finding abilities will be put to the test from here on out. The route to the top is fairly obvious, but finding the path of least resistance can be an interesting challenge. Aiming for large patches of open terrain is a good strategy. Note that you will encounter one more barbed-wire fence to climb over.

GPS users may want to use the following waypoints as guides.

1. GR970778, 1505 m, high point before losing elevation
2. GR975790, 1718 m, interesting viewpoint before the summit. You can gain the ridge, up a steep slope, to the west (left) here, or go more directly to the summit.
3. GR977795, 1810 m, Backus summit.

Depending on your route, you may encounter a few steeper slopes just before the summit. The summit view features an interesting combination of statuesque peaks to the west and prairie to the east. Mount Syncline, Mount Darrah and Crowsnest Mountain are particularly eye-catching.

Return the same way. Trying to avoid the elevation gain back to the high point by staying over to the west is self-defeating and not at all recommended.

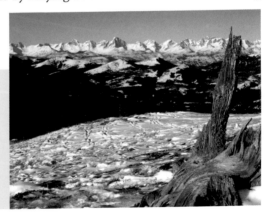

THE VIEW TO THE WEST FROM NEAR THE SUMMIT. MOUNT DARRAH IS THE PROMINENT PEAK JUST LEFT OF CENTRE.

7 CARBONDALE HILL

(MAP 3, PAGE 480)

DIFFICULTY	ADVANCED
MOUNTAIN HEIGHT	1800 M
ELEVATION GAIN	450 M
ROUND-TRIP DISTANCE	9–10 KM
ROUND-TRIP TIME	3–5 HOURS
MAP 82 G/08	BEAVER MINES

Though located at the east end of the Front Ranges, this modest peak provides comprehensive views of the surrounding area, which explains the strategic placement of the fire lookout at the summit. It is a great trip but does entail a significant amount of elevation gain. Take your snowshoes, even if the peak looks relatively dry. The trail to the lookout can hold deep snow, unseen from the trailhead.

DIRECTIONS

From Pincher Creek turn west onto Highway 507 and then turn left (south) onto Highway 774. Approximately 15 km west of the hamlet of Beaver Mines, turn right onto Range Road 3-0 (signed as the Lynx Creek turnoff). Drive 1.8 km to the gate (locked from December 15–May 1).

Snowshoe or hike for about 1 km to the Carbondale Hill trailhead on the west side of the road. It is unsigned but very obvious and has another closed gate to prevent motorized vehicle access. The trail (a fire road) starts going north and eventually swings around to the west, ascending at a gentle grade toward the south ridge of the hill.

About 45 minutes from your vehicle (longer if travel is slow), look for a small opening in the trees to your left. This opening

A CLOSE-UP OF THE SOUTH RIDGE OF CARBONDALE HILL.

grants a good view of Table Mountain and the peaks around the Castle Mountain Ski Resort, as well as an opportunity for a short break before the real work begins.

Resuming travel, you'll find the trail immediately turns northwest. Approximately 75 m from the aforementioned opening, more open slopes appear to your right. At this point you can either continue along the wide trail or head immediately to the south ridge. The south ridge route is recommended for the ascent, leaving the trail for descent. The ridge offers good views almost immediately and the tree cover is light throughout.

SOUTH RIDGE ROUTE

Leave the trail and ascend slopes to the right. This slope will be the steepest part of the trip and may require snowshoes with good crampons and heel lifts. It could also be completely wind-blown and free of snow. Upon reaching the ridge, turn north and simply follow it to the summit. Travel time along the ridge to the top can vary from 45 to 90 minutes, depending on snow conditions. There can be some decent cornice scenery higher up, along with some fairly significant drop-offs down the east face – keep your distance from the edge.

TRAIL ROUTE

Following the trail all the way to the summit is generally easy but long due to several large switchbacks, and views are limited until you get close to the top. Nevertheless, the trail route does offer an alternative to the ridge and is a pleasant affair.

The trail takes a long, ascending route up the west side of the mountain before it becomes a series of shorter, but still long, switchbacks to the summit. At one point the switchbacks reach

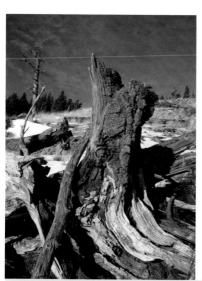

all the way to the end of the south ridge, where you may decide to follow the ridge to the summit instead. Either way, the route is very obvious.

THE SUMMIT

The top of Carbondale Hill is home to a fire lookout. As such, the summit view is very extensive in all directions. Particularly impressive are the peaks of

ONE OF THE UNEXPECTED BENEFITS OF LEAVING THE BEATEN PATH IS SOME COLOURFUL AND INTERESTING TREE SCENERY.

the Flathead Range to the west and those to the south around Mount Haig. The slightly higher hill to the east is Mount Back-us, and the prominent flat-looking peak to the southeast is aptly named Table Mountain.

For descent, the south ridge is definitely the fastest route. However, the trail is a flatter affair and has plenty of attractive features. A slight change in scenery is probably enough motivation to use this route, if you took the ridge route up. Through most of the year, the trail will be easy to follow even if you take the south ridge up. After a heavy snowfall, however, the switch-backs may not be so obvious. If this is the case, it is very important to find the main, southeast-trending section that leads back to the first opening. Missing this could mean many hours of tedious bushwhacking and side-sloping.

APPROACHING THE LOOKOUT FROM THE SOUTH RIDGE.
NOTE THE TRAIL AT THE LEFT IS STILL COMPLETELY
SNOW-COVERED. MY SNOWSHOES SAVED ME FROM SEVERAL
KILOMETRES OF INTENSE POSTHOLING ON DESCENT.

CROWSNEST PASS

The Crowsnest Pass area has a surprising amount of snow-shoeing potential, most of it being brought to my attention by Dave McMurray and his adventurous southern spirit! Dave has snowshoed, hiked or scrambled up pretty much everything in the area. Bob Spirko and Dinah Kruze have also completed a ton of interesting ascents in Crowsnest.

Unfortunately, access can be an issue in winter. Most of the backroads are not maintained. Thus when the snows comes, it sometimes stays for a very long time. Adanac (Canada, backwards!) Road is a classic example. In January of 2011, I drove my Honda Civic along an almost completely snow-free road to the trailhead of Hillcrest Mountain. Three attempts on the same road in January and February of 2016 were met with deep snow and/or sheer ice and I was forced to turn around. Only on a fourth attempt in mid-February was I able to negotiate the road back to that trailhead in my Civic (coincidentally I traded the Civic for a CR-V three days later!).

Nevertheless, there are a host of routes with less troublesome access issues and five are described here (Byron Hill and Poker are along Adanac Road). Ascents of all peaks are relatively straightforward but most will earn an Advanced rating because of high elevation gain, some steep terrain, and route-finding challenges.

Once again, the trick to enjoyable snowshoeing in this area of the province is to patiently wait until enough snow has accumulated to actually render them snowshoe ascents. Unfortunately, as fast as that snow builds, it can be picked up by the fierce southern Alberta winds and blown into Saskatchewan! Timing is everything down here.

For all ascents in the Crowsnest area it is strongly recommended that you bring your snowshoes, even if the route appears to be snow-free. Snow that doesn't make it into our neighbour province often builds up in deep pockets that may be unseen from the start of the trip, and summit ridges are often plastered in deep snow when the ascent slopes are clear. Unexpected postholing nightmares can be common for those who decide to leave their snowshoes in the car.

ROUTES

BEAUTIFUL CORNICE SCENERY ON "POKER PEAK." (DAVE MCMURRAY)

8 BYRON HILL

(MAP 4, PAGE 480)

RATING	ADVANCED
MOUNTAIN HEIGHT	1855 M
ELEVATION GAIN	510 M
ROUND-TRIP DISTANCE	8.1 KM
ROUND-TRIP TIME	3.5–5.5 HOURS
MAPS	82 G/9 BLAIRMORE

The first 20 minutes of this trip are brutal and can be very challenging. However, after that it's an easy trek up an old road to an outstanding summit panorama. Unfortunately, the very steep 70-m descent to Byron Creek near the beginning push this trip far into the advanced category. If snowshoeing or hiking down very steep terrain is not your cup of tea, pick another objective. "Poker Peak" (see page 107) is a perfect alternative, if you can drive to the trailhead.

DIRECTIONS

Driving west on Highway 3, turn left onto East Hillcrest Drive (1.2 km west of the Leitch Collieries). Drive 2.1 km on East Hillcrest Drive and take a very sharp left onto Adanac Road. Only the first kilometre of Adanac Road is maintained. Be prepared to park at the "No Winter Maintenance Beyond this Point" sign and walk the approach. It will add 1.2 km to each end of the trip. If the road is driveable, continue up for 1.2 km (from the sign) and park where the road takes a sharp turn to the right. There is lots of space to find a parking spot here.

The summit of Byron Hill is not visible from the road, but the general ascent route is (see photo). From the parking area

LOOKING DOWN TO BYRON CREEK, WITH THE OPEN AREA TO AIM
FOR ON THE OTHER SIDE AND TO THE LEFT. (DAVE MCMURRAY)

snowshoe or walk south, down through the obvious clearing to a point overlooking Byron Creek, far down below. Ignore the ATV trails. Be sure to pick out the obvious open area on the other side of the creek. This is the key to the trip.

Descend to the creek. Choose your line carefully and proceed slowly. It is very steep and can be unnerving if you take anything but the least steep route. Once at the bottom, cross the creek and make your way toward the open area, crossing a smaller creek along the way. This section can be challenging, as it is choked with deadfall. Again, go slowly and carefully. Your perseverance will soon be rewarded.

At the open area, slog your way up a steep slope to more gentle terrain above. Follow the obvious open line through the trees, eventually intersecting an old road. It is now simply a matter of following that road all the way to the summit of Byron Hill.

Several kilometres along, around GR922890, there is the option to leave the road and gain the northwest ridge. This point is fairly obvious, as another road appears to come in from the left and there is an open line through the trees, directly to the ridge. Right before you reach it, you will have curved left and ascended a noticeably steeper section of the road. This route has the advantage of revealing some of the terrific views a little earlier in the trip and is a pleasant affair in itself. Once on the ridge, turn right (south) and follow it to a small col where you will meet up with the road.

If you decided to stay on the road, it makes its way to the same col and your first view of the true summit of Byron Hill, lying farther to the east than you might have thought. The road continues, heading into the trees and traversing the northeast side of the minor bump to the south, eventually bringing you to another col, due west of the summit. The summit is quickly reached after that.

ABOVE: THE BIG ADVANTAGE OF GAINING THE NORTHWEST RIDGE RIGHT AWAY IS VIEWS LIKE THIS. (DAVE MCMURRAY) BELOW: JEFF LANG ENJOYS THE TERRIFIC VIEW TO THE NORTHWEST. HILLCREST MOUNTAIN IN THE CENTRE, TURTLE MOUNTAIN TO THE RIGHT AND MOUNTAINS OF THE FLATHEAD RANGE TO THE LEFT. (DAVE MCMURRAY)

Purely as a scenic diversion, the minor bump to the south can be ascended as opposed to following the road from the first col. From the top of the bump, descend to the next col to the east and then up to the summit of Byron Hill.

The summit view, on a clear day, is going to be spectacular, regardless of which route got you to the top. If the unique mountains of the north end of the Castle area to the south don't impress you, the striking ones of the Flathead Range to the west certainly should. And in complete contrast to those views you can look to the east to the more or less flat prairies, hosting a field of wind turbines.

Return the same way. If you did ascend the minor bump and used the northwest ridge diversion, sticking to the road throughout the descent will be the fastest route back.

9 "POKER PEAK"

(MAP 4, PAGE 480)

RATING	ADVANCED
MOUNTAIN HEIGHT	1944 M
ELEVATION GAIN	395 M FOR ROUTE A, 333 M FOR ROUTE B, 270 M FOR ROUTE C, 670 M IF YOU HIKE THE ENTIRE APPROACH
ROUND-TRIP DISTANCE	6 KM FOR ROUTE A, 4 KM FOR ROUTE B, 1.2 KM FOR ROUTE C, 16.4 KM IF YOU HIKE THE ENTIRE APPROACH
ROUND-TRIP TIME	2–6 HOURS DEPENDING ON ROUTE
MAPS	82 G/9 BLAIRMORE, G/8 BEAVER MINES

The crux of an ascent of unofficial "Poker Peak" is getting to the trailhead (unless you walk the approach road). The reward is a fun ascent up interesting terrain, an easy and scenic ridgewalk to the summit and an unbelievable view from the top that is one of the best of any peak in the Crowsnest area. Wait for a bluebird day. If the road is not driveable, Byron Hill makes an excellent alternative. Microspikes are a good idea if you intend to hike all or any portion of the road.

DIRECTIONS

Driving west on Highway 3, turn left onto East Hillcrest Drive (1.2 km west of the Leitch Collieries). Drive 2.1 km on East Hillcrest Drive and take a very sharp left onto Adanac Road. Only the first kilometre of Adanac Road is maintained. Be prepared to park at the "No Winter Maintenance Beyond this Point" sign and walk the approach. For "Poker Peak," that means an extra 5 km of waking each way. Byron Hill (see page 102) makes a great alternative if you cannot drive farther than the sign.

If the road is driveable there are three logical places from which to start the ascent. Route B is recommended if you can drive all the way to a starting point. Route A is recommended if you have to walk all or any part of the approach road. Route C is only recommended as a steep hike when all the snow in the area has completely melted.

Route A. From the "No Winter Maintenance..." sign, drive 5 km along the road and park off to the side. If you are hiking, this point lies at GR884879. You are now at the base of the far northwest end of "Poker Peak." The ascent route lies at the right side of the hill on the east side of the road (see photo). There is some deadfall and tedious terrain to contend with to get to open slopes, but once you are on them it is smooth sailing all the way up to the north end of the peak. There is some steep terrain where you'll want to put your heel lifts up.

Once you reach the ridge, turn right (south) and follow it over undulating terrain to the summit. Views and the ridgewalk are fantastic throughout and you may be treated to some terrific cornice scenery en route. See **Summit** etc. on page 112 for descriptions of the view from the top and an optional descent route. Returning the same way is of course an option and may be best if you want to take in the scenery again and/or if weather conditions improve.

Route B. From the "No Winter Maintenance..." sign, drive 5.7 km along the road and park off to the side. If you are hiking, this point lies at GR884872. You are now approximately midway between the north end of "Poker Peak" and its summit.

A drainage divides two sub-peaks of the mountain. Following the drainage up to the ridge is the safest route to travel. Persevere through the difficulties at the beginning (deadfall, unsupportive

ABOVE: THE START OF ASCENT ROUTE A. (DAVE MCMURRAY)
BELOW: THE APPROXIMATE PATH FOR ROUTE B.

FROM THE MINOR BUMP NORTH OF THE SUMMIT, THE TRUE
SUMMIT AND REMAINDER OF THE ROUTE IS VISIBLE. HOPE
YOU BROUGHT YOUR SNOWSHOES! (DAVE McMURRAY)

snow, etc.), as easier terrain is soon to be found. You don't have
to be right in the drainage. Pick the path of least resistance,
which will probably be on the left side of the drainage.

Perhaps the most interesting feature of this route is the new
growth emerging from the devastating results of the 2003 Lost
Creek fire. The stark contrast of old and new is quite beautiful.

You will cross an old logging road eventually and you can travel it for a while. The road soon disappears around the west side
of the mountain and is not worth following. Keep going, more or
less up the drainage, between the two peaks. If the slopes on the
peak to your left are snow-free and you want to gain the upper
ridge as fast as possible, cut to the left and make your way up

THE OBVIOUS ROUTE FOR ROUTE C. S=SUMMIT.

steeper terrain directly to the ridge. Otherwise, stay the course, eventually reaching a small col.

Turn right (south) and gain a minor bump north of "Poker Peak's" true summit. The view from this point is awesome on a clear day. The true summit, to the south, is obvious and easy to reach. Hopefully a few cornices along the way will add to the already terrific scenery. See **Summit** etc. on next page for a summit view description and an optional descent route. Returning the same way is, of course, an option and may be best if you want to take in the scenery again and/or if weather conditions improve.

Route C. During the winter and early spring, it is highly unlikely the road will be snow-free all the way to this starting point. But if it is, the climb will probably be a steep hike and not a snowshoe ascent. Nevertheless, this starting point offers the most direct and shortest route to the summit, with only 270 m of elevation gain. A decent pace can get you up and down the mountain in about 1 hour.

From the "No Winter Maintenance..." sign, drive approximately 7.5 km along the road to a large sign reading "Castle Special Management Area" and park off to the side, just past the barbed-wire fence (GR885860). This puts you at a point due west of the summit of "Poker Peak."

The route is obvious and easy, though steep throughout. Follow the barbed-wire fence up and east. When the fence ends, keep going up, staying on the ridge. Note the interesting juxtaposition of healthy, undamaged trees on the right side of the ridge and the victims of the 2003 fire on the left side. Follow your nose to the summit. The final trudge is particularly steep. Enjoy the magnificent view and then return the same way.

Summit and optional descent route. The number of mountains clearly visible from this viewpoint is staggering. Especially interesting is the fact that both the Crowsnest and Castle areas are featured. Due west lie some of the more statuesque peaks of the Flathead Range, including striking Mount Darrah. To the south the three summits of Syncline Mountain are close at hand, with Mount Haig towering behind. You can also see the entire north end of the Castle area, from Mount McCarthy to Prairie Bluff. Foothills and prairies to the east and the south end of the Livingstone Range to the north complete the view. And of course don't forget "Poker Peak's" nearest companions, Hillcrest Mountain and famous Turtle Mountain to the northwest. Continuing to follow the ridge to the south leads to much lower Maverick Hill.

For all routes you can return the same way or go down the

west slopes and then hike the road back to your vehicle. This optional descent is remarkably fast, at least to get down to the road. Head down the west side of the mountain, trending a little to the right. It's steepest right near the beginning. You'll soon realize you are on a wide ridge, with old, live trees on the south side and dead, burnt ones on the north side. Stay on the ridge, eventually finding a barbed-wire fence that goes all the way to the road. Follow the fence on its left (south) side to the road. With decent travel conditions this part of the descent will take a mere 15–20 minutes.

Upon reaching the road, turn right (north) and follow it, first around a dramatic hairpin loop to the west and then more or less in a straight line north and northeast back to where your vehicle sits.

10 SASKATOON MOUNTAIN

(MAP 5, PAGE 480)

RATING ADVANCED	
MOUNTAIN HEIGHT 1823 M	
ELEVATION GAIN 490 M	
ROUND-TRIP DISTANCE 7.7 KM	
ROUND-TRIP TIME 3.5–5.5 HOURS	
MAPS 82 G/10 CROWSNEST, G/9 BLAIRMORE	

Saskatoon Mountain has a little of everything: a pleasant and scenic approach, some route-finding, steep terrain alternating with gentle terrain, cool rock scenery and great views. The steep sections and lack of a definitive trail definitely push the ascent into the advanced category.

DIRECTIONS

Drive west on Highway 3 to the west end of Coleman, looking for signs to Miners Path. Turn right at the sign, then another immediate right and, shortly after, left into the parking lot. The Nez Perce Creek trail is very pleasant and easy to follow. It quickly crosses to the east side of the creek and then parallels the creek, going north. Ignore the second bridge and keep going north to a set of stairs on the right side of the trail. A small but scenic waterfall is worth a look here.

Ascend the stairs and turn left at the top. Take the right fork when the trail splits about 50 m along. Within minutes you'll see the south end of Saskatoon Mountain and approximate route up.

THE END OF THE SOUTH RIDGE. AIM FOR THE
RIGHT SIDE. SS=STEEP SLOPES.

There are trails heading in multiple directions, but the best route
is a direct one, toward the high point. There are a couple of wire
fences to climb over or go through on the way up. The second
fence lies at GR801025 and has a gap through it.

The terrain starts to steepen beyond the fence. Head toward
the top, but also start going more to the right to avoid the steepest slopes. Regardless of your route, you will still have to tackle
steep slopes. The goal now is to go around the prominent rock-
bands at the end of the ridge and gain the ridge just north of
the rock. The lichen-covered rock is quite beautiful close-up, if
you wish to detour in that direction. Note that these slopes are
very steep and there may even be some avalanche potential in
extreme conditions.

ON THE RIDGE, LOOKING TOWARD THE FIRST SUMMIT.
THE SMALL ELEVATION LOSS, WHERE YOU GO FAR TO
THE RIGHT, IS CLOSE. 1S=FIRST SUMMIT.

Once you have worked your way up to the ridge, simply follow it north, enjoying improving views to the south and west. The first summit eventually makes an appearance, but you must lose a little elevation first. Swing way around to the right as you descend, to avoid losing unnecessary elevation. Then head up, toward the obvious continuation of the ridge. Another fence must be hopped over.

The first summit is marked with a large cairn at GR804037, 1790 m. It's not the highest point of the mountain, but the views are as good as those seen from the true summit. Many will choose to make this the end of the line. Views of Crowsnest Mountain,

SOME OF THE COOL WINTER SCENERY ON THE RIDGE.
MOUNT TECUMSEH IN THE BACKGROUND.

Mount Tecumseh, and Turtle Mountain are very rewarding. Return the same way if you have had enough.

If you want to reach the true summit, continue travelling north and slightly east, through lightly treed terrain and then more open terrain. The cairnless and partially treed summit is quickly reached at approximately GR807043, 1823 m. The view is similar to that seen from the first summit. Return the same way.

11 "THE SADDLE" ("STAR CREEK HILL")

(MAP 5, PAGE 480)

RATING	ADVANCED
MOUNTAIN HEIGHT	1807 M
TOTAL ELEVATION GAIN	735 M
ROUND-TRIP DISTANCE	9.6 KM
ROUND-TRIP TIME	4.5–6.5 HOURS
MAPS	82 G/10 CROWSNEST

Another terrific little trip that you'll want to save for a clear day. Views of the entire Crowsnest area are great from the summit and it's a fun ride to get there. A few necessary elevation losses and regains increase the total elevation gain for the day, but they are required in order to experience the most enjoyable route to the summit. Locals refer to this unofficial mountain as both "The Saddle" and "Star Creek Hill."

DIRECTIONS

Drive west through Coleman and turn left at the "Coleman West Access" sign. Turn right onto 70 St. and right again onto 17 Ave. In 400 m the road veers off to the left. Turn right onto 16 Ave. and drive 1.7 km to the corner of 16 Ave. and 54 St. Park off to the side of the road here or turn left onto 54 St. and drive a short distance up the road and park off to the side before a small hill.

Hike or snowshoe up the road and hill to a large cutline running east–west. Turn left (east) and descend the cutline to Star

Creek. Cross the creek and start up the other side, staying to the right side. A short distance up, a trail veers off to the right into the trees. This is the unsigned Star Falls Viewpoint trail. Follow the trail up, as it gains elevation above Star Creek. The trail gets very icy so snowshoes or Microspikes will work well.

Eventually you will see Star Falls quite a distance below. It may be fully frozen, not frozen at all, or in a state between. Regardless, it's a beautiful little ice/waterfall and very pleasant start to the trip. Continue past the viewpoint. There are several trails that lead in various directions. You will want to keep going slightly up and in a southeasterly direction. The goal is to gain the north summit before continuing on to the south summit.

More than likely you will have to leave any trail and start through the trees more directly up. The forest here is light and easy to negotiate. Keep going up and southeast, aiming for open areas where the great views of the Flathead Range and Mount Tecumseh will be revealed. Slog your way up to the north summit at GR786992, 1709 m. With easy travel conditions expect to take 1.25–1.75 hours from car to this summit – much more if you experience tough trail-breaking conditions.

The view from the north summit is outstanding, featuring Crowsnest Mountain and Mount Tecumseh to the north and northwest respectively and a number of the striking peaks of the Flathead Range (Coulthard, Andy Good, Parrish, McLaren, Chinook and Sentry) to the southwest. In fact, calling it a day here and returning the same way may be enough for many. The view from the true summit is slightly different but not significantly better. However, the trip there is only about a kilometre and, if nothing else, is worth it for the extra exercise and an optional descent route.

For those continuing on to the true summit, getting off the north summit is not the pushover you may think. A steep

ABOVE: From the top of the hill, the descent to Star Creek, the turnoff to Star Creek Falls and northern summit are all clearly visible. NS=northern summit. (Dave McMurray) BELOW: You don't need a maximum of two legs and a social insurance number to enjoy the beauty of the mountains. This super-friendly dog followed me all the way to the summit and down the alternative descent route. Best company ever!

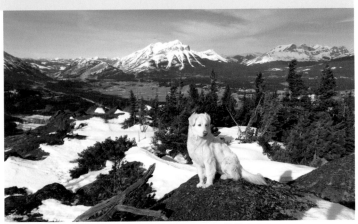

rockband lines the south face, requiring you to go way over to the left (east) to get down and around it. The terrain here is quite steep. Continue going south up to the next high point at GR791984, which probably sports the best view of the day. The goal for the day is a little farther on at GR794981, 1807 m. The highest point of the mountain (marginally) actually lies farther south but is treed and not worth the effort. Enjoy the view and then return the same way or take the recommended optional descent route, down the west side of the mountain and then back to the starting point via ATV/snowmobile trails.

The first part of the optional descent route is easy. From the summit you should be able to see an obvious ATV/snowmobile trail running south–north, at the base of "The Saddle" on the west side. Go down the west-facing slopes and route-find your way down to the ATV trail. Turn right (north) and off you go.

The second part is not as straightforward as the first, but still relatively easy. There are a maze of ATV/snowmobile trails here. You basically have to follow your nose north back to the starting area. There are many routes you can take that will lead you home. I followed the main trail over a small creek, eventually reaching an "Unsafe Bridge." I crossed the creek and then took a right turn shortly after. The route from then on was pretty obvious and I exited the forest only a few hundred metres from where I entered on the way to the Star Falls viewpoint.

12 WEDGE MOUNTAIN TRAIL

(MAP 5, PAGE 480)

RATING	EASY
ELEVATION GAIN	270 M
ROUND-TRIP DISTANCE	4 KM
ROUND-TRIP TIME	1-1.5 HOURS
MAPS	82 G/10 CROWSNEST

This easy little jaunt along the east side of Wedge Mountain grants good views of the impressive peaks of the north end of the Flathead Range, as well as the famous Turtle Mountain. From the high point of the trail, there is the option to ascend Wedge Mountain – a considerably more challenging undertaking.

DIRECTIONS

Drive west on Highway 3 to the west end of Coleman and turn right onto 61st (signed as the "McGillivray Staging" area). Immediately there is a somewhat convoluted intersection. Take the 23 Ave. fork, going up, and drive about 2.9 km to a large open area right under the southwest ridge of Wedge Mountain (you can check out the condition of the mountain on the drive in [see photo]). Park here and look for an obvious cutline where the powerlines are, running east–west.

Snowshoe or hike the cutline, going east, crossing a small bridge and a cattle guard and eventually turning northeast. The goal is to reach the high point of the trail around GR791046, 1745 m. A healthy amount of elevation gain means you'll get a decent workout along the way. While catching your breath you

ABOVE: THE SOUTHEAST FACE OF WEDGE MOUNTAIN FROM
THE DRIVE IN. WEDGE MOUNTAIN TRAIL GOES FROM LEFT
TO RIGHT, AT THE BASE OF THE PEAK. (DAVE MCMURRAY)
BELOW: CROWSNEST MOUNTAIN AND THE CROSS LOOK
TERRIFIC FROM THE SUMMIT. (DAVE MCMURRAY)

can always turn around to see the improving views of mounts Coulthard, McLaren, Parrish, Andy Good and Chinook Peak.

An open clearing marks the high point. It is worth going over to the north end, where you'll see the steep, downhill continuation of the trail and the south end of the Livingstone Range.

Return the same way or take up the challenge of an ascent of Wedge Mountain via the northeast side as described below.

WEDGE MOUNTAIN (NORTHEAST SIDE)

From the clearing, it's 190 m of elevation gain in approximately 1 km of horizontal distance to the summit of Wedge Mountain. There is one section of steep snowshoeing and a section near the summit that is more scrambling than snowshoeing. This is definitely an advanced route.

A trail does take you most of the way up if you can find it. The start, on the left (west) side of the clearing, is marked with orange flagging (GR791046). The trail winds up the mountain in a northerly direction initially. A short, but much steeper section is quickly reached and then the trail resumes at a much gentler grade. When the trail turns sharply to the right, it's time to leave it and make your way up and to the left, in order to gain the northeast ridge.

Once on the ridge follow it in a southwesterly direction toward the summit. A trail helps avoid most of the bushwhacking. Just before the summit, the terrain steepens considerably. Depending on snow conditions this will be a very steep snowshoe or an easy scramble. The summit is only a short distance away once above the steep section. You will have to continue south along the ridge for about 50 m to arrive at the summit cairn and a large wooden cross (GR786047, 1934 m).

Most will agree the summit panorama is a real bargain for the effort required to get there. The main attraction is the east side of magnificent Crowsnest Mountain, with the serrated Seven Sisters immediately north of Crowsnest. Mount Tecumseh, due west, also stands out.

For descent either return the way you came or take a shorter, more direct route down the south ridge. The south ridge is generally straightforward, but the last part of the descent is steep and will require careful route-finding to locate the line of least resistance. Consider it to be a graduation requirement before moving on to the more challenging routes in *Snowshoeing in the Canadian Rockies, 2nd Edition*!

The route goes basically as follows. Snowshoe south, down the ridge, until you arrive at the point close to but high above the parking area. Here the slopes get much steeper and you'll want to be cautious about your specific route if there exists the possibility of an unstable snowpack. If you get cliffed out, veer over to the left and find easier terrain back down to the trail. Hopefully you'll intersect the trail just east of the cattle guard, where it's a short distance back to your vehicle.

13 WEDGE MOUNTAIN (SOUTH RIDGE)

(MAP 5, PAGE 480)

RATING ADVANCED	
MOUNTAIN HEIGHT 1934 M	
ELEVATION GAIN 460 M	
ROUND-TRIP DISTANCE 3.6–4.8 KM	
ROUND-TRIP TIME 2.5–4 HOURS	
MAPS 82 G/10 CROWSNEST	

This is definitely one of the most difficult routes in this book. The steepness of the initial part of the route and the fact that there is sometimes not enough snow to snowshoe that section can add considerable challenge. However, the ascent, along with Island Ridge, is also one of the better "bangs for your buck" in the west Crowsnest area. From car to summit is less than 2 km of horizontal distance, with only 460 m of elevation gain. Views are satisfying throughout, especially of nearby Crowsnest Mountain. The south ridge offers the quickest route to the summit but a loop route is possible for those craving some extra excitement and exercise.

DIRECTIONS

Drive west on Highway 3 to the west end of Coleman and turn right onto 61 St. (signed as the "McGillivray Staging" area). Immediately there is a somewhat convoluted intersection. Take the 23 Ave. fork, going up, and drive about 2.9 km to a large open area, right under the southwest ridge of Wedge Mountain. Park here and look for an obvious cutline where the powerlines are,

ABOVE: Typical terrain on the south ridge — a combination of treed and open slopes. (Dave McMurray) BELOW: Dave McMurray manages to capture himself, The Cross and Crowsnest Mountain in a terrific selfie. (Dave McMurray)

running east–west. Check out snow conditions on the drive in (see photo in previous trip).

The goal is to gain the end of the south ridge and then follow the ridge north to the summit. Hike or snowshoe east along the cutline, across a small bridge and over a cattle guard. The steepest part of the ascent occurs next. Turn left (north) after the cattle guard and route-find your way to the end of the south ridge, through treed and open terrain. There are some fairly steep slopes here, where heel lifts and snowshoe crampons will be appreciated – provided there is enough snow. There is a trail that will be obvious if the slopes are snow-free.

Reaching the south end of the ridge is a double blessing: the views start to open up in most directions and the ascent continues at a much gentler grade. Follow the ridge north to the summit. It does get a little steeper near the summit, but nothing too nail-biting! The summit is marked by a cairn and a large wooden cross (as of late 2015). Views of Crowsnest Mountain are excellent, as are those of the Flathead Range to the south. Continue north along the ridge for about 50 m to fully take in the panorama.

The easiest way back is to retrace your steps down the south ridge. It's a fast and almost effortless descent with the right snow conditions.

LOOP ROUTE

The Loop Route descends the northeast side of the mountain and then follows a wide trail back to the parking area. It is not a faster way down but provides some variety and slightly different views.

From the summit cairn (Cross) continue going north for a short distance and then drop down the rockband on the northeast side of the ridge. This is the toughest part of the route. A narrow trail winds its way down but will be hard to follow if snow-covered. This section will probably feel more like winter scrambling than snowshoeing, and you may have to remove your snowshoes.

Once below the rockband, keep going down and northeast, looking to your right (southeast) to the open clearing and trail below. When it becomes obvious, turn southeast and make your way down to the clearing. There will be a few small steep sections. The clearing marks the high point of the trail on the east side of Wedge Mountain. Take in the interesting views to the north, east and south and then follow the wide trail southwest and around the mountain, back to the parking area.

14 ISLAND RIDGE

(MAP 6, PAGE 481)

RATING	ADVANCED
MOUNTAIN HEIGHT	1813 M
ELEVATION GAIN	440 M
ROUND-TRIP DISTANCE	8.4 KM
ROUND-TRIP TIME	3–5 HOURS
MAPS	82 G/10 CROWSNEST

Another awesome little trip, brought to my attention by Dave McMurray. An easy approach, straightforward, though at times steep, ascent, and fantastic views from the top make this one of my favourite trips in the southern Rockies. Deciding where to park may be the crux of the trip!

DIRECTIONS

Drive west past Coleman. The visitor centre is soon passed on the left (south) side of the road. About 4.5 km farther (1.3 km west of the roadside turnout at Crowsnest Lake), turn left onto unsigned Coal Road.

There are three logical places to park, depending on snow conditions on the gravel road and how comfortable you feel negotiating the road if it's snowy and/or icy: 1. Right at the turnoff. This is the safest spot – no fear of getting stuck; 2. If the road is generally snow-free or completely packed down, there is a large staging area about 480 m along the road; 3. If the road is completely snow-free and you are positive your vehicle won't get stuck, you can drive about 3 km along the road, to the unsigned Ptolemy Creek trailhead, at GR673970. This option means your roundtrip time for the trip may be closer to 1.5 hours. Personally I recommend option 1. The 6 km of easy walking option 1 adds to the trip is a small price to pay for the peace of mind of eliminating any possibility of getting your vehicle stuck in the snow.

Assuming you picked option 1, hike, Microspike or snowshoe about 3 km to the unsigned Ptolemy Creek trailhead, at GR673970. Island Ridge is on the right side throughout. Go about 50 m farther to a clearing on the right (north) side of the road (see photo). This is where you leave the road (going northwest), to route-find your way onto the south ridge and then up to the summit. There is a trail if you trend to the left as you go up. The lower slopes are fairly steep but nothing outrageous. Sentry Mountain and the peaks around Ptolemy Creek are there to keep you company.

Once you are satisfied you are on the ridge (it's a very wide ridge!), simply go up. The widely spaced trees mean that bushwhacking will not be an issue. The views really start to open up as you near treeline and include the distant but very distinctive

THE CLEARING WHERE YOU LEAVE THE ROAD AND THE APPROXIMATE ROUTE UP. (DAVE MCMURRAY)

form of Mount Washburn to the west. Just before you hit the summit, Crowsnest Mountain and Mount Tecumseh both make a triumphant appearance. Mount Erickson, stretching out to the north, and Crowsnest Lake complete the vista once you reach the spacious summit at GR673980, 1813 m. Return the same way.

THE VIEW TO THE SOUTH FROM NEAR THE SUMMIT. TENT
MOUNTAIN IS TO THE RIGHT, WITH THE NORTHWEST OUTLIERS
OF MOUNT PTOLEMY TO THE LEFT. (DAVE MCMURRAY)

HIGHWAY 541

Highway 541 is the south section of Highway 40. It starts at Longview and then runs west for about 45 km to a closed gate, just beyond the Highway 940 turnoff. Because this is a front range area, peaks and routes can be snow-free during any month of the year, or they can be absolutely plastered in snow. As a result, snowshoes may not be necessary for the four trips that follow. It's always a good idea to take them anyway.

This area may also be subject to clearer skies when cloudy conditions persist to the west.

ROUTES

WIND-RAVAGED TREES DOMINATE THE
SCENERY ON BULL CREEK HILLS.

15 BULL CREEK HILLS

(MAP 7, PAGE 481)

DIFFICULTY ADVANCED

ELEVATION GAIN 750 M

ROUND-TRIP DISTANCE 8–12 KM

ROUND-TRIP TIME 6–9 HOURS

MAPS 82 J/07 MOUNT HEAD,
GEM TREK HIGHWOOD AND CATARACT CREEK

These hills make for a great day out at any time of the year. The area is subject to very high winds, so watch for wind-loaded slopes and retreat if the winds are too strong. Violent gusts have been known to knock people off their feet! There are many routes to the summit, including ones via Grass Pass, Fir Creek and slopes near Marston Creek. Described below is the ascent near Marston Creek. Also note the huge elevation gain for this trip.

DIRECTIONS

From Longview, drive about 35 km west on Highway 541 and park just off the road at the Highwood Provincial Recreation Area parking lot.

Cross the road and start heading north. There is a trail but snow cover may make it difficult to locate. A small outlier is located to the right, and you'll want to be west of it. Ascend gentle terrain past this outlier. A barbed-wire fence will let you know if you've strayed too far east. Eventually the first major high point becomes visible, and the summit is in the background to the left of it. Make your way across open meadows toward the high point,

ABOVE: THE WIND-BLASTED SLOPES OF BULL CREEK
HILLS, AS SEEN FROM NEAR THE BEGINNING OF THE
TRIP. FH=FIRST HIGH POINT. S=SUMMIT. BELOW: A
VERY WINDY AUTUMN DAY AT BULL CREEK HILLS.

quickly arriving at a stand of trees. At this point, the trail swings sharply to the right and down before resuming its northward trend. Cross Marston Creek and emerge from the trees, again heading north. Ascend another hill, at which point the main ascent slope will become visible.

Once you're on the correct ascent slope, directions are unnecessary. Simply follow the terrain up to the first high point. From there the wide ridge descends a little, curving around to the west. Follow the ridge to the highest point of Bull Creek Hills, at 2179 m.

To descend, either return the same way or complete a loop route via Grass Pass. The Fir Creek descent is not recommended, due to avalanche concerns. Note that the Grass Pass descent makes for a very long day, and most parties will choose to return the way they came.

Grass Pass Descent

Continue west from the summit down to the next high point, about 500 m away. The high point farther west of this one is also easily reached. The trail now swings around to the southwest, descending gentle slopes toward Grass Pass. Expect the trail to be covered by snow and therefore not obvious. Some careful route-finding may be necessary. At the last high point of the day, the trail turns west and drops down to Grass Pass at GR714875. Another good trail, 3.2 km in length, goes south to the highway. From the Grass Pass trailhead, it's a 3-km hike along the road back to your vehicle.

16 GRASS PASS

(MAP 7, PAGE 481)

DIFFICULTY INTERMEDIATE FOR GRASS PASS; ADVANCED FOR THE EXTENSIONS	
ELEVATION GAIN 425 M FOR GRASS PASS; ADD 75–150 M FOR THE EXTENSIONS	
ROUND-TRIP DISTANCE 6.4–8 KM	
ROUND-TRIP TIME 2–4.5 HOURS	
MAPS 82 J/07 MOUNT HEAD, GEM TREK HIGHWOOD AND CATARACT CREEK	

The Grass Pass route can be snowshoed as a trip unto itself, or you can complete it at the beginning or end of the Bull Creek Hills trip. If you choose to tackle Grass Pass in conjunction with Bull Creek Hills, be prepared for a lengthy day with a healthy dose of elevation gain. Probably best to do the trips separately. The Grass Pass route has two worthwhile extensions that make for a very satisfying day out. Due to its easterly location, attempting the route right after a major snowfall is perhaps the best way to ensure you need your snowshoes! Although the elevation gain to Grass Pass is significant, travel is easy and therefore the trip is rated as intermediate.

DIRECTIONS

From Highway 22 at Longview, turn west onto Highway 541 and drive about 38 km to the Sentinel parking lot. The lot will be closed, but there should be some room to park near the gate. Do not block the gate.

Hike back along the road for about 300 m to the unsigned start of the trail, which is on the north side of the road, near the Sentinel sign (see photo).

THE START OF THE GRASS PASS TRAIL.

Once you find the trail, the route to the pass is obvious and foolproof. Follow the old road north, with ridges on either side, for 3.2 km to the pass. The first 2 km are in the trees, but near treeline the views to the pass are very pleasant, especially when snow covers the surrounding slopes. Sections of the trail, especially low down, are quite rocky, so watch your footing. Even when you're wearing snowshoes the terrain can be somewhat precarious. It's best to take it slow and steady all the way up and down.

Reaching the pass, you may find the views somewhat disappointing. That is, until you ascend slopes to the east, where the vista will open up almost immediately. You will only need to go up a short distance to be treated to great views of the southeast sides of Holy Cross Mountain, Mount Head and the Wileman Creek valley. To the south lies the long ridge of Mount Burke, with its former lookout atop the distant summit.

Return the way you came in. Again, unless the snow cover is deep and supportive, use care going down the rocky trail.

EXTENSION TO "BOUNDARY PINE" RIDGE

"Boundary Pine" Ridge lies east and southeast of Grass Pass and, in my opinion, represents the best way to extend your day without "killing" yourself to achieve the ambitious objective of Bull Creek Hills. There are two routes to the ridge.

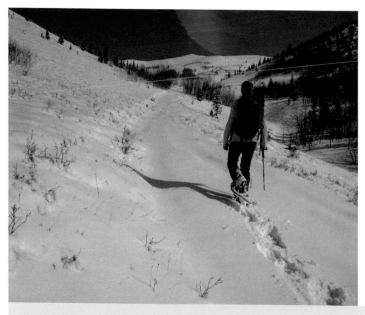

PLEASANT TERRAIN AND SNOW SCENERY NEAR TREELINE ON THE GRASS PASS ROUTE.

Directions

The easiest route is a direct, side-sloping traverse from Grass Pass, heading southeast across slopes to the obvious ridge. However, if these slopes are loaded with snow this may not be the safest option. An avalanche is very unlikely, but there's no sense tempting fate.

Using the safest route also means gaining a little extra elevation, but that just delivers more great views! Heading upslope in an east–northeasterly direction, gain about 70 m to the high point that then leads directly down to the ridge to the south.

For both routes, once you are on the ridge, follow it south and enjoy the excellent views of the statuesque peaks of the High Rock Range to the southwest. The famous Boundary Pine is quickly reached. Continue on for another 500 m or so to the open area at the south end of the ridge. Enjoy the view and then return the same way. Do not be tempted to follow this ridge back down to the road – it is heavily treed and gets very steep.

Extension to the West Ridge

The views from this ridge are much better than what you will see at Grass Pass, but a little inferior to those of Boundary Pine Ridge. Nevertheless, this is a fun extension that will bring your elevation gain to a healthy (and tiring) 500 m.

Directions

Snowshoe up increasingly steep slopes west of Grass Pass. Upon reaching the first high point, curve around to the southwest on more level terrain and then up the final slope to the summit. The last stretch of terrain is quite steep and could present an avalanche concern. To avoid this, stay to the right and ascend through the trees. There are two cairns at the summit, separated by about 100 m. The prominent peak right in front of you to the southwest is a southern outlier of Holy Cross Mountain, but it has gained the unofficial name "Gunnery Mountain," due to its proximity to Gunnery Creek. Return the same way. During the summer months it is possible to follow the ridge south, back to the road. However, because it is quite steep and also because of avalanche concerns, this route is NOT recommended as a winter snowshoe route.

Extension to Bull Creek Hills

This extension is classified as a very advanced beginner snowshoe trip because of its length, overall elevation gain and the possible need for route-finding. A trail does go all the way to the summit, but it may be snow-covered and difficult to find and follow in the winter. In general, the route goes northeast to a few high points and then heads east to the summit. A slightly shorter and easier route goes via Marston Creek and is described beginning at page 134.

Directions

From Grass Pass, snowshoe northeast up to the obvious high point. The trail (route) then turns in a more northerly direction for about 1 km before swinging around to the east and another high point. From this high point, turn east and follow the ridge down and up to another high point and then on to the summit. Return the same way you came.

17 HELL'S RIDGE (NORTH END)

(MAP 7, PAGE 481)

> RATING ADVANCED
> MOUNTAIN HEIGHT 1915 M
> ELEVATION GAIN 400 M
> ROUND-TRIP DISTANCE 6.7–7.7 KM
> ROUND-TRIP TIME 3.5–5 HOURS
> MAPS 82 J/7 MOUNT HEAD, GEM TREK HIGHWOOD
> AND CATARACT CREEK

Lengthy Hell's Ridge stretches about 9 km alongside Highway 940. Most of the ridge is treed, but the north end offers some open terrain and an almost completely open summit where you can take in the view. There is no trail to the summit so expect some route-finding. This is another good trip for the high-level beginner snowshoer to get a taste for more advanced trips.

DIRECTIONS

From Longview drive 45 km west along Highway 541 and turn left onto Highway 940. Continue for 600 m and park on the east side of the road, just past the bridge over the Highwood River. Etherington Creek is clearly visible, down the embankment to the east. If you want to get a look at the mountain and approximate route up, walk over to the west side of the road and up the embankment a short ways. Also, it may be advantageous to drive about 1 km farther up the road to get a look at the snow conditions on the open slopes of the mountain. Then return to the parking area.

HELL'S RIDGE AS SEEN FROM UP THE EMBANKMENT ON
THE WEST SIDE OF THE ROAD. THE ROUTE GOES UP THE
MOUNTAIN FROM LEFT TO LEFT AND THEN TRAVERSES
THE RIDGE TO THE TIP. S=SUMMIT. (BOB SPIRKO)

From the parking area make your way down to the creek and cross it. It usually freezes quite early in the season. Lower Etherington Creek Trail starts on the other side and is easy to find. It heads north to the Highwood River and then parallels the river going east. Note that this trail was damaged by the 2013 floods and you may encounter deadfall and have to do a little route-finding. The trail eventually swings around to the right, leaving the river, and then goes southeast, due west, due south and finally in a general south-southeasterly direction.

At this point, you can leave the trail, heading uphill to gain the ridge above, but I found it easier to keep following the main trail for about 10–15 minutes, to approximately GR678828. If you are not using GPS, it's the point where the trail levels off and then starts to lose a slight amount of elevation. Regardless of where you leave the main trail, the direction is obvious – go up and in a southeasterly direction. The terrain is not viciously steep but will get the blood pumping. A proliferation of animal trails may help along the way.

The goal now is to find several of the open areas on the side of the mountain that will grant you decent views to the west and serve as route markers: GR679827, 1616 m; GR681827, 1686 m; GR684826, 1756 m. It is not necessary that you find them all but the last one is fairly important. From GR684826 you get a great view of the remainder of the route (see photo), plus the surrounding area. Work your way up to the north end of the ridge at GR687827, 1850 m. There may be a couple of scramble-like moves near the top. Start heading southeast toward the summit.

The ridge is treed on the east side but more open on the west. At times it is easy to travel directly on the ridge and at other

FROM GR684826 THE REMAINDER OF THE ROUTE IS VISIBLE. THERE WAS A MAJOR SNOWFALL TWO DAYS BEFORE THIS ASCENT. UNFORTUNATELY IT SNOWED ONLY IN NORTHERN KANANASKIS! NR=NORTH END OF THE RIDGE. S=SUMMIT.

times it is best to stay in the trees to the left. The goal is to reach the high point at GR690820, 1915 m, approximately 600 m along the ridge. The summit is almost completely open, except for a small stand of trees to the north. As such the view is excellent in almost all directions! Although blocked a little by Coyote Hills, Three Cairns and Raspberry Ridge, peaks of the Continental Divide are still prominent and spectacular. There is a higher point on the ridge farther south, but it is some distance away, requires some elevation loss and regain and appears to be fully treed. It's probably best to just enjoy the view from the summit you have achieved. Note that you can easily drop down a few metres to the east side of the ridge to escape the wind if it is blowing hard – a good place to have lunch.

Return the same way. Once back down to Lower Etherington Creek Trail, you can shave about 1 km off the return trip by cutting through the forest in a westerly direction when the trail starts heading due north. Be prepared to hop over some deadfall and do a little route-finding if you choose this option.

18 HIGHWAY 40 SOUTH (BEYOND THE LOCKED GATE)

(MAP 7, PAGE 481)

RATING EASY	
ELEVATION GAIN VARIABLE	
ROUND-TRIP DISTANCE VARIABLE	
ROUND-TRIP TIME VARIABLE	
MAPS 82 J/7 MOUNT HEAD, GEM TREK HIGHWOOD AND CATARACT CREEK	

If the locked gate at north end of the Highway 40 road closure provides the starting point of an official snowshoe trail (Wintour Trail), why not try the south end? Another easy beginner route that can be as long or as short as you wish. Trips later in the season are recommended, when the snow has had a chance to build up on the road. Early in the season, after a major snowfall, sometimes works too.

DIRECTIONS

Turn west onto Highway 541 and drive 45 km to the locked gate (barricaded yearly from December 1–June 15). Put on your snowshoes, provided there is enough snow, and follow the road until your heart's content (or it gives out on you!).

There are a couple of destinations you can aim for. About 2.7 km along, the Fitzsimmons Creek turnoff is reached. Double that to 5.4 km and you reach Cat Creek, where you will find plenty of room to explore the area. Beyond the 6.2-km mark, the views don't change much. It's a logical place to call it a day if you haven't already.

Along the way, enjoy good views of a host of unnamed but shapely peaks on the east side of the road and the odd glance at the more striking and statuesque mountains of the Continental Divide to the west. Return the same way.

HIGHWAY 549 (SOUTH END)

Highway 549 stretches from Highway 66, near Bragg Creek, all the way to Millarville and then joins up with Highway 22 south. While certainly not a mecca for snowshoeing, there are at least two trips that are worthwhile in winter, made aware to me by the Dafferns. Wait for good snow coverage, as the area is subject to chinook melting. Both trips can be completed in the same day if time and energy are in abundance.

THE SURPRISINGLY TREE-FREE EAST FACE OF MESA BUTTE.
WAIT FOR GOOD SNOW COVERAGE FOR THIS ONE.

There are three ways to access this area:

1. *from the south end of Calgary via Highway 22X west, Highway 22 south, and then west onto Highway 549 near Millarville;*

2. *from the west side of Calgary, before December 1, via Highway 1 west, Highway 22 south to Bragg Creek, Highway 66 west, and Highway 549 south (McLean Creek Trail);*

3. *from the west side of Calgary, between December 1 and May 15, via Highway 1 west, Highway 22 south to Bragg Creek, a short section east on Highway 22, Highway 762 south, and then west onto Highway 549.*

Note that when the north end of the road is open, you can also combine either trip with an ascent of McLean Hill.

ROUTES

19 SINNOT HILL

(MAP 8, PAGE 481)

RATING INTERMEDIATE
MOUNTAIN HEIGHT 1539 M
ELEVATION GAIN 230 M
ROUND-TRIP DISTANCE 7 KM
ROUND-TRIP TIME 2.5–4 HOURS
MAPS 82 J/15 BRAGG CREEK, J/10 MOUNT RAE,
GEM TREK BRAGG CREEK AND ELBOW VALLEY
(SHEEP VALLEY)

This can be a very rewarding and straightforward snowshoe trip if there is enough snow. With an early start and good energy level both Sinnot Hill and nearby Mesa Butte can be completed comfortably in a day.

DIRECTIONS

Drive west on Highway 549 to the "Entering Kananaskis Country" sign, 2 km from the point where the paved road turns into a gravel road. You will pass a wide trail heading west from the south side of the road just before reaching the sign. Park on the side of the road and walk back to the wide trail. Follow it toward a wooden fenced corral, turn left and descend to Threepoint Creek. Cross the creek. By late December it is usually frozen. Continue along the trail to an open meadow with a trail sign (GR737248). The trail you want to be on (9999 Trail) continues on the other side of the meadow (south) and is marked with an orange diamond-shaped sign in a tree.

Once on the 9999, the ascent is straightforward, at least for

ABOVE: AT THE PASS, LOOKING UP TO THE FIRST
BUMP. BELOW: TONY DAFFERN AT THE SUMMIT
OF SINNOT HILL. (GILLEAN DAFFERN)

the first section. Follow the trail for about 1.5 km, in a south-westerly direction, up to a pass (GR729235, 1448 m) between the north outlier and the two bumps of Sinnot Hill to the southeast. Turn 90° to the southeast and ascend the first bump (see photo). There is a trail, but it may be hard to follow when snow-covered. Also, it is best to go all the way to the top of this lower summit, as opposed to trying to avoid the elevation loss on the other side by traversing around it.

Make your way over to the south side of the bump, where there is an open view of the summit of Sinnot Hill. It looks farther away than it really is and should only take about 20–30 minutes to reach. The route is obvious and leads to a mostly open viewpoint. The view to the west and southwest is quite pleasant. Return the same way.

20 MESA BUTTE

(MAP 8, PAGE 481)

RATING INTERMEDIATE
MOUNTAIN HEIGHT 1684 M
ELEVATION GAIN 235 M
ROUND-TRIP DISTANCE 4.2 KM
ROUND-TRIP TIME 1.5–3 HOURS
MAPS 82 J/15 BRAGG CREEK, GEM TREK BRAGG CREEK AND ELBOW VALLEY (SHEEP VALLEY)

Mesa Butte is a fairly popular trip year-round. The terrain is interesting and the ascent is fun and stress-free. I love the view of the east-facing, barren slopes of the summit block.

DIRECTIONS

Drive west on Highway 549, 4.1 km past the "Entering Kananaskis Country" sign and park at the locked gate on the right side of the road. Snowshoe up the road as it curves to the right. Quickly you'll arrive at a fenced gas plant, where lies a wide trail going up on the left side of the fence. Follow this trail to a view of the southwest side of Mesa Butte (see photo). The trail soon narrows and heads into the trees but is generally easy to follow.

An important junction is reached at GR715277, 1533 m, and is marked with an orange diamond-shaped sign in a tree, identifying it as the "Mesa Grind" trail. Take a hard right here and follow the trail, as it traverses around to the south side of the mountain. About 350–400 m later another sign is reached at GR719276, 1556 m. This one reads "Mesa Grind 800 m to Summit." Take a

A SHORT DISTANCE IN, THE SOUTHWEST SIDE OF THE
MOUNTAIN IS REVEALED. ONCE IN THE TREES THE ROUTE
SWINGS AROUND TO THE RIGHT. (BOB SPIRKO)

hard left. A few hundred metres up, the view opens up and the
remainder of the ascent can be seen (see photo).

The ascent does get a little steeper for the final slope. The best
view actually occurs at the top of this slope and includes an array
of distant peaks stretching from the Elbow Valley area down to
peaks around Highway 541. The trail continues to a higher point
at GR720282, 1684 m, but is also heavily treed. A fire pit sits just
inside the trees if you have a few marshmallows to roast! Return
the same way.

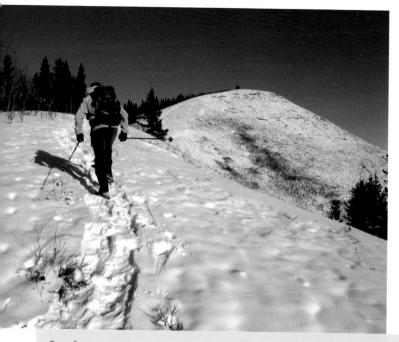

BOB SPIRKO EMBARKS ON THE FINAL PUSH TO THE SUMMIT,
VISIBLE AT THE RIGHT. NOT ENOUGH SNOW FOR SNOWSHOES
ON THIS DAY, BUT WHAT SNOW THERE IS CERTAINLY
RENDERS THE SCENE A BEAUTIFUL ONE. (DINAH KRUZE)

BRAGG CREEK AND ELBOW VALLEY

Bragg Creek's close proximity to Calgary and the nature of the terrain around and to the west of the hamlet make it an ideal area to explore in the winter. Unfortunately its easterly location also welcomes snow-eating chinook winds. Picking an appropriate time of year to put on the snowshoes can be the biggest challenge for trips around Bragg Creek. January through March are generally the most reliable months for good snow, although a warm stretch of weather can melt most of the snow at any time of the year. Conversely, a heavy snowfall may allow trips in December or April. A good strategy is to pick a trip in this area immediately after a major snowfall. Needless to say, this may render the drive difficult and/or dangerous. Be sure to check the AMA road reports before setting out.

If you are doing any trips in the vicinity of the seasonal road closure just beyond the Elbow Falls parking lot (December 1 to May 15 each year), consider an enjoyable winter walk around the falls as a finish to your day. Although they won't be giving Niagara Falls a run for their money, Elbow Falls look fantastic in the dead of winter when there have been enough cold hours for the spray from the falling water to create fascinating ice sculptures alongside the river. You can complete the entire falls walk in 5 minutes if time is a concern. However, better to take your time and enjoy the scenery. Note that this is not a snowshoe trip and can easily be completed in hiking boots.

ROUTES

ENJOYING THE VIEW FROM MUSTANG HILLS.

21 SNOWSHOE HARE LOOP

(MAP BELOW)

DIFFICULTY INTERMEDIATE	
ELEVATION LOSS/GAIN MINIMAL	
ROUND-TRIP DISTANCE 5.4 KM	
ROUND-TRIP TIME 1.5–2.5 HOURS	
MAPS 82 J/15 BRAGG CREEK, GEM TREK BRAGG CREEK AND ELBOW VALLEY (SHEEP VALLEY)	

This is an official snowshoe trail that provides a pleasant up-and-down stroll through forest. Don't expect any far-reaching views, and given the easterly location of the route, snowshoes may not be necessary at any time of the year. Note that because the trail is in an environmentally sensitive area, it is closed from April 1–November 30.

DIRECTIONS

Drive west on Highway 22 to Bragg Creek and turn right, onto Balsam Avenue, following the sign to West Bragg Creek. In 500 m turn left on Centre Avenue and drive 8.7 km to the trailhead. Park at the east end of the large parking lot.

The loop can be done in either direction: counter-clockwise, starting from the east end of the parking lot, or clockwise, starting nearer the west end. Toss a coin to pick one.

Route descriptions for both directions are unnecessary, as it is simply a matter of following the orange snowshoe signs. If you go in a clockwise direction, be careful not to jump onto one of the ski trails when you arrive at a couple of junctions early on. Other than that, route-finding is not an issue and travel is generally very easy. A few steeper sections that give the trip its intermediate rating may require some extra care, but they are very short.

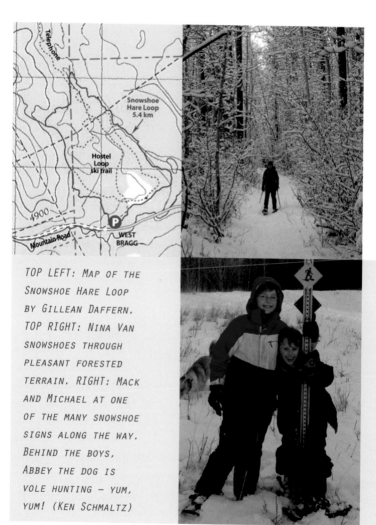

TOP LEFT: MAP OF THE SNOWSHOE HARE LOOP BY GILLEAN DAFFERN. TOP RIGHT: NINA VAN SNOWSHOES THROUGH PLEASANT FORESTED TERRAIN. RIGHT: MACK AND MICHAEL AT ONE OF THE MANY SNOWSHOE SIGNS ALONG THE WAY. BEHIND THE BOYS, ABBEY THE DOG IS VOLE HUNTING — YUM, YUM! (KEN SCHMALTZ)

22 SNOWY OWL

(MAP BELOW)

RATING INTERMEDIATE
ELEVATION GAIN 80–200 M
ROUND-TRIP DISTANCE 5.4–12.2 KM
ROUND-TRIP TIME 1.5–3.5 HOURS
MAPS 82 J/15 BRAGG CREEK, GEM TREK BRAGG
CREEK AND ELBOW VALLEY (SHEEP VALLEY)

Kudos go to the Greater Bragg Creek Trails Association for designing this delightful snowshoe trail. The scenery and terrain are varied and interesting throughout. As well, there are options to do a quick 1.5-hour trip or a longer more involved one, up to 4.5 hours. The best time to do the trip is right after a major snowfall, and Alberta Parks recommends that you not snowshoe or hike the trail before November 30 and after April 1. Bring Microspikes if you have them, just in case the trail is more Icy Owl than Snowy Owl (groan!).

DIRECTIONS

Drive west on Highway 22 to Bragg Creek and turn right, onto Balsam Avenue, following the sign to West Bragg Creek. In 500 m turn left on Centre Avenue and drive 8.7 km to the trailhead. Park at the west end of the large parking lot. Hike out onto the main road (blockaded during the winter) and turn right (west), reaching the first snowshoe sign in about 100 m, on the left side of the road. From here on in, a detailed route description is unnecessary, due to the terrific placement of snowshoe signs. Some 1.4 km down the trail you will have to decide on your specific route. There are three potential routes to take from here (see map):

MAP OF ALL THE SNOWY OWL ROUTES
(MAP COURTESY OF KANANASKISTRAILS.COM).

Route 1: A small loop via the first section of Snowy Owl and then Snowy Shortcut back to the main trail – 5.4 km and approximately 1.5–2 hours.

Route 2: Snowy Owl to its end and then back the same way, but using Snowy Shortcut – 12.2 km and approximately 3.5–4.5 hours.

Route 3: A big loop via Snowy Owl to its end and then Strange Brew and Boundary Ridge, all the way back to the parking lot – 9.2 km and approximately 2.5–3.5 hours.

The big loop (Route 3) is highly recommended. This route allows you to see the most and get a good workout.

Here are a few points to keep in mind for all routes:

- Trail signs and snowshoe signs are plentiful and easy to follow.
- The first section of the Snowy Owl is arguably the most interesting part of the day, so don't skip it.
- Fat-tire bikers often use the trail. Be on the lookout for them and give them the right of way as they pass.
- The trail throughout can get very icy at any time during the snow season. If there is not enough snow to snowshoe, at least bring another type of traction device such as Microspikes.
- If you choose Route 3, follow Strange Brew and Boundary Ridge (north) and avoid using the ski trails.

A TRIP AT DUSK YIELDS SOME INTERESTING CLOUDS AND LIGHTING.

23 MCLEAN HILL

(MAP 9, PAGE 482)

> DIFFICULTY ADVANCED
> HILL HEIGHT 1722 M
> ELEVATION GAIN APPROXIMATELY 350 M
> ROUND-TRIP DISTANCE 8.8 KM
> ROUND-TRIP TIME 3–5 HOURS
> MAPS 82 J/15 BRAGG CREEK, GEM TREK BRAGG
> CREEK AND ELBOW VALLEY (SHEEP VALLEY)

McLean Hill does not stand out in the least as you drive west on Highway 66. However, the route up the hill is enjoyable and interesting and the summit view is surprisingly good. Several steep sections and the possibility of route-finding challenges if the trail is not broken push this trip into the advanced category. Be aware that ATVers use this area frequently.

DIRECTIONS

From the four-way stop in Bragg Creek, drive south on Highway 22 for a few kilometres and turn right (west) onto Highway 66. Drive 8.3 km and turn left at the McLean Creek Recreational Area sign. Drive another 1.5 km and take another left, onto Highway 549, which is closed December 1–April 30. Park near the closed gate but do not block it.

Hike or snowshoe south on the road for 1 km. Just past the yellow 1-km sign, a trail heads east (left) into the forest. The first 300 m moves along due east, but after that, the trail goes every which way. Nevertheless, it is relatively obvious and easy to follow. After the first 300 m, the trail takes a 90° turn to the left and heads steeply uphill, swinging around to the west and then back to the east, losing a little elevation. A northerly direction is soon resumed. The trail goes up and down and has a few sharp turns now and then. Watch for another 90° turn to the left at one point and a hairpin turn to the right, where the trail descends.

Eventually you'll find yourself grinding your way up a wide, steep hill. At the top of the hill a 90° turn to the right (south) is required. There are two signs in the trees here indicating that four-wheel motorized vehicles are not permitted but two-wheeled ones (motorbikes) are. The signs are not clearly visible at first, as they are on the opposite side of a tree.

The general direction of the trail from the 90° turnoff is south and then southeast. When the trail intersects a cutline, cross to the other side of the cutline and continue going southeast, following the motorbike signs. From the cutline, the summit is about 700 m away. The views finally start to open up a short distance from the top, and you are treated to a beautiful panorama at the high point. Trees block much of the view to the east, but

MARK NUGARA AND NINA VAN AT THE SUMMIT OF MCLEAN HILL.

the north, west and south are fully open. Moose Mountain, Prairie Mountain and the "Group of Four" (Glasgow, Cornwall, Outlaw and Banded) are particularly noteworthy. After taking in the spectacle, return the same way.

ABOVE: AN ATMOSPHERIC VIEW TO THE SOUTHEAST. BELOW: A LITTLE BLAST OF WINTER THE NIGHT BEFORE COVERED THE TREES IN A BEAUTIFUL LAYER OF FRESH SNOW.

24 RANGER RIDGE

(MAP 9, PAGE 482)

> DIFFICULTY INTERMEDIATE
>
> ELEVATION GAIN APPROXIMATELY 300 M
>
> ROUND-TRIP DISTANCE 8 KM
>
> ROUND-TRIP TIME 2.5–4.5 HOURS
>
> MAPS 82 J/15 BRAGG CREEK, GEM TREK BRAGG CREEK AND ELBOW VALLEY (SHEEP VALLEY)

Ranger Ridge is a short extension of the very popular Fullerton Loop route. As such the Fullerton section is often well packed down, and snowshoes may not be necessary. That being said the well-travelled terrain often becomes icy. Snowshoes or spikes can be useful if that is the case.

DIRECTIONS

From the four-way stop in Bragg Creek, drive south on Highway 22 for a few kilometres and turn right (west) onto Highway 66. Drive 9.7 km to the Allen Bill parking lot. Park at the east end of this popular starting point.

The trail starts at the east end, going east and then turning north, under the highway, alongside the Elbow River. After paralleling the river for a short distance, the trail veers a little to the left and passes through a cattle gate. More easy snowshoeing/hiking leads to the well-signed Fullerton Loop, 1.1 km from the parking lot. Turn left onto the wide trail.

After crossing the first bridge and just before the second bridge, the trail forks (300 m from the Fullerton Loop turnoff and unsigned as of 2012. Either fork goes, as they are both part of the same loop, but a clockwise direction is preferable. Turn left onto the fork and snowshoe or hike the easy-to-follow trail, taking in improving views to the southwest as you gain elevation.

When you arrive at the second wooden bench, you've also attained the high point / viewpoint of the loop. From here you can continue to follow the loop as it turns east, or for a little more exercise and some additional views, complete the short extension of the trip up the west side of Ranger Ridge.

EXTENSION UP THE WEST SIDE OF RANGER RIDGE

Leave the main trail at the loop high point and travel northwest up and through a brief section of light forest to an open area. Continue up to the treed ridge above and travel along the edge of the trees. This eventually leads to another open area that you will probably want to call your high point for the day. The views aren't much different from those at the loop high point, so you'll be

doing this extension mostly for the exercise. An option does exist to continue on to the high point to the northwest, but it is fully treed and has very limited views. Most parties will choose to turn around and complete the remainder of the Fullerton Loop back to the Allen Bill parking lot.

NOT ENOUGH SNOW ON THE TRAIL FOR SNOWSHOEING, BUT THE ATMOSPHERIC CLOUDS MADE UP FOR THAT.

25 PADDY'S FLAT INTERPRETIVE TRAIL

(MAP 9, PAGE 482)

DIFFICULTY EASY

ELEVATION GAIN APPROXIMATELY 50 M

ROUND-TRIP DISTANCE APPROXIMATELY 4 KM

ROUND-TRIP TIME 1–2 HOURS

MAPS 82 J/15 BRAGG CREEK, GEM TREK BRAGG CREEK AND ELBOW VALLEY (SHEEP VALLEY)

With good snow coverage, this interpretive trail is a wonderful introduction to beginner snowshoeing and also to the beautiful environs of the Elbow River.

DIRECTIONS

From the four-way stop in Bragg Creek, drive south on Highway 22 for a few kilometres and turn right (west) onto Highway 66. Drive 13.1 km west and park near the locked gate of the Paddy's Flat Campground turnoff.

Snowshoe through the campground, heading southwest and then following the signs to Loop C. After you've entered Loop C and passed a playground, the trailhead can be seen on your right. This is actually the end of the trail, but the route is described in reverse direction here.

The trail curves to the right, paralleling the river but some distance away from it. You will soon arrive at a shortcut trail that leads down to the river. Ignore this and keep going straight. An orange sign in the trees ahead points you in the right direction. Keep going through light forest, eventually arriving at another important intersection. The right fork goes back into the campground. The left takes a hairpin turn down toward the river. Take the left fork.

Reaching the river, you can now change direction and snowshoe or hike downstream. Hopefully there will be tons of cool snow and ice scenery. The interpretive trail follows the river for a fair distance before going over a couple of bridges and then swinging around to the left and uphill, back to the campground. Upon reaching the campground road, follow it back to Highway 66 and your vehicle.

26 RIVERVIEW TRAIL

(MAP 9, PAGE 482)

DIFFICULTY INTERMEDIATE

ELEVATION GAIN APPROXIMATELY 70 M

ROUND-TRIP DISTANCE APPROXIMATELY 7 KM

ROUND-TRIP TIME 2–3 HOURS

MAPS 82 J/15 BRAGG CREEK, GEM TREK BRAGG
CREEK AND ELBOW VALLEY (SHEEP VALLEY)

Riverview Trail takes in beautiful scenery along the Elbow River, which, along with the Bow, provides Calgary's drinking water. Options exist to simply enjoy Riverview Trail or complete a loop route via Sulphur Springs Trail or Elbow Valley Trail. Wait for good snow coverage so you don't have to snowshoe over rocky terrain.

DIRECTIONS

From the four-way stop in Bragg Creek, drive south on Highway 22 for a few kilometres and turn right (west) onto Highway 66. Drive 13.1 km west and park near the locked gate of the Paddy's Flat Campground turnoff.

Snowshoe through the campground, heading southwest to Loop E. Turn left (south) into Loop E, quickly finding the trailhead sign. Turn left onto the trail and then take the right fork only a few metres later. The trail drops a little and within minutes spits you out at the Elbow River's edge.

Turn west and follow the beautiful shoreline. Throughout the trip extreme caution should be taken about getting too close to the edge of the river. Starting from the shore, ice sheets form over the river during the winter season. They can hold huge amounts of weight or collapse under the slightest pressure, sending whatever or whoever is on top into the icy water.

For the most part you can stay near the water, but, depending on ice and snow conditions, you may have to move away from the shore to get around certain sections. If any sections appear too difficult or potentially dangerous, it's time to turn around.

For those who want to complete the entire river walk (snowshoe), follow the river for about 2.5 km. Along this distance the river bends right, with a wall of impressively vertical rock on the opposite side. About 500 m beyond that feature, start looking for a fairly obvious ramp to your right (see photo on page 173). This is where the trail leaves the river and ascends to a bench high above. There is a fair amount of elevation gain and the trail becomes indistinct in places. Don't stop at the first bench, but continue upward until the river is far below.

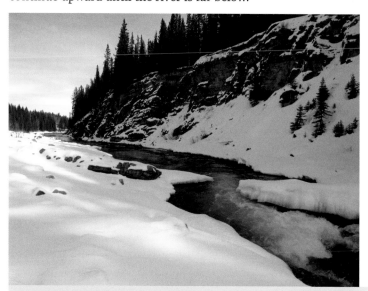

TYPICAL SCENERY AROUND THE ELBOW RIVER DURING WINTER.

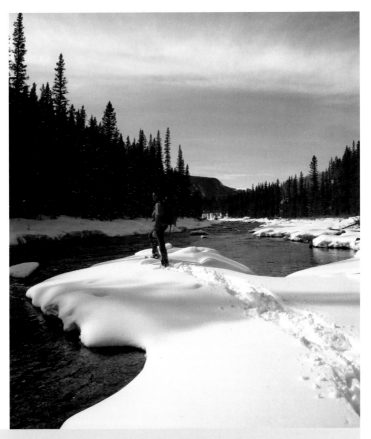

THE SNOW AND ICE ALLOW US TO EXPLORE AREAS THAT WOULD BE INACCESSIBLE IN SUMMER (WITHOUT YOUR SWIMSUIT, ANYWAY!).

Once you reach the upper bench, walk along it, going southwest again. A few hundred metres along, the trail veers off to the right, heading northwest to the highway. Upon reaching the highway, look for a pedestrian crossing and make your way over

THE OBVIOUS RAMP THAT YOU MUST FOLLOW.

to it. With some luck, you will emerge from the trees right at the crossing.

You now have to decide whether to hike along the road back to your vehicle or continue on to Sulphur Springs Trail (see next trip, page 174). If you are done for the day, there is the option to retrace your steps back to the Paddy's Flat Campground. However, most parties will choose to hike about 3 km east on Highway 66 back to their car.

27 SULPHUR SPRINGS TRAIL

(MAP 9, PAGE 482)

> DIFFICULTY INTERMEDIATE
>
> ELEVATION GAIN APPROXIMATELY 330 M
>
> ROUND-TRIP DISTANCE APPROXIMATELY 10 KM
> (INCLUDES RIVERVIEW TRAIL)
>
> ROUND-TRIP TIME 3.5–6 HOURS
>
> MAPS 82 J/15 BRAGG CREEK, GEM TREK BRAGG
> CREEK AND ELBOW VALLEY (SHEEP VALLEY)

This is a continuation of Riverview Trail. It is a nice stroll, mostly through forested terrain, with a decent amount of elevation gain and one viewpoint. Upon reaching the road after snowshoeing Riverview Trail, if you have the extra time and energy, this trip is a great way to complete a loop route and get the old heart pumping.

DIRECTIONS

Complete Riverview Trail as described on page 170. Cross the road to the sign and map on the other side. The trail, through lightly treed terrain, generally winds its way north with some trending to the left (west). You'll soon arrive at a major, signed, four-way junction. At this point you can go north on Sulphur Springs Trail or east on Elbow Valley Trail. Sulphur Springs is described as follows. Go north, looking for and following the small orange and red diamond markers on the bare aspen trees.

The trail makes a string of large, sweeping curves up the hillside toward the high point. At one point it swings over to the right (northeast), seemingly heading away from the high point,

ON THE LOWER SECTION OF SULPHUR SPRINGS TRAIL. THE HIGH POINT IS OUTSIDE THE PHOTO, TO THE LEFT.

but then abruptly turns to the left. The viewpoint is reached soon after. The view from the high point is pleasant, although it may not have you breaking out your hula hoop in a celebratory dance! Prairie Mountain is the prominent peak to the west.

Leaving the high point, the trail continues north, losing a little elevation before crossing Moose Mountain Road. A northerly direction is resumed for several hundred metres before the trail swings around to the east. Staying on the trail should not be too difficult, and the occasional red marker in the trees is present to guide you. Expect some ups and downs and a crossing of what

THE VIEW FROM THE HIGH POINT OF SULPHUR SPRINGS
TRAIL. PRAIRIE MOUNTAIN IS TO THE RIGHT.

appears to be an old road. The trail meanders north and then goes east again. This section of the trail is relatively long (approximately 3 km), so expect to take some time to complete it (45 to 90 minutes).

Finally, you will see a bridge on your right side that marks the end of Sulphur Springs Trail. Cross the bridge and then make your way left, over to the road. A 700-m hike along Highway 66 completes the loop.

28 BEAVER LODGE INTERPRETIVE TRAIL

(MAP 10, PAGE 482)

DIFFICULTY EASY	
ELEVATION GAIN APPROXIMATELY 30 M	
ROUND-TRIP DISTANCE APPROXIMATELY 4 KM	
ROUND-TRIP TIME 1–2 HOURS	
MAPS 82 J/15 BRAGG CREEK, GEM TREK BRAGG CREEK AND ELBOW VALLEY (SHEEP VALLEY)	

This is a delightful and interesting little trip at any time of year. As usual for trips in this area, it is a good idea to wait for a significant snowfall event so that you can use your snowshoes.

DIRECTIONS

From the four-way stop in Bragg Creek, drive south on Highway 22 for a few kilometres and turn right (west) onto Highway 66. Drive about 18.4 km west to the road closure and park on the side of the road but not in front of the gate.

Hike or snowshoe the road west for about 400 m, quickly arriving at a parking area on the south side of the road and a big sign reading "Beaver Lodge." The trail starts at the sign and descends immediately to the valley below. Follow the trail southwest, ignoring a trail branch heading off to the left. Cross a small bridge over Powderface Creek, eventually emerging from the forest to a pleasant view of the first pond.

The time of year and amount of snowfall will determine if you are looking at open water or snow-covered ice. The open water is usually preferred because it yields better photo opportunities. Attempts later in the season favour ice-free ponds, but the downside may be a lack of snow. Regardless of the condition of the ponds, the imposing form of Iyahe Ipan above them will hopefully be enough to impress you.

Continue along the trail, taking time to check out the varied scenery. After crossing another small bridge you will suddenly pop out of the trees at the Beaver Flats Campground. This marks the end of the interpretive trail. Options here are to return the way you came, snowshoe around the campground to Highway 66 and then hike back along the road to your car, or continue the trip alongside the Elbow River.

IYAHE IPAN TOWERING ABOVE ONE OF THE PONDS.

For the latter option, turn left and follow the road toward the Elbow River. A trail soon intersects the road, on your left. Take this trail, paralleling the campground, as opposed to following the campground road. At the far end of the campground, the narrow trail continues south. Follow it through a cattle gate and then down to the Elbow River. Snowshoe or hike along the riverbank until you encounter cliff-bands on the west side of the river. At that point it is time to turn around. You can simply retrace your steps or ascend steepish slopes to the west, making your way up to the road. An easy road hike north takes you back to your vehicle.

29 PRAIRIE MOUNTAIN

(MAP 10, PAGE 482)

RATING ADVANCED

MOUNTAIN HEIGHT 2210 M

ELEVATION GAIN 700 M

ROUND-TRIP DISTANCE 7 KM

ROUND-TRIP TIME 4–6 HOURS

MAPS 82 J/15 BRAGG CREEK, GEM TREK BRAGG CREEK AND ELBOW VALLEY (SHEEP VALLEY)

A snowshoe ascent of Prairie Mountain is a terrific way to transition from beginner snowshoeing to intermediate snowshoeing. The ascent has no avalanche risk and is not committing in any way. However, it has a decent amount of horizontal distance to cover, a relatively large elevation gain and enough steep terrain to acquaint the beginner snowshoer with some of the elements of higher-level snowshoeing. Yet again the crux of the trip is waiting for enough snow to accumulate so that snowshoes are actually necessary. Best to make an attempt right after a big dump of snow. Take Microspikes, as an alternative to snowshoes.

DIRECTIONS

From the four-way stop in Bragg Creek, drive south on Highway 22 for a few kilometres and turn right (west) onto Highway 66. Drive about 18.4 km west to the road closure and park on the side of the road, but not in front of the gate. Walk or snowshoe west for about 100 m to a point just before Prairie Creek flows under the road. Gaining Prairie Mountain's south ridge here may

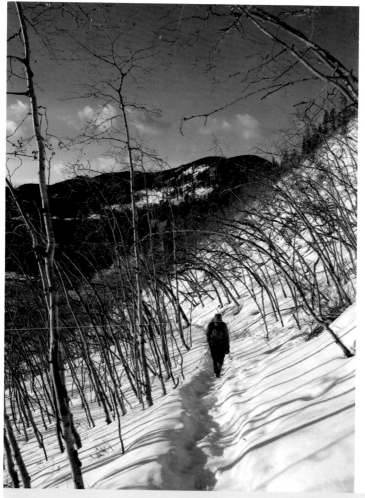

DINAH KRUZE TAKES THE ALTERNATIVE ROUTE
TO GAIN THE PLATEAU. (BOB SPIRKO)

actually be the crux of the trip. Turn sharply right (northeast) and make your way up steep, potentially rocky terrain to gain the plateau above. There is also a less steep but longer route that side-slopes the ridge, eventually arriving at the same plateau (see photo).

The trail now heads north, through treed terrain for a fair distance. Throughout, the route is obvious and probably well-travelled. Open areas occasionally reveal sections of the upper part of the mountain to the northwest.

Eventually the trail turns more northwest and starts up much steeper terrain, again through the trees. This is where your snowshoes will be very helpful for traction if the trail is icy or snowy. Grind your way up the steep slopes, popping out in open terrain about 1 km south of the summit. Turn right (north) and

DINAH REACHES AN OPEN AREA ALONG THE WAY. THE ROUTE ASCENDS THE TREED SLOPE IN FRONT FROM RIGHT TO LEFT AND THEN GOES NORTH TO THE SUMMIT. (BOB SPIRKO)

make your way to the huge cairn at the top. This part of the trip is prone to be wind-blasted and snowshoes will probably not be necessary.

The summit view features Moose Mountain to the north, Powderface Ridge and Nihahi Ridge to the southwest, and the Banded Peak quartet farther southwest. Return the way you came. Descending the steep sections will be much easier with snowshoes.

THE CLASSIC CURVE OF PRAIRIE'S UPPER RIDGE. (BOB SPIRKO)

30 POWDERFACE RIDGE

(MAP 10, PAGE 482)

RATING ADVANCED
MOUNTAIN HEIGHT 2210 M
ELEVATION GAIN 850 M
ROUND-TRIP DISTANCE 18 KM
ROUND-TRIP TIME 6–8 HOURS
MAPS 82 J/15 BRAGG CREEK, GEM TREK BRAGG
CREEK AND ELBOW VALLEY (SHEEP VALLEY)

18 km is a fairly lengthy distance to traverse on snowshoes. Fortunately, this increasingly popular route to the summit of Powderface Ridge is often well packed down, taking all the "punch" out of any potentially strenuous trail-breaking. As on nearby Prairie Mountain, Microspikes may be a good alternative to snowshoes, although I would take both. Snowshoes can certainly speed up the descent in certain conditions. Route-finding is generally straightforward and the summit view is very pleasant.

DIRECTIONS

From the four-way stop in Bragg Creek, drive south on Highway 22 for a few kilometres and turn right (west) onto Highway 66. Drive about 18.4 km west to the road closure and park on the side of the road but not in front of the gate.

The first goal is to reach a pass northwest of Powderface Ridge. It's about 7.5 km from car to pass. Walk or snowshoe a few hundred metres down the road into the Powderface parking lot, on the right side. The trailhead at the end is obvious, going uphill immediately. That elevation will soon be lost, as you descend to Prairie Creek. Continue along the easy trail, eventually crossing to the north side of the creek on a wooden bridge. You'll encounter a cattle gate. Be sure to close it behind you. The trail generally stays close to the creek, but when it veers away, there are usually orange diamond-shaped signs in trees to mark the route.

About 50–60 minutes into the trip, when you reach an open area with a trail sign (GR525367), keep travelling west. Eventually the trail crosses back to the south side of the creek. Shortly after, the work begins, as the grade of the trail increases. After gaining a good chunk of elevation, the trail suddenly swings over to the right (GR509360), crossing the creek again and then going up and traversing the hillside to the north. A similar, though less dramatic situation occurs shortly after. This creek is very small, so with heavy snow cover you may not even be aware you crossed

A SECTION OF PLEASANT SCENERY EN ROUTE. POWDERFACE RIDGE IN THE DISTANCE. (MATTHEW CLAY)

it. Route-finding to the pass from this point gets a little trickier. Look for orange diamond-shaped signs in the trees as you continue to gradually side-hill up and to the west. The bottom of the valley you are in is now down and to your left.

The pass is marked with a trail sign at GR500354, 2015 m. A decent view waits here, but the view from the ridge is far superior. Turning to the southeast, you'll see an outlier close by and it's a pleasant detour if not snow loaded. There is some minor avalanche concern if you decide to ascend the outlier. The summit of the western outlier lies at GR503350, 2155 m, and the route up is obvious (see photo).

Most will bypass the outlier, in favour of the longer but safer route through the trees and onto scenic Powderface Ridge. Head toward the trees in a southeasterly direction, looking for orange

AT THE PASS, LOOKING TOWARD THE WESTERN OUTLIER. BR=BYPASS ROUTE. WOR=WESTERN OUTLIER ROUTE. WO=WESTERN OUTLIER. (MATTHEW CLAY)

flagging. Once you find the flagging, the route is fairly obvious. It gains some elevation and then turns left, basically traversing at the same level for a good distance through the trees. Eventually, the trail starts to gain elevation, heading more to the right and up to the low point between the outlier and Powderface. Once out of the trees, the route to the summit at GR514348, 2207 m, is very obvious and straightforward.

There is a great deal to see from the summit. I'll refrained from describing everything – best to go see it for yourself! Return the same way. Even if you hiked up or used Microspikes, snowshoes can be great for making the descent a speedy one.

31 HIGHWAY 66 (BEYOND THE LOCKED GATE)

(MAP 10, PAGE 482)

RATING EASY

ELEVATION GAIN VARIABLE

ROUND-TRIP DISTANCE VARIABLE

ROUND-TRIP TIME VARIABLE

MAPS 82 J/15 BRAGG CREEK, GEM TREK BRAGG CREEK AND ELBOW VALLEY (SHEEP VALLEY)

This route is similar to Wintour Road on Highway 40, in that you are simply travelling along a wide road that is closed during the winter. It's a great beginner trip that can be as long or as short as you wish. The snowpack on this road eventually gets hammered down to the point where snowshoes may be unnecessary. However, there are innumerable points along the way, where you can leave the road to do some exploration, so take the shoes anyway. The trip is technically available from December 1–May 15. Realistically, however, the window is much shorter. Right after a heavy snowfall is the ideal time to do the trip.

DIRECTIONS

From the four-way stop in Bragg Creek, drive south on Highway 22 for a few kilometres and turn right (west) onto Highway 66. Drive about 18.4 km west to the road closure and park on the side of the road but not in front of the gate. Snowshoe west along the road – that's it!

Enjoy the scenery and views of some of the big hills, such as Mustang Hills and Rainy Summit, and then some of the big mountains, such Banded Peak and Forgetmenot Ridge. There are several open, relatively flat areas where you can leave the road to explore.

Go as far as time, energy and/or motivation allow and then turn around. If you have legs like Arnie (Schwarzenegger) and the cardio of your average gazelle, you can snowshoe all the way to the end of Highway 66 and then back – most will stop long before that lofty goal is reached!

Upon returning to your vehicle, a quick stop at Elbow Falls is certainly a good way to end (or begin) the day. The falls are very pretty when frozen. Directions are obvious. Stay on the designated path.

SOME OF THE TERRIFIC WINTER SCENERY AT ELBOW FALLS.

32 MUSTANG HILLS

(MAP 10, PAGE 482)

RATING ADVANCED

MOUNTAIN HEIGHT 1813 M

ELEVATION GAIN 300 M

ROUND-TRIP DISTANCE 3.2 KM (ADD 7 KM IF THE WINTER GATE IS CLOSED)

ROUND-TRIP TIME 2.5–4 HOURS (ADD 1.5 HOURS IF THE WINTER GATE IS CLOSED)

MAPS 82 J/15 BRAGG CREEK, GEM TREK BRAGG CREEK AND ELBOW VALLEY (SHEEP VALLEY)

There are three summits that make up Mustang Hills. This route goes to the centre and east summits. The view from the highest (west) summit is somewhat lacklustre and not really worth the effort. The best time to attempt the trip is any time before December 1, and right after a major snowfall. Our mid-November ascent in 2015 was perfect for snowshoes and terrific, snowy scenery. After December 1 the closed road will necessitate an extra 3.5 km (one way) of walking/snowshoeing to the start of the route.

DIRECTIONS

From the four-way stop in Bragg Creek, drive south on Highway 22 for a few kilometres and turn right (west) onto Highway 66. Drive 18.4 km to the winter gate. If it is still open, continue driving for 3.5 km past the winter gate and park at the wide pullout on the east side of the road. After December 1 you will have to hike or snowshoe this part of the road. From the parking area, walk back along the road about 50 m to the "Caring for Alberta Highways" sign. Look up and to the east, through the trees, for the large patch of clear terrain on the west side of one of the hills. This is what you are aiming for.

Snowshoe east, through the trees and down to the creek. Cross the creek and continue up the other side. There is some steep terrain here but nothing too sustained. The summer trail can be very difficult to find. Best to just keep going up and east, looking for the aforementioned clearing.

The grade gets a little steeper at the clearing. Hopefully the improving views behind you will keep upward progress steady. Upon reaching the top of the clearing, turn right (south), following the ridgetop. The trail goes back into the trees. Look for flagging here. The trail is not too difficult to follow.

AT THE SUMMIT. FORGETMENOT RIDGE AND MOUNTAIN TO THE LEFT. (NICOLE LISAFELD)

NICOLE JUMPING FOR JOY UPON REACHING THE ELUSIVE SUMMIT!

At one point, around GR548342, the trail keeps going straight but appears to start going down ahead. Here, look left where you'll see more open terrain going slightly uphill. Go in this direction and follow your nose to the summit at GR549342, 1813 m. The summit view is pretty decent for a low summit. Forgetmenot Ridge and Mountain stretch out to the west. The familiar quartet of Glasgow, Cornwall, Outlaw and Banded peaks lie to the distant right.

The east summit is only about a 10-minute trek away and is worth the effort for a marginally better view of the mountain quartet mentioned above. The route there is obvious and the summit lies at GR552341, 1810 m. Return the way you came. The descent can be surprisingly fast.

When the powder is deep and the slope is steep, it can be sublime to descend a different line. (Take that, T.S. Eliot!) Our uptrack on the left, my descent track in the middle, Nicole making her own to the right.

HIGHWAY 68

Like Bragg Creek, trips along Highway 68 (Sibbald Creek Trail) are mostly along the far eastern edge of the Rockies and therefore susceptible to poor snow conditions or a complete lack of snow. Having said that, the snowy spring of 2012 and great December of 2015 enabled me to snowshoe each of the following routes in their entirety (with the exception of the stairs down to Moose Loop). Be patient and wait for the right time to attempt these routes on snowshoes – each trip can be rewarding.

ROUTES

SNOWSHOES WERE MANDATORY FOR ASCENDING THIS TYPE
OF TERRAIN ON COX HILL IN LATE MARCH 2012.

33 MOOSE CREEK LOOP AND PINE WOODS LOOP

(MAP 11, PAGE 483)

DIFFICULTY INTERMEDIATE; TWO SHORT, STEEPER SECTIONS ON MOOSE CREEK

ELEVATION GAIN 122 M

ROUND-TRIP DISTANCE 6 KM

ROUND-TRIP TIME 1–2.5 HOURS FOR BOTH LOOPS

MAPS 82 O/02 JUMPINGPOUND CREEK, GEM TREK BRAGG CREEK AND ELBOW VALLEY (SHEEP VALLEY)

These two loops can easily be combined for an enjoyable half-day out, or you can tackle each one separately. Perhaps some of the most interesting scenery of the day occurs near the beginning, around Jumpingpound Creek.

If both loops are on the agenda, you have two options in regard to route direction. If you do Pine Loop first, complete Moose Loop in a counter-clockwise direction. If Moose Loop goes first, do it in a clockwise direction. The first option is described below.

DIRECTIONS

From Highway 1, turn south onto Sibbald Creek Trail (Highway 68). Drive 18.3 km and turn left (south) onto Jumpingpound Demonstration Forest South Loop road. About 3.8 km along that road you will arrive at the large Moose Creek Trails parking lot. If you are driving from the west, the turnoff is 19.4 km east on Highway 68 (2.7 km east of the Sibbald Viewpoint turnoff).

Don't put your snowshoes on right away, because the trail almost immediately descends a long set of stairs. The stairs may be completely clear of snow. If snowy, the crampons on your snowshoes may make the descent easier, so put them on. Getting down the stairs may be the crux of the trip!

At the bottom of the stairs, cross Jumpingpound Creek on a bridge. Surprisingly, the scenery around the bridge can be some of the best of the entire trip. If conditions permit, it is worthwhile to snowshoe west along the shoreline for a short distance to check out the terrain.

After crossing the bridge, turn right and snowshoe south for about 400 m to an important three-way junction. Follow the sign to Pine Woods Loop. The trail nears a road and then runs parallel to it and northwest. A few hundred metres farther, look for a bridge on the road. Cross the bridge and over to the other side of the road and another trail sign. This is the start of Pine Woods Loop.

THE RUSTY BRIDGE OVER JUMPINGPOUND CREEK.

The loop is easy to follow at first. It ascends to the hilltop, where there are sporadic views of Moose Mountain to the south. Start looking for a Pine Woods sign that will direct you to turn right, into the forest. From that point on, blue flagging will guide you through the trees and around the loop. Don't freak out when you suddenly notice the eerie alignment of all the trees. You have not slipped into the Twilight Zone – after clear-cutting, this area was replanted in 1974.

Eventually you will arrive back at the main trail. Turn left (east) onto it and snowshoe back to where you left the main trail. The remainder of the return route is the same way you came up. Return to the aforementioned three-way junction.

From the three-way junction, Moose Loop is also relatively easy to follow. However, the unusually strong winds of the fall of 2011 and winter of 2012 knocked down many trees in the area. Expect some awkward moves as you climb over the fallen trees. Perhaps they will have been cleared away by the time you attempt the trip.

The trail goes uphill immediately, paralleling the road below and heading south. Eventually a sign will direct you to trend left (east), away from the road, gaining a little more elevation in the process. Views are limited, but the scenery is varied and very pleasant. A small jaunt to the east precedes a steepish descent to Moose Creek. Upon reaching the creek, the trail takes a hard left turn, now going north alongside the creek. Again, expect some fallen trees blocking the path as you travel back toward Jumpingpound Creek. Watch for a trail sign that keeps you travelling north instead of detouring west. About 700–800 m after reaching Moose Creek you will find yourself back at the bridge over Jumpingpound Creek and a short hike from your vehicle.

Reminder: for those who want to do Moose Creek Loop first,

it is better to do it in a clockwise direction. For this route, simply turn left after crossing the bridge and follow the trail.

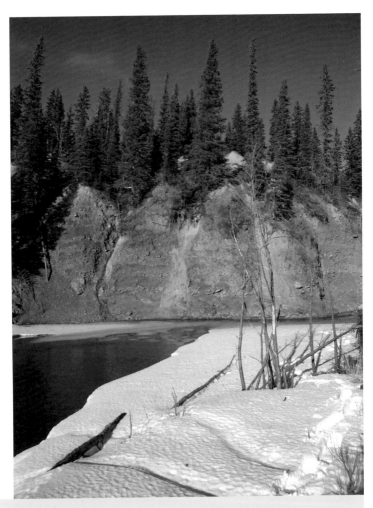

SOME INTERESTING CLIFFS JUST WEST OF THE BRIDGE.

34 DEER RIDGE

RATING INTERMEDIATE
MOUNTAIN HEIGHT 1698 M
ELEVATION GAIN 229 M
ROUND-TRIP DISTANCE 4.6 KM
ROUND-TRIP TIME 1.5–2.5 HOURS
MAPS 82 O/02 JUMPINGPOUND CREEK, GEM TREK
BRAGG CREEK AND ELBOW VALLEY (SHEEP VAL-
LEY)

Varied terrain and an interesting summit view make this one of my favourite trips along Highway 68. The return to Sibbald Lake at the end of the trip provides a perfect place to relax and take in the beautiful surroundings.

DIRECTIONS

From Highway 1, turn south onto Sibbald Creek Trail (Highway 68). Drive approximately 22 km to the Sibbald Lake turnoff and follow the road to the day use parking lot near Sibbald Lake. Hike back along the road for about 50 m to the trail sign on the west side of the road. Hopefully there'll be enough snow to warrant putting on the shoes at this point. Snowshoe in a clockwise direction around the hill to your right. There are two interpretive trail signs along the way. You will quickly reach Moose Pond, at which point you can decide if you want to stay on the trail southeast of the pond or follow the pond shoreline. Provided it is sufficiently frozen, the pond shoreline is recommended.

Staying on the southeast shore of the pond, make your way

over to the other side. Leave the pond and find the trail that now follows the south side of the pond. About 100 m along, the trail veers off to the left and soon starts to go gently uphill, eventually turning south. Follow it up to an important junction, marked with a trail sign, around GR489567. Turn 90° to the right (west).

The trail now goes west for a while, switchbacks a couple of times and then takes a hard turn to the left. You'll soon get some partial views to the left, as you side-hill on the south side of the mountain. A very pleasant stint through spruce forest follows, with another switchback that leads up to the ridge proper at around GR485567.

Follow the wide ridge. It undulates a little and soon offers a partial view of Moose Mountain to the southeast and the east

JACK TANNETT TIMES AN ASCENT PERFECTLY! GREAT SNOW COVERAGE FOR THE SUMMIT OF DEER RIDGE. (JACK TANNETT)

summit of Deer Ridge straight ahead. The route from here goes around the north (right) side of the east summit, eventually arriving at another important junction, with a horse-post. Take a sharp left here, traversing around to the northwest side of the summit. Make your way up steeper terrain to the summit at GR459579, in short order.

The summit view is far from open and expansive in all directions, but is intriguing nonetheless. A wildly meandering creek below is perhaps the best feature of the view. Hopefully the creek is not hidden under a thick blanket of snow. A discerning eye will pick out Mount Yamnuska to the north and the distinctive summit block of Tiara Peak to the southwest, though both are small and distant. Much bigger is Cox Hill, immediately south (see page 204).

Return the same way. If you want some extra exercise you can easily ascend the slightly higher west summit, upon returning to the junction with the horse-post. Unfortunately this summit is completely treed and doesn't offer any good views. Instead, I would probably settle for a relaxing visit to Sibbald Lake.

35 COX HILL

(MAP 11, PAGE 483)

(MAP 11, PAGE 483)

DIFFICULTY ADVANCED; POTENTIAL AVALANCHE TERRAIN

MOUNTAIN HEIGHT 2217 M

ELEVATION GAIN NET 700 M; TOTAL APPROXIMATELY 900–1000 M

ROUND-TRIP DISTANCE 13.2 KM

ROUND-TRIP TIME 4.5–7 HOURS

MAPS 82 O/02 JUMPINGPOUND CREEK, 82 J/15 BRAGG CREEK, GEM TREK BRAGG CREEK AND ELBOW VALLEY (SHEEP VALLEY)

Cox Hill is a fairly popular hike year-round, as chinook winds can clean snow off the mountain very quickly. In those conditions the trip is mostly a moderate hike with a few sections of steep terrain. However, heavy snow years can also transform the hill into a high-end snowshoe trip that will definitely push the limits of the beginner. Such was the case on March 31, 2012, when only those on snowshoes were able to negotiate the deep snow to the summit. Note that when such conditions are present there is some potential avalanche danger on the final ascent slope. The push to the summit should be undertaken only by those with experience on avalanche terrain and who have avalanche equipment and are comfortable on steep terrain.

DIRECTIONS

From Highway 1, turn south onto Sibbald Creek Trail (Highway 68). Drive about 23 km and turn left (south) onto Powderface Trail. Follow the Powderface for 2.9 km and turn left into the Dawson parking lot. Note that this road is not maintained during winter and may be dangerous or impassable after a heavy snowfall.

The signed trailhead sits near the entrance of the parking lot. Hike or snowshoe about 100 m and cross Jumpingpound Creek on a bridge. In another 200 m arrive at an important, signed, three-way junction. Turn right. After some 100 m of flat terrain along a straight trail, there begins an onslaught of approximately 800 m of elevation gain up a barrage of switchbacks that meander up the north ridge of the hill.

The trail is generally easy to follow, even when covered with snow. At times it goes along the hillsides, but it always ends up on the ridge via switchbacks. Heel lifts on your snowshoes will help to ease the calf burn you are bound to experience during the first part of the ascent. Expect a few minor downhill sections along the way. The occasional open section allows you to see some of the surrounding area, but for the most part the ascent is through view-blocking trees.

There are two fairly obvious areas where short detours to your left take you to open high points that permit good views of Moose Mountain. The second detour (around GR480513 for those using GPS) allows you to see the summit block to the southwest (see photo on next page). From this point the trail goes south for a few hundred metres and then turns southwest (right) into the forest. A big chunk of elevation gain ensues.

Higher up, the trail swings around to the west, avoiding very steep terrain to the south by going under the north side of the summit block. The trees start to thin and the crux of the trip appears to your left (south). The steep, open slopes of the north face can have some avalanche potential in certain conditions. A switchbacking trail does make the ascent more bearable, but in winter this trail may be difficult or impossible to find. If these

THE SNOW-COVERED SUMMIT BLOCK TO THE SOUTHWEST. ALTHOUGH IT APPEARED A LITTLE DICEY FROM THIS DISTANCE, THE ASCENT WAS ACTUALLY STRAIGHTFORWARD, WITH NO AVALANCHE DANGER.

slopes are completely plastered in snow it is best to play it safe and call it a day. Otherwise, switchback your way up or go straight up, whereupon you'll quickly arrive at the east summit.

Another strategy for tackling the summit block is to go to the west end of the slope. Although it appears to be even steeper here, that is the case only for a short section. Gentler terrain then leads to the summit.

Regardless of your route to the top, you are bound to be elated when finally arriving. The view from the east summit is excellent, with a vast array of peaks stretched out to the west, northwest and southwest. Take a few moments to catch your breath and

ABOVE: Snowshoeing to the true summit. Note the cloudy conditions to the west, while Cox Hill remains bathed in sunlight. BELOW: Part of the extensive view from the true summit. The mountain catching the sun at the right is Tiara Peak.

then snowshoe or hike west to the slightly higher true summit. This high point offers a completely unobstructed view of the area and is bound to have your camera working overtime.

If you are a true glutton for punishment and really want your money's worth, continue south along the wide ridge down to the next high point about 500 m away. The views are not significantly different from this point, but you do all of a sudden seem to be very close to Jumpingpound Mountain to the southwest. When enough is enough, return the same way you came in. The descent is generally quite fast, and with snowshoes on you can be confident in deep snow and on icy terrain.

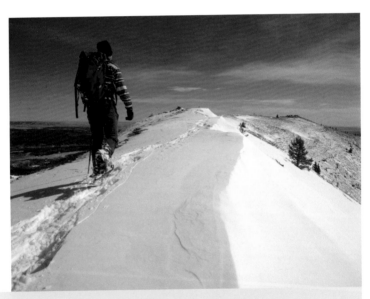

HEADING BACK TO THE EAST SUMMIT OF COX HILL.

36 EAGLE HILL

(MAP 11, PAGE 483)

DIFFICULTY INTERMEDIATE
HILL HEIGHT 1713 M
ELEVATION GAIN 300 M
ROUND-TRIP DISTANCE 8.2 KM
ROUND-TRIP TIME 3–5 HOURS
MAP 82 0/02 JUMPINGPOUND CREEK

Eagle Hill offers a unique experience in a somewhat secluded area. If you are looking for a little solitude and serenity, and good views to go with them, this is a terrific trip. Snow conditions on the mountain can vary wildly from one week to the next. Mid-March and April are your best bets, and attempting the route right after a snowfall is often a good idea. Even if the area appears dry, it is a good idea to take your snowshoes along. The logging road and trail often hold deep snow, even when the surrounding slopes are snow-free.

DIRECTIONS

From Highway 1, turn south onto Sibbald Creek Trail (Highway 68). Drive about 27 km and park on the north side of the road near a bike sign (4.1 km west of the Powderface Trail turnoff). If you are approaching from the west side of Highway 68, it's about 9.7 km from where you turn off Highway 40 onto 68.

The route starts at the bike sign and goes up an old logging road. You shouldn't have any route-finding difficulties, following the wide path in a northerly direction. The trail slowly gains elevation on the hillside and then levels out, going around the hill. The combination of aspens and evergreens on either side of the track provide some very pleasant scenery.

About 1.5 km along, a not-so-obvious cutline marked with pink flagging veers off to the right. If you are looking for the fastest route to the top with the least amount of elevation gain, the cutline is the route to take. However, the scenery along the trail is better, so that is the route I recommend.

Stay on the trail, soon reaching a yellow sign that reads "2823 RD." The trail forks here and you should take the right fork. A few hundred metres later another sign ("2328") appears and the trail starts to drop and curve to the right, down into the base of the valley. Before it drops there is a good view of the objective straight ahead of you.

Now in the valley, the trail crosses the cutline (more flagging where the cutline comes out of the forest), heading east, and then curves back around to the north. A path through light trees continues north, eventually joining up with the aforementioned cutline. Snowshoe 400 or so horizontal metres along the cutline and arrive at the base of Eagle Hill and an important unsigned junction. Hopefully the junction is clear, but snow cover may hide it to some degree.

It is possible at this point to take a more direct line north to the summit. Better is the circuitous route via the southeast

DON'T FORGET TO LOOK UP ONCE IN A WHILE.

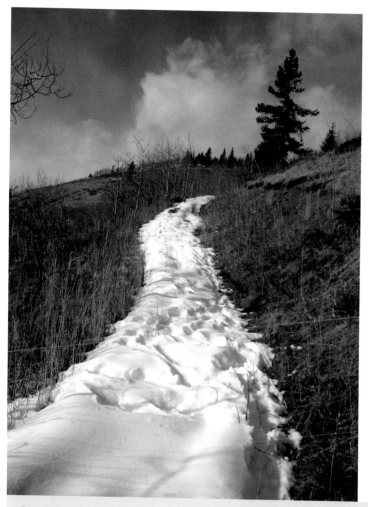

THE TRAIL HOLDS SNOW WELL, WHILE THE SURROUNDING
SLOPES ARE COMPLETELY CLEAR. DESCENDING THIS
TRAIL ON SNOWSHOES WAS FAST AND FUN.

FROM NEAR THE VALLEY BOTTOM, LOOKING TOWARD THE SUMMIT
OF EAGLE HILL. IT'S HARD TO BELIEVE THAT SNOWSHOES WERE
NEEDED ON THIS MARCH DAY, BUT THEY WERE INVALUABLE.

slope's trail. From the junction, turn right (east) and follow the trail as it gently ascends the hill, going more or less away from the summit. About 300 m along, the trail turns sharply to the northwest, zigzagging a little near the top before you reach a barbed-wire fence. This marks the summit, but to get the best view, hop over the fence and walk or snowshoe a few metres northwest. A unique view toward Mount Yamnuska and company awaits.

Return the way you came in or take the cutline route if you feel comfortable descending a different route than you ascended for several sections.

37 SEVENTY BUCK VIEWPOINT

(MAP 11, PAGE 483)

RATING ADVANCED
MOUNTAIN HEIGHT 1756 M
ELEVATION GAIN 293 M
ROUND-TRIP DISTANCE 2.2 KM
ROUND-TRIP TIME 1.5–2.5 HOURS
MAPS 82 0/02 JUMPINGPOUND CREEK,
GEM TREK BRAGG CREEK AND ELBOW VALLEY
(SHEEP VALLEY)

Steep terrain, mostly without a trail, to a cool viewpoint atop a significant band of vertical rock are the selling points for this terrific little Daffern trip. If you are looking for a little taste of what intermediate/advanced snowshoeing, more characteristic of trips in Snowshoeing in the Canadian Rockies, 2nd Edition, *involves, this trip is the ticket! Be patient and wait for good snow coverage.*

DIRECTIONS

From Highway 1, turn south onto Sibbald Creek Trail (Highway 68). Drive about 27.6 km (4.6 km west of the Powderface Trail turnoff) and park on the side of the road, just past a distinctive group of rocks on the side of the mountain. If you are approaching from the west it's 1.8 km east of the turnoff to Sibbald Meadows Pond.

The route goes up the right side of the shallow gully that lies to the left of the rocks (see photo). "Go up" would be the only necessary words to describe the first part of the ascent. There may be

FROM THE ROAD, THE START OF THE ROUTE BY
THE DISTINCTIVE ROCKS. R=ROCKS.

trails but if snow-covered they will be difficult to follow. Pick the line of least resistance. Almost immediately you will be aware of the steep grade of the slope. Snowshoes with good crampons and heel lifts will be mandatory here. Go north and aim for the end of the south-southeast ridge, around GR459579, 1609 m.

At this point the terrain gets easier and the views open up as you go northwest to the viewpoint. The left side of the mountain eventually disappears, leaving only a vertiginous drop on that side – be careful you don't get too close to the edge. There is a trail more to the right of the edge. Follow it easily to the delightful high point of the cliff at GR454583, 1756 m.

The summit view features good but distant views of Mount

Yamnuska and company to the north, as well as Mount Baldy and the Mount McGillivray massif to the west. Return the same way.

A CLOSE-UP OF ICONIC MOUNT YAMNUSKA.

38 KANANASKIS INTEGRATED FOREST INTERPRETIVE TRAIL (KIFIT)

(MAP 12, PAGE 483)

DIFFICULTY INTERMEDIATE

ELEVATION GAIN APPROXIMATELY 120 M

ROUND-TRIP DISTANCE 5.0–6.1 KM, DEPENDING ON RETURN ROUTE

ROUND-TRIP TIME 2–4 HOURS

MAPS 82 O/03 CANMORE; GEM TREK CANMORE AND KANANASKIS VILLAGE

When there is enough snow, this is a great trip with surprisingly good views and interesting terrain. Wait for good snow coverage to attempt the trip. The interpretive trail signs provide an interesting overview of forest management in the area.

DIRECTIONS

From Highway 40 south, turn east onto Highway 68 and drive 1.3 km. Park on the south side of the road (200 m west of the Lusk Creek parking lot). If this is unsafe, drive 200 m east and park in the Lusk Creek parking lot and hike over to the embankment.

Snowshoe up the embankment on the south side of the road and look for the wide path through the trees to the west. Snowshoe along the path, reaching the first of seven informative signs

RELAXING (SNOOZING) AT THE END OF THE TRAIL.
SNOWSHOES MAKE GOOD FOOT RESTS!

in about 300 m (actually it's the second – the first is in the Lusk Creek parking lot).

Continue to the second sign, 400 m west of the first. This is where the interpretive trail turns south into sparse forest. If the trail is broken and easy to follow, turn left and snowshoe in the general directions southwest, then south, then southeast. It is a good idea to take a good look at the trail map on the back of the interpretive sign before you go into the forest. If the trail is not obvious, it is easier, and perhaps a little more scenic, to follow the alternative route described below.

For the normal route, the next sign is about 200 m SSE of where you left the main trail, and the one after that is 300 m farther in the same direction. Hopefully, following the winding path will be straightforward, but if at any point you become disoriented, turn right and head for the open cutblocks to the west. Once in the cutblocks, go south for a while and then look left for the interpretive signs.

Once out into open terrain, following the path from sign to sign is much easier and the views really open up. The end of the interpretive section of the trail is marked with two wooden benches and two signs. Take a breather to read the signs and enjoy the views of Mount Baldy to the west and Goat Mountain, Mount Yamnuska and Association Peak to the north.

ALTERNATIVE ROUTE

From the second sign, reading "Growth in Progress," continue going west on the main trail for another 100–150 m, to the obvious hiking sign indicating the start of Baldy Pass Trail (sometimes identified as Old Mill Road). Snowshoe south along the wide path until you arrive at another hiking sign a few hundred metres later. Here, Baldy Pass Trail continues south and a large cutblock appears on your left (to the southeast). Turn left into the cutblock and make your way up and southeast.

The pleasant aspect of this route is that you are treated to good views almost right away. Be sure to turn around periodically and look north to Goat Mountain, Mount Yamnuska, Association Peak and Black Rock Mountain.

Elevation gain up the cutblock is very gentle and the panorama further unfolds. Eventually you'll want to start looking left for the back of an interpretive sign. When you see the sign, make your way over and up to it to join the interpretive trail. Follow the trail southeast to its termination, where you will find two signs and two benches.

Conclusion for Both Routes

At the end of the interpretive trail you can return the way you came in or continue south to higher ground (highly recommended). If you choose to extend the trip, the trail continues south, although it may not be as obvious in places. It trends in a southwesterly direction for about 400 m and then south for another 400 m, eventually running into Baldy Pass Trail. Throughout, views to the south continue to improve, featuring the unnamed but impressive outliers and peaks south of Mount Baldy.

Upon reaching Baldy Pass Trail you again have two options for return: go back the same way you came up, or make it a loop route by taking Baldy Pass Trail back to the start of the interpretive trail. The loop route is enjoyable but not terribly scenic. Trees on both sides of the trail block most of the views. Also, a loop route will probably not save you any time, as the trail first goes west, then north, taking a couple of switchbacks en route. Variety will probably be the primary motivation for using Baldy Pass Trail as a return route.

PEAKS SOUTH OF MOUNT BALDY.

HIGHWAY 40 SOUTH

Highway 40 South does not boast the same number of snow-shoe routes as its counterpart to the west – Highway 742 (Smith–Dorrien) (see page 244). Nevertheless, there are several worthwhile trips in the area and, like the Highway 541 area (page 133), the easterly location of this road makes it a good place to find good weather when the situation is more dismal farther west. This is especially true of the north section of the road, which may be basking in sunlight while clouds consume more westerly peaks. The north section is also subject to snow-eating blasts from chinook winds. You may end up carrying your snowshoes as much as you wear them.

ROUTES

Nakiska
Ski
Area

N

0   0.5   1.0   1.5   2.0
Kilometres

Kananaskis Village Inset

Centennial Drive

Troll Falls Trail ①
1.7 km one-way
from Stoney Trail
Parking Lot; 60 m
of elevation gain.

Troll
Falls

Hey
Meadow

1.7 Troll Falls

**Highway #1
23 km**

Aspen

Terrace

Terrace Drive

**3.3
Ribbon Creek**

Stoney
Trail
Parking
Lot

Kovach

**2.5
Village
Loops**

Village
Sportsfield
Parking Lot

Ribbon Creek
Parking Lot

Avalanche Danger
Beyond This Point

Emergency
Centre

Sports Field

Village Rim
Trail

Terrace

Heli-pad

Kovach

Terrace

**Ribbon Creek
Snowshoe trail** ②
3.3km trail follows
picturesque Ribbon Creek.
60m of elevation gain.

Aspen

Kananaskis
Village

Heli-pad

Legend

👣 Trailhead
— — — Snowshoe Trail
· · · · · · Cross-country
       Ski Trail

0   125 250 Metres

Kovach

Village
Sportsfield
Parking Lot
(See Inset)

Avalanche Danger
Beyond This Point

**Village
Loops
2.5**

Avalanche Danger
Beyond This Point

40

**Peter Lougheed
Provincial Park
Turn-off 26 km**

Terrace Trail south and Ribbon Creek trail beyond the Link and
Ribbon Creek Ski trail juntion are not maintained for winter use,
and are not recommended due to avalanche hazards in the area.

Village Loops Trail ③
2 loops totaling 2.5 km with 40 m of elevation gain,
starts at Village Sports Field Trailhead.

ABOVE: THE EASY SNOWSHOE ROUTES AROUND KANANASKIS
VILLAGE (MAP COURTESY ALBERTA PARKS, KANANASKIS).
BELOW: NINA VAN SNOWSHOES THE SCENIC KANANASKIS
VILLAGE TRAIL. THE AWESOME FORM OF MOUNT KIDD IS TO
THE LEFT. THE HILL ABOVE NINA'S HEAD IS THE FORMER
MOUNT KIDD FIRE LOOKOUT — ANOTHER ADVANCED TRIP
DESCRIBED IN SNOWSHOEING IN THE CANADIAN ROCKIES.

39 TROLL FALLS

(MAP 13, PAGE 484)

DIFFICULTY EASY	
ELEVATION GAIN 60 M	
ROUND-TRIP DISTANCE 3.7 KM	
ROUND-TRIP TIME 1.5–2 HOURS	
MAPS 82 J/14 SPRAY LAKES RESERVOIR, GEM TREK CANMORE AND KANANASKIS VILLAGE	

This short trip goes to a small frozen waterfall. It is an ideal trip for the family and young children. Yet again, waiting for sufficient snow coverage will be the key to making this a snowshoe trip instead of an icy hike.

DIRECTIONS

Drive south on Highway 40 for about 25 km to the Kananaskis Village turnoff. Turn right and drive about 1 km up the road. Turn right on the gravel road, signed "Stoney Trailhead." The parking area is a few hundred metres down the road.

Snowshoe north on Stoney Trail for about 1.2 km. At the intersection with Hay Meadow Trail, turn left and snowshoe a few hundred metres to Troll Falls Trail. A short section of the trail is groomed for cross-country skiers, so stay to the side. Follow the trail and signs to Troll Falls in about 600 m. At the falls, you can actually crawl right behind the frozen water! Return the same way you came in.

ABOVE: THE FROZEN FORM OF TROLL FALLS.
BELOW: MARK CRAWLS BEHIND THE FALLS.

40 KANANASKIS VILLAGE SNOWSHOE TRAIL

(MAP 13, PAGE 484)

DIFFICULTY INTERMEDIATE

ELEVATION GAIN APPROXIMATELY 100 M

ROUND-TRIP DISTANCE 2.7 KM, FIGURE 8 LOOP

ROUND-TRIP TIME 45–90 MINUTES

MAPS 82 J/14 SPRAY LAKES RESERVOIR, GEM TREK CANMORE AND KANANASKIS VILLAGE

This short loop route through the forests above Kananaskis Village has several pleasant viewpoints. Even though snow may be scarce at various times of the year and/or after a chinook, the trail tends to get icy. Therefore, snowshoes or spikes are recommended for the entire trip. Consider combining this short jaunt with another trip in the area, or just relax in Woody's Pub for refreshments afterward (no minors!).

DIRECTIONS

Driving south on Highway 40, turn right at the Nakiska turnoff. Shortly after, turn left toward Kananaskis Village. Just before the village, turn right at the sign for Mount Kidd Manor and follow the road to the public parking lot. From the parking lot you'll be able to take in a good view of Mount Kidd.

The loop can be completed in either direction. The north loop has the most elevation gain but the south has better views. To start with the north loop, find the trailhead at the west end of the parking lot and look for the first orange snowshoe sign on a light-blue pole. (The south loop starts with a similar marker but it is slightly to the south (left) of the west end of the parking lot.) Go to the start of the north loop and follow the snowshoe signs through the trees in a northwesterly direction. The remainder of the route is simply a matter of following a string of snowshoe signs and orange and pink flagging in the trees.

The high point of the north loop has a good view of the northeast side of Mount Kidd and of the ascent slopes to Mount Kidd Lookout (a trip to which is described in *Snowshoeing in the Canadian Rockies*). The trail soon swings around to the south and descends to a junction where the south loop starts.

FAMILY SNOWSHOEING AROUND KANANASKIS VILLAGE. MOST OF THE TIME ROGAN ENJOYS RIDING IN THE CHARIOT, BUT SOMETIMES HE JUST WANTS TO DO THE WORK HIMSELF.

LOOKING SOUTHEAST ACROSS KANANASKIS VALLEY
TOWARD THE WEDGE. (GILLEAN DAFFERN)

Again, follow signs and flagging around the shorter south loop, enjoying some very respectable views of mountains to the south and east. At the south end of the loop, do not be tempted to follow the ski tracks going south. This path may put you in avalanche danger.

41 EVAN-THOMAS CREEK

(MAP 13, PAGE 484)

DIFFICULTY EASY	
ELEVATION GAIN MINIMAL	
ROUND-TRIP DISTANCE 8–10 KM	
ROUND-TRIP TIME 3–5 HOURS	
MAPS 82 J/14 SPRAY LAKES RESERVOIR, GEM TREK CANMORE AND KANANASKIS VILLAGE	

Evan-Thomas Creek is a very popular destination because there are four easily accessible ice climbs on the west side of the creek. Although far-reaching mountain views are largely absent throughout as you snowshoe this trail, the creek and canyon are very interesting and definitely worth a visit. Ice climbers certainly appreciate a few snowshoers packing down the approach trail to the climbs!

DIRECTIONS

Park at Evan-Thomas Creek parking lot, 27.2 km south on Highway 40.

From the south end of the parking lot find the trailhead, snowshoe a few hundred metres to a T junction, turn left and continue on for another 1.5 km to a major intersection. At this intersection, left goes toward Evan-Thomas Pass and right leads down to Evan-Thomas Creek and the connector trail to Wedge Pond. Turn right, arriving at the creek and a bridge across it in short order.

Don't cross the creek, as the trail usually starts on the east side of it before switching over to the west side some distance along. Where it crosses, and if multiple crossings are necessary, may change from year to year. In any case the water underneath the ice flows quite fast and can therefore erode and weaken the ice surface at any point. Caution is required for any crossing along the way.

The first frozen waterfall (Chantilly Falls) appears on the west (right) side of the creek, about 1.2 km from the bridge. A slight detour to the west, from the main trail, takes you directly under the wall of ice, where you are quite likely to see ice climbers working their way up the falls. As with all frozen waterfalls, be careful about getting too close – standing in the firing line of a 5-kg chunk of ice moving at 160 km/h may not be the best thing for your health!

Snowshoe another 700 m along the main trail to reach the very popular trio of ice climbs Snowline, Moonlight and 2 Low 4 Zero. Once again you must leave the creek and head west to see these impressive cascades of ice.

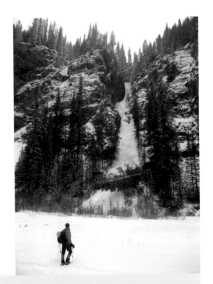

Most parties will choose to return at this point. However, it certainly is possible (and desirable) to continue up the creek in a southeasterly direction for another kilometre or so. You have reached the end of the line when the creek turns

CHECKING OUT CHANTILLY FALLS FROM A SAFE DISTANCE.

INTERESTING ICE FORMATIONS ALONG EVAN-THOMAS CREEK. MATTHEW CLAY TELLS ME THESE ARE THE RESULT OF SMALL FLUCTUATIONS IN RIVER FLOW, CAUSING THE BOTTOM OF ICICLES TO GROW AS WATER SPLASHES ON THEM, BUT NOT THE TOP. (MATTHEW CLAY)

a sharp left. Travel beyond this point is not possible, as the canyon narrows and steepens to the point where it becomes impassable. Just before you get to that point, however, the third interesting detour of the day pops up on the east side of the creek in the form of a pleasant and narrow canyon leading to a small ice climb. The canyon is not obvious from the creek but can be located with a little searching. It's definitely worth checking out if you have made it this far. When you've had enough, return the way you came in.

42 WEDGE POND

(MAP 13, PAGE 484)

DIFFICULTY EASY

ELEVATION GAIN MINIMAL

ROUND-TRIP DISTANCE 1 KM (POND); ADD 4 KM RETURN TO EVAN-THOMAS CREEK

ROUND-TRIP TIME 0.5–1 HOUR; ADD 1–2 HOURS FOR EVAN-THOMAS CREEK

MAPS 82 J/14 SPRAY LAKES RESERVOIR, GEM TREK CANMORE AND KANANASKIS VILLAGE

The best time of the year to visit Wedge Pond is in the fall, when the leaves are changing colour. Clear, calm weather attracts photographers hoping to capture that sweet image of Mount Kidd and The Fortress reflected perfectly in the waters of the pond. Winter – more accurately, snow – unfortunately deprives us of that reflection, but the scenery around the pond is still worth a look. This very short trip can easily be combined with trips nearby, such as Evan-Thomas Creek, for a fuller day.

DIRECTIONS

Park at Wedge Pond, 29.6 km south on Highway 40.

The pond is visible through the trees. Make your way down to the shoreline and snowshoe around the perimeter of the pond, taking in good views of the surrounding mountains. Mount Kidd, to the west, is the most prominent peak, but the unique form of The Fortress, to the southwest, will likely garner as much if not more attention.

If the trip around the pond is not enough, trekking along nearby Evan-Thomas Creek should do the trick. From the south

MOUNT KIDD PROVIDES AN IMPRESSIVE
BACKGROUND FOR WEDGE POND.

end of the parking lot, a trail (bike path) heads east and slightly
north. Ignore a couple of left-turning paths but follow the third
one, which goes left to a T junction. At the junction turn right
and follow the path uphill to a high point and another T junction. This time, stay left and descend to Evan-Thomas Creek in a
few hundred metres. Cross the creek and pick up the trail on the
other side. For the remainder of the route, see the description for
Evan-Thomas Creek on page 227.

43 WINTOUR ROAD

(MAP 17, PAGE 486)

DIFFICULTY EASY

ELEVATION GAIN APPROXIMATELY 120 M

ROUND-TRIP DISTANCE 10 KM

ROUND-TRIP TIME 2.5–4 HOURS

MAPS 82 J/14 SPRAY LAKES RESERVOIR,
82 J/11 KANANASKIS LAKES,
GEM TREK KANANASKIS LAKES

The Wintour Road snowshoe trail is as easy a route-finding challenge as there is, simply because there is no route-finding and therefore no challenge. Unless you decide to try it blindfolded, you cannot get lost or disoriented on this trip! The primary motivation for completing the 10-km route is for the exercise and pleasant views of the north end of the Elk Range and peaks around Elk Lakes. Trail-breaking will likely be easy, as the trail is often packed down by skiers and other snowshoers, as well as ice climbers heading to Whiteman's Falls. This is not the most exciting trip in the area, so bring some friends for conversation. Also, don't try this trip before December 1 – the road will still be open at that time of the winter and driving the length of the route pretty much kills the exercise element!

DIRECTIONS

Drive the 49-km length of Highway 40 south to the Kananaskis Trail junction, where Highway 40 is barricaded.

Strap on your snowshoes and enjoy 5 km (one way) of easy snowshoeing beyond the closure. Throughout, the entire length of Mount Wintour is there to keep you company, on your left

THE PEAKS AROUND ELK LAKES: FROM LEFT TO RIGHT, AOSTA, FOX, FOCH AND SARRAIL.

side, with good views of the peaks around Elk Lakes making an appearance early on. Later on, diminutive but striking Gap Mountain appears, south of Wintour.

The Elpoca turnoff marks the end of the route. You can only snowshoe up that road for a very short distance until you reach the "End of the Trail" sign.

Of course, ambitious snowshoers can stay on Highway 40 and continue along the road. An additional 5 km will get you a magnificent view of Elpoca Mountain's stunning west face. However, that brings the round-trip distance to 20 km – a significant distance on snowshoes, even if the trail is packed down. Most parties will call it a day at Elpoca and then return the same way.

THE HIGHWOOD

The window for snowshoeing in The Highwood is a very small one: any time before December 1. However, an area that boasts such consistently spectacular scenery and views warrants a visit or ten, whether there is enough snow to snowshoe or not! Fortunately the wickedly high starting elevations for most trips in The Highwood means that snow is often abundant before the road closes at midnight on December 1 of each year. Unfortunately most of the ascents are steep and challenging and therefore appear in Snowshoeing in the Canadian Rockies, 2nd Edition. *Two exceptions are described in this volume. Usually by mid-November, but sometimes before, the snow has piled up enough to make snowshoeing worthwhile and fun.*

ROUTES

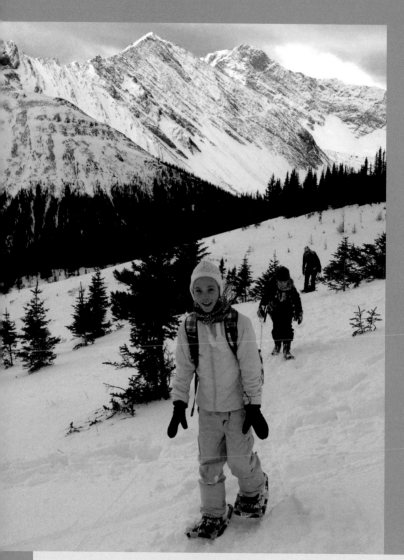

TIA MCCARTNEY, DANICA BATEMAN AND JACKIE BATEMAN
SNOWSHOE INTO PTARMIGAN CIRQUE. (TANYA KOOB)

44 ELBOW LAKE AND RAE GLACIER TRAIL

(MAP 14, PAGE 484)

RATING intermediate to Elbow Lake, advanced to Rae Glacier	
HIGH POINTS 2088 m at Elbow Lake, 2215 m at Rae Glacier	
ELEVATION GAIN 137 m to Elbow Lake, add 230 m for Rae Glacier	
ROUND-TRIP DISTANCE 2.8 km for Elbow Lake, 5.2–7.2 km for Rae Glacier	
ROUND-TRIP TIME 3–5 hours	
MAPS 82 J/11 Kananaskis Lakes, J/10 Mount Rae, Gem Trek Kananaskis Lakes	

The source of Calgary's drinking water, Elbow Lake, is a fantastic destination any time of the year. The relatively short but steep trail is ideal for beginner snowshoers looking to move up to more challenging routes, without anything too dramatically difficult. Once at the lake there are a couple to options to extend the trip. This route is very popular with skiers. Fortunately there is tons of room for everyone. I have seen people toboggan down the trail!

DIRECTIONS

Drive 12.3 km south of the winter gate and park in the Elbow Pass parking lot. The 1.4-km trail to Elbow Lake is obvious, wide and generally easy to negotiate. The steep sections are perfect for snowshoes, going up and coming down. At the lake, enjoy the terrific view of a few of the innumerable outliers of massive

Mount Rae to the northeast and the formidable face of Elpoca Mountain's south side to the northwest. The south end of Tombstone Mountain will become visible to the north if you go around the right side of the lake.

At this point, you have three options: 1. Return the way you came; 2. Snowshoe around the west side of the lake to get a better view of the valley to the north; 3. Snowshoe Rae Glacier Trail to a very scenic high point (highly recommended).

RAE GLACIER TRAIL

To find the Rae Glacier Trail, snowshoe along the east shore (right side) of the lake or follow the trails through the campground. Once out of the campground, the trail continues alongside the lake. About 5–10 minutes past the campground, Rae Glacier Trail veers off to the east (right). It is generally easy to find, usually due to heavy human traffic, but if you can't find it just go east until you intersect a creek. Stay on the south side of the creek and start following it in a southeasterly direction.

WHEN THE SUN DOESN'T COME OUT TO PLAY, HOT PINK PANTS CAN SAVE THE DAY! NICOLE AT ELBOW LAKE.

If you do find the trail, follow it in an easterly direction until you reach an open area, around GR414119. Here the trail turns southeast, paralleling the wide creek that originates from Mount Rae and its glacier. The creek eventually narrows into a small canyon. DO NOT go into the canyon unless you are planning to take a frigid swim in the water hidden by the snow! Instead, follow the trail as it ascends slopes on the right side of the canyon.

Time to gain some elevation. The trail goes steadily uphill, through the trees, soon coming to an open area and high point with an amazing view of the surrounding area (GR418114, 2215 m). This, more than likely, will be the end of the trail for beginners. The terrain beyond this point gets more complex and if the slopes on either side of the valley are snow-loaded, serious avalanches can occur. Take in the view and then return the way you came. Hopefully you will enjoy the ease of the descent, especially plunge-stepping down the trail from Elbow Lake.

NICOLE MAKES HER WAY TOWARD THE HIGH POINT OF THE TRAIL (CENTRE OF PHOTO) ON A GLOOMY BUT ATMOSPHERIC DAY. NO CHANCE OF AVALANCHES IN THESE CONDITIONS, BUT IF THE SLOPES WERE SNOW-LOADED, AVALANCHE GEAR WOULD BE NECESSARY.

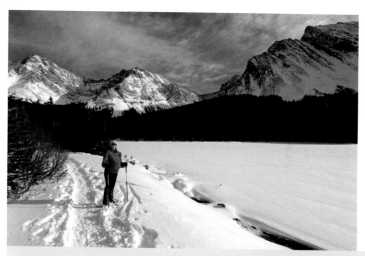

SNOWSHOEING IN YOUR THIRD TRIMESTER OF PREGNANCY MAY NOT BE FOR EVERYONE (SPECIFICALLY MALES!), BUT SARAH MCLEAN MANAGES TO GET OUT TO ENJOY THE SUPERB ENVIRONS OF THE WEST SIDE OF ELBOW LAKE. (SCOTT MCLEAN) BELOW: MASSIVE TOMBSTONE MOUNTAIN DOMINATES THE VIEW TO THE NORTH.

If the slopes on either side of the valley are NOT snow-loaded, then it is possible for beginners to continue to the end of the Rae Glacier Trail. Note, however, that the rocky and undulating terrain may be tricky to negotiate, due to a lack of snow.

Continue going southeast on the trail, eventually descending to the rocky drainage and then following it up. Several hundred metres up the drainage you will take the right fork and make your way up to a cairned high point at GR421106, 2360 m. The actual high point of the trail can be seen up a hill to the right. A large cairn marks the spot. Snow conditions make dictate if you go to this point or not. The view from both is excellent, although the panorama from the higher point is a little more comprehensive. Return the same way.

WEST SIDE OF ELBOW LAKE

Instead of visiting the Rae Glacier, there is the option is snowshoe around the west side of Elbow Lake and continue on the wide trail, heading north. This takes you into a spectacular valley, featuring Tombstone Mountain (north), Elpoca Mountain (northwest) and the outliers of Mount Rae (northeast). Follow the trail around the left (west) side of the lake to the lake outlet. Cross the outlet on a log and then turn north and continue following the trail as it parallels the Elbow River. It's up to you how far you go down the valley but the scenery doesn't change much beyond 300 m past the lake outlet (GR410122). Here you will get the best views of Elpoca and Tombstone. Note that you are actually descending the valley from here, so the return trip will be a little more work.

Return the same way when satiated or dog-tired, whichever comes first! You can return via the east side of the lake if you want to see some extra scenery. Unless you are 100% sure that the lake is fully frozen (and I wouldn't bet a stick of licorice on it!), follow the easy trail near the lakeshore.

45 PTARMIGAN CIRQUE

(MAP 14, PAGE 484)

RATING INTERMEDIATE
HIGH POINT 2438 M
ELEVATION GAIN 229 M
ROUND-TRIP DISTANCE 3.6 KM
ROUND-TRIP TIME 2–4 HOURS
MAPS 82 J/11 KANANASKIS LAKES, J/10 MOUNT
RAE, GEM TREK KANANASKIS LAKES

*At 2206 m, Ptarmigan Cirque boasts the highest starting eleva-
tion of any trip in Kananaskis. In fact, upon stepping out of the
car you are already higher than the summit of Mount Baldy, one of
the first significant peaks off Highway 40 south. In extreme conditions there could some minor avalanche concerns, but they are
unlikely to occur before the road closes.*

DIRECTIONS

Park at the Highwood Meadows – Ptarmigan Cirque parking lot,
just south of Highwood Pass. Don't put on your snowshoes yet.
It is easiest to carry them and walk 300 m back up the road to the
signed crosswalk. Ptarmigan Cirque Trail starts here on the east
side of the road. Snowshoe up the embankment, trending left.
The trail quickly turns right, into the trees, heading northeast.
It soon starts to gain elevation more steeply, turning north and
eventually taking a sharp, uphill turn to the east.

When the view begins to open up, the trail goes north and
then northwest. Choosing a route into the cirque becomes a

little more obvious from here. Either stay high, to the left and then turn northeast toward the cirque or take a more direct route that may have some minor ups and downs. The end of the official Ptarmigan Cirque Trail lies around GR429079. Beyond that you are heading up Alan Kane's scramble route for Mount Rae – highly unadvised when snowy. Return the same way. The summer trail makes a loop, but when snow covers everything, the trail will be very difficult to follow and trying to do so may take you needlessly into dangerous terrain.

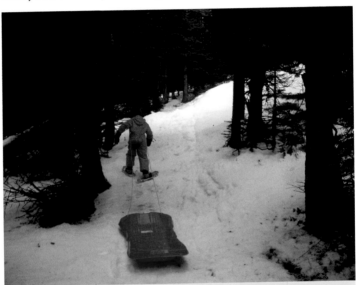

NOAH KOOB DRAGS HIS SLED UP THE PTARMIGAN CIRQUE TRAIL. (TANYA KOOB)

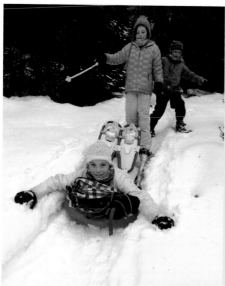

ABOVE: MARK KOOB, NOAH KOOB AND SEBASTIAN MARKS MAKE THEIR WAY INTO THE CIRQUE. (TANYA KOOB) LEFT: WHAT A GENTLEMAN! IT APPEARS NOAH HAS GIVEN HIS SLED TO TIA MCCARTNEY. MACKENZIE AND DANICA BATEMAN BRING UP THE REAR. CHIVALRY IS NOT DEAD! (TANYA KOOB)

HIGHWAY 742 (SMITH–DORRIEN)

This stretch of highway from Canmore to the Kananaskis Lakes Trail turnoff is an absolute gold mine of snowshoeing potential. I think it is the best location in the southern end of the Canadian Rockies for snowshoeing. You can park your vehicle almost anywhere along this road and find an interesting route or area to snowshoe in; just don't park in any of the "no stopping" zones because they are avalanche areas. Returning to find your vehicle buried in several metres of avalanche debris may put a damper on your day!

When other areas of the Rockies, especially those to the east, are struggling to maintain a good base of snow, the routes along the Smith–Dorrien are usually swimming in the white stuff. Great snowshoeing snow is almost guaranteed, especially from January to May. If you are looking for deep snow and lots of it, this is the place to go.

In this section of the book, I have identified several places as good snowshoeing areas but I haven't provided route descriptions or destinations. These areas, mainly on the west side of the road, are perfect for random exploration and more specifically for engaging in some serious trail-breaking. If you are after some strenuous exercise and/or are looking for less-crowded areas in which to snowshoe, try one of these trips. They are marked by the highway number and then a letter, from 742-A to 742-J. All these areas automatically earn an intermediate rating, due to a strong possibility of trail-breaking and lack of a specific trail or route.

Highway 742 can be accessed from the southwest end of Canmore or via Highway 40 South and Kananaskis Trail. If you are coming from Calgary, the driving time to Chester Lake and Burstall Pass parking lots is about the same using either route. Therefore any routes north of those parking lots can be more quickly accessed by going through Canmore, and routes to the south from Highway 40 South and Kananaskis Trail.

Also, note that Highway 742 is a gravel road and can be quite snowy and slippery after a snowfall. And then when all that snow melts, the road gets muddy and slippery – an equally bad combination.

ROUTES

EVEN THE SNOWMEN NEED SNOWSHOES IN THIS AREA! MICHELLE MARCHE, NICOLE LISAFELD AND THEIR NEW BUDDY MAKE THEIR WAY ACROSS BURSTALL FLATS. (SADLY, ABOUT A MONTH LATER, THE SNOWMAN DROWNED IN HIS OWN BODILY FLUIDS.)

46 CANMORE PARK

(MAP 15, PAGE 484)

DIFFICULTY EASY
ELEVATION GAIN MINIMAL
ROUND-TRIP DISTANCE VARIABLE
ROUND-TRIP TIME VARIABLE
MAPS 82 O/03 CANMORE,
GEM TREK CANMORE AND KANANASKIS VILLAGE

There is no easier trip in this book than this one. The park is a great area to practise basic skills and get the feel for walking with

VERY EASY SNOWSHOE TERRAIN BELOW HA LING PEAK
(RIGHT) AND MOUNT LAWRENCE GRASSI.

snowshoes on your feet. It is also ideal for quick and convenient family trips and outings with young children. You can walk around, mainly on hard-packed ground, for 10 minutes or an hour. Excellent views of the east face of Ha Ling Peak, Mount Lawrence Grassi, the East End of Rundle (EEOR) and Mount Lady MacDonald are constant companions. Due to its popularity, waiting until right after a big snowfall can be the best time to visit the park. Otherwise, expect icy conditions.

DIRECTIONS

From the southwest end of Canmore, turn onto Highway 742 (Smith–Dorrien) and drive 500 m to the park entrance. Turn left into the parking lot.

Put on your snowshoes and explore the area at your leisure.

MORE EASY TERRAIN AND THE EAST END OF RUNDLE.

47 CANMORE NORDIC CENTRE SNOWSHOE

(MAP 15, PAGE 484)

RATING INTERMEDIATE	
NET ELEVATION GAIN APPROXIMATELY 100 M	
ROUND-TRIP DISTANCE 3 KM	
ROUND-TRIP TIME 1–2 HOURS	
MAPS 82 O/03 CANMORE, GEM TREK CANMORE AND KANANASKIS VILLAGE	

This relatively new loop route is surprisingly enjoyable and a little more physically taxing than I was expecting. It earns an intermediate rating because of several steep slopes that must be ascended and descended. At a fast pace the loop can be completed in about an hour. Better, however, to take your time and enjoy the ride. Wait until the area is under a deep blanket of snow. Also, follow the snowshoe signs carefully, as they are not always obvious and route-finding is perhaps more tricky than you would expect from a signed route.

DIRECTIONS

Near Canmore, drive 2 km on Highway 742 and turn right, into the Canmore Nordic Centre. Find the Bill Warren Training Centre and park on the east side of it. You should see the snowshoe trail sign at the east end of the parking lot.

From the snowshoe trail sign, drop down and to the left, to the beginning of the loop route. Although either direction is fine, a clockwise route is recommended. Both ends of the loop are visible from the starting point. Take the lower trail. It gently descends, goes under a bridge, turns to the left and then descends quite steeply. Just beyond the low point of this steep descent, look for a snowshoe sign on the right side of the trail that will lead you into the trees, on a much narrower trail (Orchid bike trail).

Follow Orchid Trail for a few hundred metres until you arrive at an important intersection. Here, you have the option to keep following the loop or to take a side trip to a very pleasant viewpoint. For the side trip, turn left at the snowshoe sign and descend switchbacks to Georgetown Trail. Turn right onto Georgetown Trail and follow it for another couple of hundred metres to the obvious viewpoint of Canmore and the Bow River. Be careful near the cliff edge. It's a straight drop down if you go too far!

DO NOT continue farther along Georgetown Trail, even though it is easy to do so. Instead, retrace your steps back up to the aforementioned important intersection and continue following the snowshoe trail, now on the other side of Canmore Trail.

kananaskistrails.com

MAP OF THE ROUTE. A CLOCKWISE DIRECTION IS RECOMMENDED (MAP COURTESY OF KANANASKISTRAILS.COM).

Once again the trail descends a short way and starts winding its way across a hillside. There are no snowshoe signs for the next long stretch, but the path is obvious.

Eventually you'll pop out of the trees to see power lines and another open view. Turn right (sign on a tree), go uphill for about 15 m and then take another sharp right back into the trees. As of April 2015 there was no snowshoe sign directing you back into the trees. Once you're back in the trees, however, the snowshoe signs soon appear and it's an easy, though uphill, jaunt back to the start.

742-A

(MAP 15, PAGE 484)

DIFFICULTY INTERMEDIATE
ELEVATION GAIN VARIABLE
ROUND-TRIP DISTANCE VARIABLE
ROUND-TRIP TIME VARIABLE
MAPS 82 O/03 CANMORE,
GEM TREK CANMORE AND KANANASKIS VILLAGE

742-A is the northernmost snowshoeing area on the Smith–
Dorrien. It lies just north of Goat Pond.

A VERY PLEASANT AREA TO ENCOUNTER SOME EASY TERRAIN,
UNDER THE NORTHERN SECTION OF THE GOAT RANGE.

DIRECTIONS

Drive approximately 1.1 km north of the bridge over the canal. There is a small pullout on the west side of the road where you can park.

Snowshoe in the open area to the west and southwest, as conditions dictate. If the snow is not deep in this area, consider picking a location farther south, along Highway 742.

742-A

HIGHWAY 742

DIFFICULTY INTERMEDIATE

ELEVATION GAIN VARIABLE

ROUND-TRIP DISTANCE VARIABLE

ROUND-TRIP TIME VARIABLE

MAPS 82 J/14 SPRAY LAKES RESERVOIR,
GEM TREK CANMORE AND KANANASKIS VILLAGE

A DOGSLED TEAM STARTS ITS JOURNEY ACROSS SPRAY LAKE.
MOUNT SPARROWHAWK IS IN THE BACKGROUND. THE SMALL,
POINTED PEAK AT THE LEFT IS LITTLE LOUGHEED, WHICH
SNOWSHOERS CAN ASCEND ON AN ADVANCED SNOWSHOEING/HIKING
TRIP, DESCRIBED IN SNOWSHOEING IN THE CANADIAN ROCKIES,
THAT FEATURES AN AWESOME VIEW OF MOUNT LOUGHEED.

Near the north end of Spray Lake sits a large staging area for dog-sleds. Needless to say, this is also an ideal spot for snowshoeing around and across that part of the lake, as long as the lake is sufficiently frozen. If you see a sled with 10 dogs and a rider bounding across the surface, you should be good to go!

The prominent mountain to the south, on the other side of the lake, is Old Goat Mountain. More to the southeast stand the massive forms of Mount Lougheed and Sparrowhawk Mountain. From the other side of the lake you can turn around to see The Rimwall, several outliers and the south side of Big Sister.

DIRECTIONS

Park at the Driftwood Day Use parking lot, about 3 km south of the Spray Lake Campground turnoff.

Snowshoeing across the lake to the other side grants excellent views of Big Sister, The Rimwall and other peaks on the north-east side of the lake. Alternatively, you may wish to follow the east shoreline northwest and/or southeast.

742-C

(MAP 16, PAGE 485)

DIFFICULTY INTERMEDIATE

ELEVATION GAIN VARIABLE

ROUND-TRIP DISTANCE VARIABLE

ROUND-TRIP TIME VARIABLE

MAPS 82 J/14 SPRAY LAKES RESERVOIR,
GEM TREK CANMORE AND KANANASKIS VILLAGE

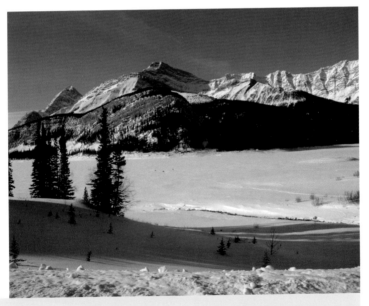

LOOKING SOUTH DOWN SPRAY LAKE. OLD GOAT MOUNTAIN AND
MOUNT NESTOR ARE ON THE OTHER SIDE OF THE LAKE.

A little farther south of 742-B is another easy-access point to Spray Lake. This area is popular with ice fishers. Views are similar to those of 742-B, if slightly better and with the added bonus of the striking Mount Nestor, south of Old Goat Mountain. Snowshoeing along the lakeshore or across the lake can be very rewarding on a sunny day.

DIRECTIONS

Park on the west side of the road, across from the small Spurling Creek sign, approximately 2.3 km south of the Driftwood turnoff.

742-C

51 742-D

(MAP 16, PAGE 485)

DIFFICULTY INTERMEDIATE

ELEVATION GAIN VARIABLE

ROUND-TRIP DISTANCE VARIABLE

ROUND-TRIP TIME VARIABLE

MAPS 82 J/14 SPRAY LAKES RESERVOIR,
GEM TREK CANMORE AND KANANASKIS VILLAGE

Only about 1 km south of 742-D, yet another open area grants easy access to the lake and wonderful views of the surrounding mountains. The profile of Mount Nestor is bound to impress you.

DIRECTIONS

Park on the west side of the road, about 1 km south of the small Spurling Creek sign, approximately 3.3 km south of the Driftwood turnoff.

MOUNT NESTOR, IN ALL ITS GLORY! NOTE THE SMALL WHITE ICE-FISHING HUT ON THE LAKE.

52 FORBES CREEK GROTTO

(MAP 16, PAGE 485)

RATING	INTERMEDIATE
ELEVATION GAIN	APPROXIMATELY 100 M
ROUND-TRIP DISTANCE	5.4–6.4 KM
ROUND-TRIP TIME	1.5–3 HOURS
MAPS	82 J/14 SPRAY LAKES RESERVOIR, GEM TREK CANMORE

Just so you know, the simplest definition for "grotto" is "cave," and that's exactly where this neat little trip takes you. The route is actually a very small section of the High Rockies Trail, still in development as of early 2016. Gillean and Tony Daffern have snowshoed a great deal of the trail (if not all of it by now), and credit goes to them for bringing this little gem to my attention.

DIRECTIONS

The trip starts at Spencer Creek (not marked on some maps), about 2.8 km south of Spurling Creek (small sign), on the Smith-Dorrien Highway. Park on the east side of the road. The summer trail winds east alongside the creek and sometimes at a greater distance from it. It soon enters a delightful area where a small, mossy stream runs. After that the trail returns to Spencer Creek and comes to a bridge spanning the creek (about 350 m from the road).

Turn right (south), cross the creek and follow the obvious trail on the other side. Don't expect any mind-blowing scenery for a while – just trees and more trees. Nevertheless, it's a pleasant

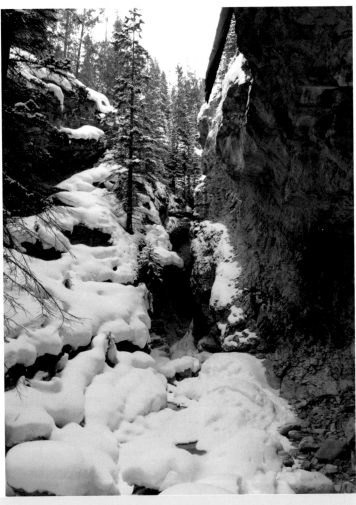

APPROACHING THE GROTTO. NOTE THE BUILT-UP SNOW ABOVE
THAT COULD FALL INTO THE GROTTO AND ONTO THOSE IN IT!

and easy jaunt. This trail will probably become popular with ski-ers. Try to stay to the far right as much as possible and create a separate snowshoe trail if one doesn't already exist.

About 1 km along, a second bridge, this time over Forbes Creek, is reached. Cross the bridge and turn left (east) at the end of it, making your way up the south bank of Forbes Creek. Soon it becomes easier to cross to the north bank of the creek and continue up. The grotto is close now.

Exercise caution as you enter the grotto. Footing can be tricky, depending on the snow coverage, and there is potential for clumps of snow to fall from the overhead features. Work your way to the back of this short but fascinating canyon and then return the way you came.

ROCKS AND BUBBLES IN THE ICE. IF YOU TOOK HIGH SCHOOL PHYSICS, YOU MAY FIGURE OUT THAT "REFRACTION" AND "TOTAL INTERNAL REFLECTION" CAUSE THE ICE ON THE ROCKS TO ACT AS A MIRROR WHEN VIEWED AT CERTAIN ANGLES — HENCE THE GLOSSY LOOK. YET ANOTHER SWEET VICTORY FOR THE AWESOME POWER OF PHYSICS!

Back at the Forbes Creek bridge you can return to your vehicle or continue the trip (recommended). The High Rockies Trail continues south for approximately another kilometre, eventually interesting the Sparrowhawk Creek Trail. There's a decent view of some of Spray Lake and Mount Nestor here and two new log benches from which to relax and admire the view. Continuing south along the High Rockies Trail, at this point, is an option. However, the recommended route descends west, all the way down onto Spray Lake. There is a trail down to the highway, but it is just as easy to point your snowshoes west and descend the embankment high above the deep canyon to the south.

Highway 742 and an even better view of the lake, with Nestor and Old Goat Mountain towering above it, is quickly reached. Of

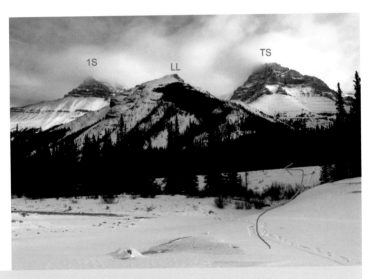

THE SECOND AND BEST ROUTE BACK TO HIGHWAY 742.
1S=FIRST SUMMIT OF MOUNT LOUGHEED. LL=LITTLE
LOUGHEED. TS=TRUE SUMMIT OF MOUNT LOUGHEED.

course you can hike along the highway directly to your car from here. It's an easy 1.7 km.

A much better option is to go across the highway and down to Spray Lake. Turn right (north) when you get to the lake and complete the 1.7 km back to your car directly on the lake or along the lakeshore. Take some time to look for areas where the ice is exposed. I saw some of the most amazing ice and rock scenery I'd ever seen around this part of the lake.

Throughout, you are accompanied by the awe-inspiring forms of Mount Nestor and Old Goat Mountain on the west side of the lake, with Big Sister and The Rimwall to the north. Turn around to see Mount Buller, Tent Ridge, Mount Smuts and Shark Mountain to the south. If you venture toward the middle of the lake, excellent views of The Windtower, Mount Lougheed, "Little Lougheed," Mount Sparrowhawk and Read's Tower to the east abound.

There are two places to make a quick and easy escape back to the road. Both are tree-free and obvious. Best to skip the first opening and go up the second (see photo), where your vehicle will only be 100 or so metres farther north on the highway.

53 742-E (BULLER POND)

(MAP 16, PAGE 485)

DIFFICULTY INTERMEDIATE

ELEVATION GAIN MINIMAL

ROUND-TRIP DISTANCE VARIABLE

ROUND-TRIP TIME VARIABLE

MAPS 82 J/14 SPRAY LAKES RESERVOIR,
GEM TREK CANMORE AND KANANASKIS VILLAGE

*You don't have to do any work to get a killer view from this vantage
point by Buller Pond. All can be seen from the road. Snowshoeing*

around or across the pond is a great way to spend some time, but if you want an even more spectacular view, consider the Beyond Buller Pond trip (page 266). January, February and early March are the best times of the year for a strong ice surface on the pond.

DIRECTIONS

A few hundred metres south of the Buller Mountain turnoff, park on the side of the road, where there is a great view to the west. Snowshoe around and/or across the pond.

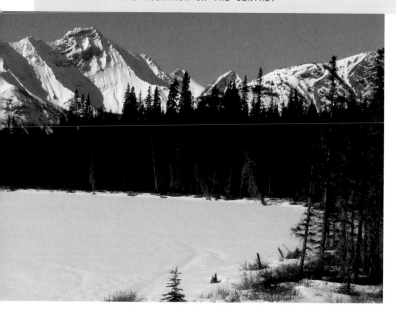

THE WONDERFUL ROADSIDE VIEW OF BULLER POND.
MIGHTY MOUNT ASSINIBOINE AT THE DISTANT LEFT
AND MASSIVE CONE MOUNTAIN IN THE CENTRE.

54 BEYOND BULLER POND

(MAP 16, PAGE 485)

HIGHWAY 742

DIFFICULTY INTERMEDIATE
ELEVATION LOSS/GAIN 100 M
ROUND-TRIP DISTANCE MINIMUM 3 KM
ROUND-TRIP TIME MINIMUM 1 HOUR
MAPS 82 J/14 SPRAY LAKES RESERVOIR,
GEM TREK CANMORE AND KANANASKIS VILLAGE

This is one of my favourite trips around Spray Lake. A pleasant jaunt down to the lake leads to fantastic views. Once there you can wander around to your heart's content (just leave before the ice melts!). Definitely a trip you'll want to save for a clear day.

DIRECTIONS

A few hundred metres south of the Buller Mountain turnoff, park on the side of the road, where there is a great view west.

Provided the pond is frozen and covered in snow, snowshoe across it and into the parking area on the other side. Turn right (north) and snowshoe to the north parking lot. Just before arriving there, look to the left and turn onto the obvious path heading down through the trees. It veers slightly to the right a few metres down.

Follow the path in a northwesterly direction for 1.1 km down toward Spray Lake. You'll lose 100 m of elevation en route. At least be thankful that you are easily breaking trail for the tougher return route uphill. The trail spits you out near a small but fascinating inlet. It's only about 100 m to Spray Lake from here,

ABOVE: HEADING DOWN TO THE LAKE IN THE EARLY MORNING HOURS, WE SAW THE SUN MANAGE TO CATCH CONE MOUNTAIN, MOUNT FORTUNE AND FORTULENT PEAKS ON THE OTHER SIDE OF THE LAKE. BELOW: A DARING SNOWSHOE JUMP OF ENORMOUS VERTICAL MAGNITUDE. EDDIE THE EAGLE WOULD BE PROUD!

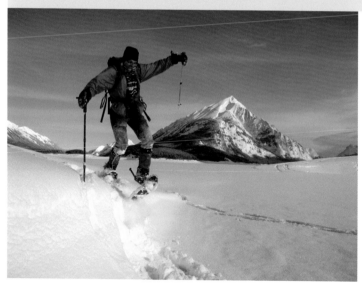

although you may want to spend some time checking out the inlet. Be careful about crossing the inlet, as the running water beneath the ice weakens the surface.

There is a lot of interesting scenery to explore around the inlet, but eventually you'll probably want to go south along the lakeshore or right out onto the lake. The views of Shark, Turner, Cone, Fortune, Fortulent (attached to Fortune) and Nestor are magnificent. As you travel farther south, mighty Mount Assiniboine makes a welcome appearance, sitting proudly between Turner and Cone.

Explore this wonderful environment for as long as you like before returning the same way you came in.

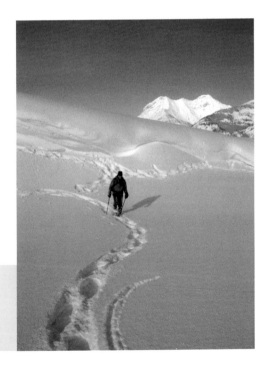

FASCINATING AND BEAUTIFUL TERRAIN AROUND THE LAKESHORE.

55 742-F

(MAP 16, PAGE 485)

DIFFICULTY INTERMEDIATE

ELEVATION GAIN MINIMAL

ROUND-TRIP DISTANCE VARIABLE

ROUND-TRIP TIME VARIABLE

MAPS 82 J/14 SPRAY LAKES RESERVOIR,
GEM TREK CANMORE AND KANANASKIS VILLAGE,
KANANASKIS LAKES

*THE AMAZING ENVIRONS OF THE NORTH END OF SMUTS
CREEK. NOTABLE PEAKS, FROM RIGHT TO LEFT,
INCLUDE TENT RIDGE, MOUNT BIRDWOOD, PIG'S TAIL,
COMMONWEALTH PEAK AND COMMONWEALTH RIDGE.*

Smuts Creek is one of many tributaries flowing into Spray Lake. It parallels Highway 742 for much of its length. The scenery and views around the creek are fabulous and worth multiple visits in multiple areas. The creek is also the gateway to several advanced snowshoeing trips described in Snowshoeing in the Canadian Rockies. *Pick a clear day to do any trip in this outstanding area of the Rockies.*

DIRECTIONS

Park at the south end of the road barrier on the west side of the road, 500 m north of the Mount Shark – Engadine Lodge turnoff.

You can snowshoe north or south, but a southerly route is far more scenic. Be careful around the creek – snow bridges across it may collapse. Expect trail-breaking to be strenuous.

742-G

(MAP 16, PAGE 485)

DIFFICULTY	INTERMEDIATE
ELEVATION GAIN	MINIMAL
ROUND-TRIP DISTANCE	VARIABLE
ROUND-TRIP TIME	VARIABLE
MAPS	82 J/14 SPRAY LAKES RESERVOIR, GEM TREK KANANASKIS LAKES

The farther south you drive on Highway 742, the more breath-taking the scenery is. Route 742-G hits the open area east of Tent Ridge. Expect deep snow, lots of intense trail-breaking and plenty of jaw-dropping scenery to keep you entertained.

ENDLESS ACRES OF PRISTINE OPEN TERRAIN TO ENJOY.

DIRECTIONS

Turn west onto the Mount Shark – Engadine Lodge road and drive a few hundred metres to a bridge over Smuts Creek.

There should be plenty of places to park on either side of the bridge. Care must be taken when you step out into the open to get across Smuts Creek. Be sure snow bridges over the waterway are solid. Snowshoe in any direction, but most will want to head south.

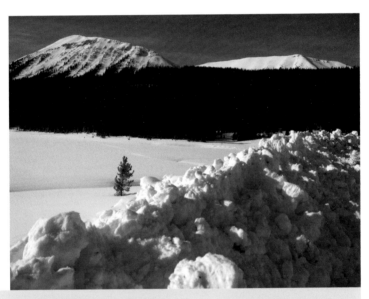

THE TWO ARMS OF TENT RIDGE, AS SEEN FROM THE BRIDGE OVER SMUTS CREEK. THE CRUX OF THE TRIP MAY BE TO GET OVER THE SNOWBANK IN THE FOREGROUND!

57 RUMMEL LAKE

(MAP 16, PAGE 485)

> DIFFICULTY INTERMEDIATE
> ELEVATION GAIN 350 M
> ROUND TRIP DISTANCE 10 KM
> ROUND TRIP TIME 5–7 HOURS
> MAPS 82 J/14 SPRAY LAKE RESERVOIR, GEM TREK CANMORE, GEM TREK KANANASKIS LAKES

Rummel Lake is an excellent destination for snowshoers and skiers alike. Its popularity means that a trail will most likely be broken for you, but if not, be prepared for some serious work. Take along a companion (or four) to ease the strain! There is a winter backcountry campground at Rummel Lake for those who wish to make this a multi-day trip. A permit to camp is required and can be picked up at any national or provincial park information centre.

DIRECTIONS

Park on the east side of Highway 742, opposite the turnoff to Engadine Lodge, about 6.3 km north of the Chester Lake parking lot.

The trail quickly ascends into the trees and then parallels the highway, heading SSE. After several hundred metres it turns back on itself, now heading northeast. There is a small shortcut before the turn that you may be able to take if the trail is broken. Soon the terrain opens up a little, revealing pleasant views to the west.

The trail then swings around and heads southeast. Eventually it goes back into the trees, following a ridge high above Rummel Creek. Stay on this ridge as it starts to curve around to the east toward Rummel Lake, losing a little elevation along the way.

Cross to the north side of Rummel Creek, around GR192324, and follow the creek or perhaps a well-packed snowshoe trail east of the west side of Rummel Lake. Return the same way you came in. Note that extending your day by going into the beautiful valley to the northeast exposes you to avalanche terrain and is therefore not recommended for beginners without avalanche training and equipment.

THE VIEW TO THE NORTHWEST FROM NEAR THE TOP OF THE SECOND CUTBLOCK. (GILLEAN DAFFERN)

ABOVE: THE VIEW TO THE SOUTHWEST. THE BIG PEAK
AT THE FAR RIGHT IS MOUNT BIRDWOOD. (MARKO
STAVRIC) BELOW: RUMMEL LAKE. (MATTHEW CLAY)

(MAP 16, PAGE 485)

DIFFICULTY INTERMEDIATE
ELEVATION GAIN MINIMAL
ROUND-TRIP DISTANCE VARIABLE
ROUND-TRIP TIME VARIABLE
MAPS 82 J/14 SPRAY LAKES RESERVOIR,
GEM TREK KANANASKIS LAKES

AT ONLY 11 KG, ROGAN COULD GET AWAY WITHOUT SNOWSHOES.
MUM AND UNCLE, HOWEVER, COULD HAVE BROKEN THROUGH THE
CRUST AT ANY TIME, LEAVING THEM WAIST-DEEP IN SNOW OR
FLOATING IN THE LESS THAN TEPID WATERS OF SMUTS CREEK.

Whereas you may have the area around 742-G all to yourself, the flats around H and I provide gateways to Commonwealth Creek and Smuts Pass beyond that. Thus the area sees more traffic and often has a multitude of trails, and skiers and snowshoers, heading toward Commonwealth Creek. Not surprisingly, the views to the west, southwest and south are terrific anywhere in this area.

DIRECTIONS

Drive about 800 m south of the Mount Shark – Engadine Lodge turnoff and park at the side of the road, where access to Smuts Creek valley is easy.

Snowshoe down into the valley and choose a route in any direction. The three striking peaks to the south are Commonwealth Peak, Pig's Tail and the awesome Mount Birdwood.

59 COMMONWEALTH CREEK LOGGING ROAD

(MAP 16, PAGE 485)

DIFFICULTY INTERMEDIATE

ELEVATION GAIN MINIMAL

ROUND-TRIP DISTANCE 4.8–8 KM

ROUND-TRIP TIME 1.5–3.5 HOURS

MAPS 82 J/14 SPRAY LAKES RESERVOIR, GEM TREK KANANASKIS LAKES

Compared to the 742-X routes in the area, this trip is somewhat lacklustre in scenic potential. What the logging road does provide is easy travel in a controlled environment. This popular route will probably be well trodden, eliminating all your trail-breaking concerns. Of course, if the only trail there is a ski trail, you will have to break a new snowshoe trail! A loop route does exist for the more adventurous and those with energy to spare.

DIRECTIONS

Turn onto the Mount Shark – Engadine Lodge road and drive about 1 km before turning left onto a side road. Park a few hundred metres up the road.

Hop the snow barricade and begin a 2.4-km snowshoe, heading south. At the 1.9-km mark a not-so-obvious trail branches off to the west. This is the easy route to scenic Tryst Lake, described in *Snowshoeing in the Canadian Rockies, 2nd Edition*. However, there are avalanche concerns along this route and therefore it is not recommended unless you have avalanche gear and training. Instead, enjoy decent views of Commonwealth Peak and Ridge, farther up the trail. Note that Commonwealth Lake (page 294) can be accessed from this trail.

Approximately 2.4 km along, the tracks starts curving to the right (west). At this point, unless you are going to Commonwealth Lake, it's time for the novice snowshoer to stop. The trail farther up gets much steeper and enters avalanche terrain. Return the same way you came in or backtrack, looking for one of several paths heading east through the trees. These paths all lead to the flats of Smuts Creek. Once down onto the flats you can snowshoe east to the road and then hike about 3 km back to your car or follow Smuts Creek north to reach the bridge across the creek by Engadine Lodge. The latter is the preferred route but may involve strenuous trail-breaking and travel.

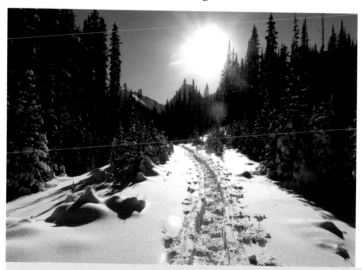

PLEASANT WINTER SCENERY ALONG THE ROAD. THE MOUNTAIN IN THE DISTANCE IS COMMONWEALTH PEAK.

60 MARUSHKA LAKE

(MAP 16, PAGE 485)

DIFFICULTY INTERMEDIATE
ELEVATION LOSS/GAIN 36–68 M
ROUND-TRIP DISTANCE 8 KM
ROUND-TRIP TIME 3.5–5 HOURS
MAPS 82 J/14 SPRAY LAKES RESERVOIR,
GEM TREK KANANASKIS LAKES

This trip has respectable views of the Spray Lake area en route to Marushka Lake, although they are inferior to those experienced from the middle of Spray Lake. The route steers clear of the avalanche terrain on Tent Ridge, is generally easy to follow and provides a few hours of good exercise. The scenery at Marushka Lake is somewhat anticlimactic, as snow cover will hide the wonderful colours of the water. To see those colours and complete the extension to Kirsten Tarns, see Gillean Daffern's Kananaskis Country Trail Guide, Volume 1, *and do the trip in the summer. Also note that the net elevation loss for this trip does not necessarily mean you will race to the lake in record time. If you are breaking trail, the trip can be more strenuous than expected.*

DIRECTIONS

Drive south on Highway 742, and turn right at the Engadine Lodge turnoff; then drive 1.8 km to a small parking area on the right side of the road.

Hike about 100 m farther up the road, put on your snowshoes and turn left onto the obvious logging road. This route is also the start of the path to Tent Ridge and is very popular with backcountry skiers. Stay off their ski tracks, even if this means a

ON A CLEAR DAY, THE VIEW TO MOUNT SHARK
IS EXCELLENT. (BERNIE NEMETH)

strenuous trail-break of your own. There's tons of room for both sets of tracks.

Snowshoe the logging road for about 20 minutes to where the road forks. Stay on the main road (right fork). The left fork leads to Tent Ridge. Stay right again, about 20–25 minutes later, when another path drifts off to the left. There is flagging on the trees here to guide you. The trail eventually curves around the hillside and becomes less obvious where the trees are starting to reassert themselves. Stay at more or less the same elevation, taking a path of least resistance in a southwesterly direction, toward the large and wonderful form of Mount Shark.

Finding the lake can be a little tricky if the trail hasn't been previously broken. Keep going southwest, sometimes gaining a little elevation and finally losing elevation to the east shore of the lake. As stated, the view at Marushka may fail to impress, but the lake is worth a visit at least once. Return the same way you came in.

ON A NOT SO CLEAR DAY THERE STILL MAY BE SOME INTERESTING VIEWS TO TAKE IN. LOOKING EAST FROM THE TRAIL: MOUNT BULLER AT THE LEFT AND MOUNT BOGART ENJOYING SOME SUN, TO THE RIGHT.

61 SOUTH END OF SPRAY LAKE

(MAP 16, PAGE 485)

DIFFICULTY EASY

ELEVATION LOSS/GAIN APPROXIMATELY 100 M

ROUND-TRIP DISTANCE APPROXIMATELY 4–8 KM

ROUND-TRIP TIME 2 HOURS

MAPS 82 J/14 SPRAY LAKE RESERVOIR,
GEM TREK CANMORE

The scenery around the southwest end of Spray Lake is anywhere from excellent to astonishing on a clear day. If you are lucky, the frozen surface of the lake may be wind-blasted clean in some areas, revealing outstanding ice scenery. Even if it isn't, the surrounding mountains will be fantastic.

DIRECTIONS

Driving south on Highway 742, turn right at the Engadine Lodge turnoff and follow the road to the Mount Shark parking lot.

The first order of business is to make it down to Spray Lake. This can be accomplished by following a maze of ski trails. Be considerate to skiers on these groomed trails and stay off to the side. You need to locate the Watridge Lake trailhead, which is at the northwest end of the parking lot. The trail descends immediately for a few metres and then heads west in a straight line. Follow this for about 500 m. Turn right at the first intersection, ascend a short hill and then turn left onto a trail that immediately descends toward Spray Lake. Follow this down, and when it curves around to the west (left), turn right, into the trees, and make your way to the lake in a matter of minutes.

At the shore of Spray Lake, Mount Fortune is immediately visible across the lake, appearing as a low, rounded hump. Aiming for Fortune is a good impulse but you can generally go in any direction. Point yourself toward Fortune (NNW) and off you go. There are several small islands in the middle of the lake, so don't be alarmed when you start going slightly uphill.

The southwest end of Spray Lake can be an interesting and fulfilling adventure in itself, depending on the weather and the state of the ice. Windblown sections of the lake surface may be free of snow, revealing huge cracks in the ice, as well as air bubbles and other fascinating phenomena. In other parts, huge slabs of ice may have collided with each other as they expanded while freezing, pushing each other up in a process similar to that of mountain building. Of course, the lake may be covered in

APPROACHING ONE OF THE ISLANDS IN THE MIDDLE OF THE LAKE. FROM LEFT TO RIGHT THE PEAKS ARE TENT RIDGE, MOUNT SMUTS AND MOUNT SHARK.

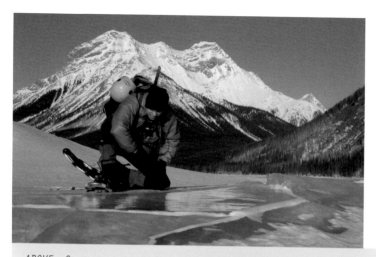

ABOVE: CHECKING OUT THE ICE, WITH CONE MOUNTAIN IN THE BACKGROUND. RIGHT: CRACKS AND BUBBLES IN SPRAY LAKE'S ICE.

deep snow with no exposed ice at all, in which case you'll have even more time to enjoy magnificent panoramas of the surrounding mountains. Tent Ridge, Smuts, Shark, Morrison, Turner and Cone may be particularly eye-catching, especially on a clear day.

62 WATRIDGE LAKE

(MAP 16, PAGE 485)

RATING EASY TO THE LAKE, ADVANCED TO KARST SPRINGS, INTERMEDIATE FOR THE SPRAY RIVER EXTENSION

LAKE HEIGHT 1800 M

ELEVATION GAIN 60 M

ROUND-TRIP DISTANCE 7.4 KM

ROUND-TRIP TIME 2.5–4 HOURS

MAPS 82 J/14 SPRAY LAKES RESERVOIR, GEM TREK CANMORE, GEM TREK KANANASKIS LAKES

This is a terrific beginner trip on a "highway" of a trail that is super easy to follow. After a rewarding view of Watridge Lake, backdropped by shapely Cone Mountain, a quick visit to Karst Springs is sweet icing on the cake! And for those who really want to experience the area, the Spray River extension is outstanding.

DIRECTIONS

Driving south on Highway 742, turn right (west) at the Mount Shark – Engadine Lodge turnoff and follow the road to the Mount Shark parking lot. Follow the signs to Watridge Lake on the very wide, often groomed trail. The trail is about 30 m from the parking area. As always, DO NOT step on any ski tracks. There is tons of room to make a separate snowshoe track.

Additional instructions are not required once you are on your way. Simply follow the signs to Watridge Lake, turning around once in a while to admire the peaks to the east and north. The peak straight ahead is Mount Shark. Alan Kane describes an excellent scramble route up this interesting peak.

A good pace will get you to the turnoff to the lake in about an hour (GR110344). There is the sign with a map on the right side of the trail. Take a sharp left turn and go downhill to reach the shores of Watridge Lake within minutes.

The view to the northwest of Cone Mountain's striking southeast end will likely be the highlight of the view from the lake. To the west sit the duo of Mount Turner (north) and Mount Morrison (south). They maybe look like one long mountain but have been given two names, in honour of Sir Richard Turner and Sir Edward Morrison, lieutenants who fought side by side in 1900 with the Royal Canadian Dragoons during the South African War. Mount Shark now lies to the southeast. Return the same way (once you have completed the mandatory extension to Karst Springs!) and/or do the Spray River/Lake extension, as described after the Karst Springs description.

THREE SNOWSHOERS MAKE THEIR WAY TO WATRIDGE LAKE. THE STUNNING FORMS OF OLD GOAT MOUNTAIN AND MOUNT NESTOR PROVIDE A MAGNIFICENT BACKDROP. (PETER HOPKINS)

KARST SPRINGS

Some 400 horizontal and 75 vertical metres – for what you will see during the course of this short trip this is the "best bang for your buck" around! Karst Springs is not to be missed.

Directions

A large sign, by the lake, points you in the right direction. Cross the lake outlet on a narrow, wooden bridge and then continue following the trail into the forest. There is a boardwalk here to reduce damage to the fragile foliage, however it may be snow-covered. More than likely the trail will be broken, as this is a very popular destination year-round.

The trail meanders through the forest until it joins up with Karst Springs (to your left). Hopefully the snow coverage will not

HOPEFULLY SNOW COVERS THE ENTIRE KARST SPRINGS AREA EXCEPT THE VIBRANT GREEN MOSS IN THE CREEK. (NICOLE LISAFELD)

be so great as to completely hide the amazingly vibrant green moss that covers almost everything in the spring (creek). Continue up the trail, taking in more terrific "mossy" scenes.

Quickly, the trail starts to gain elevation. Your snowshoe crampons will be a blessing here as you effortlessly ascend the often icy terrain that may thwart those who are simply on foot. Arrive at a wooden bench for another breathtaking view of the upper springs.

From the bench, the trail gets quite a bit steeper, as it switchbacks to the spring outlet. Those not used to such angles on snowshoes may want to call it a day at the bench. However, a good set of snowshoe crampons will make easy work of the ascent for those who are comfortable with the terrain. Use caution when reaching the end of the trail. There is a fence to prevent you from falling into the spring, but the snow can be piled high enough to render that fence completely ineffective. Enjoy the view looking down the spring and then return the same way.

Spray River and Spray Lake

This is a totally amazing extension of the Watridge Lake trip and highly, highly recommended. The route takes you down to Spray River and then onto Spray Lake, where you can follow the lake back to the parking lot. It's a fantastically scenic loop route. Don't underestimate it, however. Round-trip it's about 14 km (without Karst Springs) and will take approximately 4.5–6.5 hours, with 226 m of total elevation gain. A GPS will come in handy for finding the ski trail back to the parking lot, near the end of the trip, as will a few friends for trail-breaking duties.

Directions

After visiting Watridge Lake (and possibly Karst Springs) return up the hill to the main trail. Turn left and follow it for several kilometres, all the way down to a bridge over the Spray River. You will lose about 100 m of elevation along the way and may be wishing you had skis (at least for this part). Hopefully you have been blessed with clear skies, because the view of the river and Cone Mountain, from the middle of the bridge, is breathtaking – far better than the similar view from Watridge Lake.

Return to the east side of the bridge and start following the river downstream (north). Be prepared for some strenuous trail-breaking if a trail has not already been carved out. Stay as close to the river as possible, without putting yourself in danger. Thankfully, an ice shelf along the river's edge soon appears. Travel will hopefully be much easier at this point, as the shelf gets blasted by the wind, reducing snow levels. The ice scenery by the river can be outstanding.

And so is the mountain scenery! The prominent mountain to the west is Mount Turner, but as the river turns east, a host of other magnificent mountains appear, seemingly in pairs:

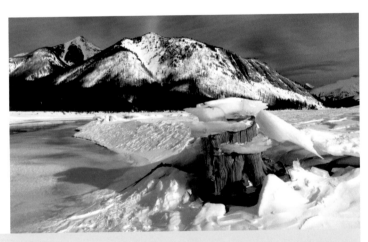

A SMALL TASTE OF SOME OF THE WONDERFUL SCENERY WHERE THE RIVER MEETS THE LAKE. MOUNT FORTUNE AND FORTULENT PEAK ARE ASCENTS DESCRIBED IN THE ADVANCED SNOWSHOEING BOOK.

Fortune and Fortulent, Nestor and Old Goat, Buller and Engadine. There is never a dull moment at this end of the lake.

Depending on snow and ice conditions, you will soon realize that you are no longer following the river but are on the lake. A group of tree stumps (hopefully not snow-covered) at GR112369 marks this spot wonderfully. Continue going east, staying closer to the south side of the lake. As of early 2016, thin wooden stakes marked the route.

This part of the trip is deceivingly long. Snowshoe east until it is possible to turn south (GR128370), toward the southernmost point of the lake. Keep going south, aiming for GR135360. Upon reaching that point, head into the trees, looking for one of the ski trails. If your route-finding is good, it's only about 30 m through the trees onto a trail. Once you've found the ski trail, turn left and then follow your nose back to the Watridge Lake Trail and then back to the parking lot. These are dedicated ski trails and you should avoid being on them for too long.

PICTURESQUE MOUNT ENGADINE KEEPS YOU COMPANY AS YOU SEARCH FOR THE SPOT TO ENTER THE TREES WHERE THE SKI TRAIL LIES. P=APPROXIMATE POINT TO GO BACK INTO THE TREES.

742-I

(MAP 16, PAGE 485)

DIFFICULTY INTERMEDIATE

ELEVATION GAIN MINIMAL

ROUND-TRIP DISTANCE VARIABLE

ROUND-TRIP TIME VARIABLE

MAPS 82 J/14 SPRAY LAKES RESERVOIR,
GEM TREK KANANASKIS LAKES

742-I lies a few hundred metres south of 742-H (see page 276). This launching point is the most direct route to Commonwealth Creek and the extraordinary valley above. You can expect several trails to be fully broken.

DIRECTIONS

Drive about 1.1 km south of the Mount Shark – Engadine Lodge turnoff and park at the side of the road, where access to the Smuts Creek valley is easy.

Snowshoe down into the valley and choose a route in any direction.

OPPOSITE: The superb environs around the south end of Smuts Creek. The prominent peaks in the background include Mount Murray, Mount French and Mount Burstall. The prominent humans in the foreground include Keri Nugara, Rogan Nugara and Mark Nugara.

64 COMMONWEALTH LAKE

(MAP 16, PAGE 485)

RATING INTERMEDIATE

LAKE ELEVATION 2042 M

ELEVATION GAIN 200 M

ROUND-TRIP DISTANCE 4.6 KM

ROUND-TRIP TIME 2–4 HOURS

MAPS 82 J/14 SPRAY LAKES RESERVOIR, GEM TREK KANANASKIS LAKE

The highlight of the trip will be the beautiful form of Commonwealth Peak behind its namesake lake. It is a short trip that can be completed in under 2 hours round-trip if the trail is well broken and packed down. For additional views and some pretty stunning scenery you can go beyond the lake, but this will take you into avalanche terrain if you go too far up the valley.

DIRECTIONS

Note that this trip can also be accessed from Commonwealth Creek Logging Road (page 278).

Drive 2.2 km south of the Mount Shark – Engadine Lodge turn-off and park on the west side of the road, around GR176312. Look west, across the flats of Smuts Creek, for a small gap in the trees (see photo). Snowshoe across the flats and go through the gap. The path trends slightly right before arriving at a "No Camping/Fires" sign. This is a very popular area so expect there to be a multitude of trails. As you approach the sign, go slightly left into the trees and head southwest. You'll soon arrive at another popular trail that runs north–south. The terrain opens up a little and the route should become more obvious.

At this point you should look for a cutline running southwest, south of Commonwealth Creek. To find it, follow the trail going toward the distinctive form of The Fist. The trail soon swings around to the left and then arrives at an open area, where it forks (GR168304). This fork is not always obvious. There are two routes to the lake from this important junction: via the summer trail or via a creek that drains the north end of the lake. For ascent, the summer is recommended.

Summer trail

At the junction, take the left fork. If the trail is broken it will be easy to follow as it steeply winds its way uphill, traverses to the right for a short distance and then switchbacks up to a higher elevation. Eventually the trail turns right again and traverses the northwest slopes of Commonwealth Ridge, heading south. If you

THE GAP IN THE TREES IS VISIBLE FROM THE PARKING AREA. G=GAP. S MOUNT=SMUTS. TF=THE FIST. TLR=TRYST LAKE RIDGE. ETR=EAST SUMMIT OF TENT RIDGE.

are breaking new trail do your best to pick the safest line. This may entail gaining more elevation onto less steep slopes. Continue south for several hundred metres and then start to look to your right to spot the lake through the trees. Invariably you will have to lose a little elevation to reach the lake. You will probably descend to the east side of the lake around GR166297.

Creek route

At the junction, take the right fork. This is the trail that more or less follows the left bank of Commonwealth Creek all the way up and into the Commonwealth valley. Follow this trail for a few hundred metres, at one point crossing a subsidiary creek coming down from the left. Shortly after crossing this creek, look for another less obvious creek at GR164301. This is the creek you will want to follow all the way up to the north end of Commonwealth Lake. At first it is best to follow the right bank of the creek, but higher up you will be forced right into the creek. Work your way up steeper slopes to the lake.

For both routes

Hopefully clear skies will grant you a terrific view of Commonwealth Peak and Pig's Back to the right of the peak. The best views are from the east and north sides of the lake so be sure to visit each side. At an elevation above 2000 m the lake will probably be frozen well into spring and can usually be crossed right down the middle.

For return either go back the way you came or use the route you didn't ascend. The advantage of the Creek Route is that it is downhill all the way. To use that route go to the north end of the lake and snowshoe right down the middle of the creek. There are steep sections and you'll have to duck under a fallen tree or two, but travel is generally fast and easy. When the creek bed becomes less confined move over to the left side of the creek and snowshoe along the bank. You'll eventually run into the trail that parallels Commonwealth Creek. Turn right and follow that trail back to the important junction.

If you came up via the Creek Route, using the Summer Trail really doesn't offer any advantages – scenic or otherwise. I would use the Creek Route for descent also.

EXTENSION

It is definitely worthwhile to extend the trip a little beyond the lake, as long as you avoid venturing into avalanche terrain. Snowshoe to the south end of the lake and continue going south, through light trees, staying toward the left side of the valley. Although steep slopes start to rear up on either side of you, the mature trees in the valley bottom show that in general avalanches do not reach this area.

Directions:
The terrain soon opens up and now you will see several obvious avalanche slopes coming down from Commonwealth Ridge to

COMMONWEALTH PEAK (LEFT) BACKDROPS COMMONWEALTH LAKE. PIG'S BACK TO THE RIGHT.

your left. This will be the end of the line for you if you do not having avalanche training. Take in the scenery and return the way you came.

If you do have avalanche training and feel confident that continuing on is safe, you can reduce the risk by going over to the right side of the valley, but this by no means will put you in a completely safe place. Continue up the valley. If you turn around you will see the familiar forms of Mount Nestor and Old Goat Mountain, towering above Spray Lake.

When you start to see large boulders to your right, turn in that direction, gain some elevation and make your way up and over to them. Here, the scene really opens up: numerous huge boulders strewn across the landscape, steep, snow-covered slopes all around, and Commonwealth Peak standing proudly above the whole scene. On a clear day the adjective "breathtaking" won't do it justice!

The continuation of this trip to Pig's Back is an advanced snowshoeing route, described in the second edition of *Snowshoeing in the Canadian Rockies*. Return the same way to the lake. Remember that once back at the lake, there are two options for descent.

THE EXQUISITE SCENERY NEAR THE BOULDER FIELD.

65 742-J (GR184294)

(MAP 16, PAGE 485)

A little farther down the road from 742-I, another open stretch of serene beauty awaits exploration. Sitting under the east face of Commonwealth Ridge, this area eventually leads to the north end of Hogarth Lakes.

DIRECTIONS

Drive 4.2 km south of the Mount Shark – Engadine Lodge turn-off or 2.1 km north of Burstall Pass parking lot, and park on the west side of the road. Snowshoe south toward Hogarth Lakes.

FAMILIAR PEAKS OF THE SPRAY MOUNTAINS PROVIDE A SPECTACULAR BACKDROP FOR SNOWSHOEING IN THIS AREA.

66 CHESTER LAKE

(MAP 16, PAGE 485)

DIFFICULTY	ADVANCED
ELEVATION GAIN	310 M
ROUND TRIP DISTANCE	8 KM
ROUND TRIP TIME	3–5 HOURS
MAPS	82 J/14 SPRAY LAKES RESERVOIR, GEM TREK KANANASKIS LAKES

Chester Lake is without question the most popular snowshoeing destination in Kananaskis. The lake is reached via a good snowshoe trail and is surrounded by spectacular mountains. Due to the sheer volume of skiers, snowboarders and snowshoers making their way to Chester Lake, it is imperative that snowshoers use the official snowshoe trail and avoid the ski trail, except on those few short sections where the trail is shared.

DIRECTIONS

Drive 6.3 km south of the Engadine Lodge turnoff or 6.2 km north of the Sawmill turnoff and turn east into the Chester Lake parking lot.

THE MAGNIFICENT ENVIRONS AROUND CHESTER LAKE. VIEWS LIKE THIS EXPLAIN THE POPULARITY OF THE AREA.

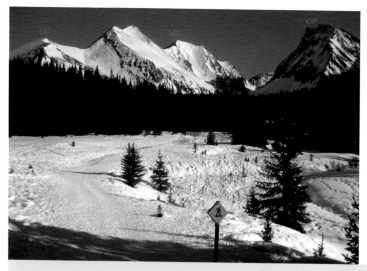

SOME OF THE OUTSTANDING VIEWS EN ROUTE TO THE LAKE. CHESTER LAKE IS NOT VISIBLE BUT LIES TO THE RIGHT OF THE PHOTO. LG=LITTLE GALATEA. MG=MOUNT GALATEA. GP=GUSTY PEAK. (JACK TANNETT)

The first 400 m of the snowshoe trail is shared with the ski trail. It starts at the north end of the parking lot. Follow the trail for a short distance and take the left fork at the first intersection (well signed). After going over a bridge, look for the snowshoe-trail sign on your right. Turn right onto this trail and follow it through forest and open areas to the beautiful environs of Chester Lake. There are trail signs on trees throughout to guide you. This trail gets very well packed down, and although some will opt to carry their snowshoes on their backpacks, I recommend that you wear snowshoes throughout. Your snowshoe crampons will make the steep sections easy on ascent and descent.

ABOVE: Matthew Clay and Sandra Jacques at Chester Lake. The prominent peak to the left is the southwest end of Gusty Peak, and The Fortress sits in the distant centre. (Matthew Clay) BELOW: Sometimes, in favour of the grand views, we forget to notice the small stuff. Matthew Clay beautifully captures the exquisite detail of frozen water near the lake. (Matthew Clay)

Detour to Elephant Rocks

If you have made it to Chester Lake, a quick detour to Elephant Rocks is almost mandatory. The small amount of elevation that you must gain in the trip to the rocks allows the views to open up a fair amount, and the rocks themselves are fascinating. The turnoff for the valley is a few hundred metres along the northwest shore of Chester Lake. Turn left and snowshoe in a northwesterly direction, arriving at Elephant Rocks in short order.

NICOLE LISAFELD ENJOYING THE STRIKING SCENERY AT ELEPHANT ROCKS.

67 LOWER CHESTER LOOP AND MOUNT MURRAY VIEWPOINT

(MAP 16, PAGE 485)

DIFFICULTY EASY

ELEVATION GAIN 70 M FOR THE LOOP; ADD 130 M FOR THE VIEWPOINT

ROUND-TRIP DISTANCE 4.4 KM FOR THE LOOP; ADD 2.4 KM FOR THE VIEWPOINT

ROUND-TRIP TIME 1–2.5 HOURS

MAPS 82 J/14 SPRAY LAKES RESERVOIR, GEM TREK KANANASKIS LAKES

On this trip you won't enjoy the same kind of outstanding scenery as you would experience at Chester Lake, but this loop makes for a relatively short and easy day. Likely, the traffic around the loop will be a fraction of the line of snowshoers and skiers making their way to the lake. The loop can be done in either direction, but clockwise is a little easier in regards to finding the route and is the direction described below. If you are blessed with clear skies, the extension to the Mount Murray Viewpoint is worth the extra effort, but again, don't expect the views to knock you off your snowshoes!

DIRECTIONS

Drive 6.3 km south of the Engadine Lodge turnoff or 6.2 km north of the Sawmill turnoff and turn east into the Chester Lake parking lot.

From the parking lot follow the normal route to Chester Lake for about 100 m until the trail splits at a major and well-signed junction. Take the right fork and follow it for about 700 m to another junction. This one is unsigned. One fork goes to the left (northeast) up a fairly steep-looking hill. Take the right fork. Snowshoe another 1.4 km to the signed southeast end of the loop.

If you are only doing the loop, take a sharp right and head downhill to complete the loop. The only place where you might encounter a route-finding issue is a sharp turn to the right as you cross a creek a few hundred metres from the parking lot. You'll emerge from the forest at the opposite end of the parking lot from which you departed.

EXTENSION TO MOUNT MURRAY VIEWPOINT

Directions

Even if you don't go all the way to the Mount Murray Viewpoint, the 600-m trek to the next major junction provides a decent view – perhaps even better than one from the viewpoint. Along the way, there are a few brief views to enjoy of the steep east face of Mount Murray. At the signed junction, the scenery opens up quite a bit, especially to the northeast. On a clear day the views of Mount Chester are very pleasant.

An additional 600 m and about 70 m of elevation are required to finish the job. The obvious trail heads up to the viewpoint in a northwesterly direction. An orange snowshoe sign directs you to turn west (left) for the final 50 m. The viewpoint sits amid a fair number of trees, so some walking about is required to get all the views. In terms of spectacular vantage points, it's not exactly the Canadian equivalent of the summit of Everest, so try not to be disappointed! Nevertheless, a good camera will be able to capture some good, zoomed-in shots of Mount Murray, Mount Birdwood, Commonwealth Peak and Mount Chester. Return the same way when you tire of the "walkabout." For variety, the lower leg of the Lower Chester Loop, as described above, is recommended.

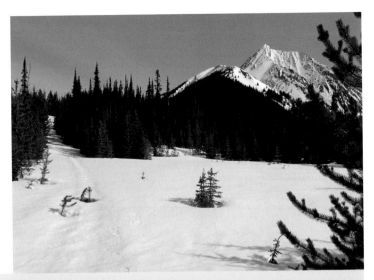

ABOVE: THE PATH UP TO THE VIEWPOINT LIES AT THE LEFT. MOUNT
CHESTER AT THE RIGHT. (JACK TANNETT) BELOW: A ZOOMED-IN
PHOTO OF THE EAST FACE OF MOUNT BIRDWOOD. (JACK TANNETT)

68 HOGARTH LAKES

(MAP 16, PAGE 485)

DIFFICULTY EASY

ELEVATION GAIN MINIMAL

ROUND-TRIP DISTANCE 4.5-KM LOOP

ROUND-TRIP TIME 1.5–2.5 HOURS

MAPS 82 J/14 SPRAY LAKE RESERVOIR,
GEM TREK KANANASKIS LAKES

The area around Hogarth and Mud lakes is a great route for beginners to get acquainted with snowshoeing in Kananaskis. The loop route has a negligible amount of elevation gain and there are infinite opportunities for exploring, should you feel like leaving the beaten path.

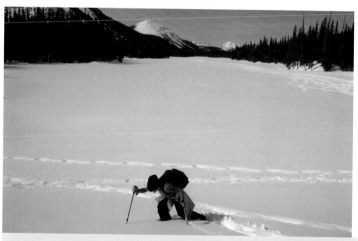

NICOLE LISAFELD WADES THROUGH DEEP SNOW SOUTH OF MUD
LAKE. THE ROUTE TO HOGARTH LAKES LIES TO THE LEFT.

Drive 6.3 km south of the Engadine Lodge turnoff or 6.2 km north of the Sawmill turnoff and turn west into the Burstall Pass parking lot.

Snowshoe the common trail southwest for 100 m or so, looking for the first orange snowshoe marker on the right side. Once you've found it, simply follow the markers as they take you west and then northwest toward Hogarth Lakes. For those who want to experience the joys (?) of trail-breaking, leave the well-trodden path at any time to do some exploring.

The markers take you to the northeast end of Hogarth Lakes in about 2 km. At this point, the official trail turns south, following the east edge of both Hogarth Lakes. Follow the trail, as it heads in easterly and southerly directions back to Burstall Pass Trail, a few hundred metres from where you left the main trail initially.

THE OFFICIAL START OF THE HOGARTH LAKES LOOP.
MOUNT BIRDWOOD, COMMONWEALTH PEAK AND COMMONWEALTH
RIDGE PROVIDE AN EXCELLENT BACKDROP.

69 BURSTALL LAKES

(MAP 16, PAGE 485)

DIFFICULTY EASY

ELEVATION GAIN APPROXIMATELY 100 M

ROUND-TRIP DISTANCE 10 KM

ROUND-TRIP TIME 3–5 HOURS

MAPS 82 J/14 SPRAY LAKE RESERVOIR,
GEM TREK KANANASKIS LAKES

The strategic location of this string of lakes makes it an ideal destination to see some great mountain scenery. Clear skies will reward those who make the trip. You should have excellent views of peaks of the Spray Range, including the awesome south sides of Mount Birdwood, Pig's Tail and Commonwealth Peak.

DIRECTIONS

Drive 6.3 km south of the Engadine Lodge turnoff or 6.2 km north of the Sawmill turnoff and turn west into the Burstall Pass parking lot.

From the north end of the parking lot, snowshoe southwest on the obvious trail past Mud Lake and the turnoff to Hogarth Lakes. You are on the Burstall Pass hiking trail, and in winter this is a very popular route for snowshoers and skiers. It is imperative that you do not snowshoe on any ski tracks. The path is wide and there is plenty of room for everyone. If no snowshoe trail exists when you get there, you and your party have been granted the honour of breaking one!

Ignore the snowshoe signs as you continue southwest. The trail turns south (left), ascending a small hill, and then curves around to the west (right). French Creek Trail stems off at this point, heading southeast. Ignore that trail too, and continue following Burstall Pass trail, at first west and then southwest. Although the trail is never steep, it does gain and lose elevation along the way. Prepare for a little huffing and puffing.

There are three Burstall Lakes, and although you can certainly visit all three, the suggested route makes a quick stop at the second and then goes right to the third and most westerly lake. Snowshoe the Burstall Pass trail for about 35–50 minutes (approximately 2 km from the parking lot). Start looking for a fairly obvious path to your right (north). That path leads very quickly to the second lake and is worth a quick look. The lake is surrounded on all sides by trees but has good views of the southeast sides of Commonwealth Peak and Mount Birdwood.

Return to the main trail and snowshoe another 400–500 m, where another path breaks off to the north. This one goes to the third lake and a wide-open view of the area. This is a great place to take a lunch break and absorb the excellent views. After fuelling up on both, you can return to the parking lot the same way you came in or continue southwest for even better views. If you do decide to call it a day, don't try any alternative routes back. You may end up below avalanche slopes and/or on very steep and dangerous terrain.

Hopefully you and your party have decided to continue southwest for approximately 1 km. The impressively long ridge in front of you and to your left (southwest) is called Whistling Rock Ridge and it terminates in a magnificently statuesque pile of Rockies rubble called Mount Sir Douglas – the 34th highest mountain in the Canadian Rockies. As you snowshoe southwest, this terrific mountain will come into view, as well as Robertson Glacier and an even more striking (but lower) mountain to the east of the glacier, named Mount Robertson. Don't stop until you can see Robertson – it will be worth it. Throughout, the views of Birdwood, Pig's Tail and Commonwealth continue to change and improve.

You can take your second break of the day when Robertson appears. Travel beyond this point is possible but not recommended. The trail goes west, up and through trees into the upper valley. Eventually you end up in avalanche terrain near Burstall Pass. While the scenery here is fantastic, you should not approach this area without avalanche training and gear. Stick to the

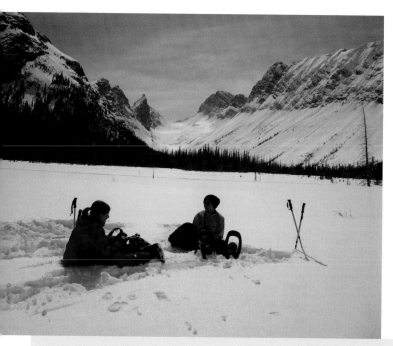

BREAK TIME AT BURSTALL FLATS. MICHELLE AND NICOLE ENJOY A REST AND THE MAGNIFICENT SCENERY. MOUNT ROBERTSON IS THE POINTY PEAK AT THE LEFT, SIR DOUGLAS SITS TO THE RIGHT AND ROBERTSON GLACIER SEPARATES THEM.

lower valley, where there should be enough to ogle at for some time, and then return the same way you came in. Again, don't try any alternative routes or shortcuts.

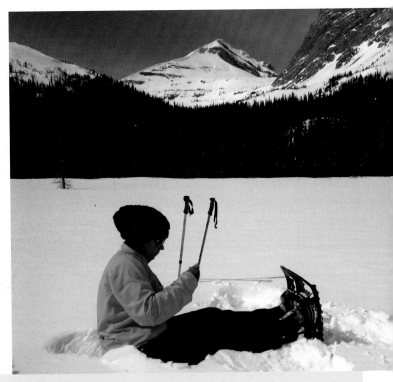

NICOLE AND SNOW PEAK. NO CELL RECEPTION YET, BUT WAIT A FEW YEARS!

70 FRENCH CREEK (TO THE FIRST WATER/ICEFALL)

(MAP 16, PAGE 485)

RATING	INTERMEDIATE
HIGH POINT	APPROXIMATELY 1975 M
ELEVATION GAIN	APPROXIMATELY 75 M
ROUND-TRIP DISTANCE	4.3 KM
ROUND-TRIP TIME	2–3 HOURS
MAPS	82 J/14 SPRAY LAKES RESERVOIR, GEM TREK CANMORE, GEM TREK KANANASKIS LAKES

If you are looking for a short and generally straightforward trip, perhaps to extend your day or as a trip on its own, the trek to the first water/icefall along French Creek is a good choice. Although clear skies are always the preference, this is also a good candidate for those not-so-good weather days. Cloudy skies will not be as detrimental to the scenery on this trip, as they would be for others.

DIRECTIONS

Park at the Burstall Pass parking lot. Snowshoe the Burstall Pass hiking trail for a few hundred metres. It soon turns left and goes uphill to a hiking sign. Don't follow the hiking trail that goes right (leads to Burstall Pass), but instead keep going straight on a narrower trail. This trail is very popular with ski mountaineers, doing the magnificent French/Haig/Robertson glacier loop (described in Chic Scott's *Summits and Icefields*). For most sections of the trail there is enough room for a separate snowshoe trail. Make the effort to create one if it doesn't already exist.

The trail slowly gains elevation (ignore the path that forks off to the right) and then gets steeper to the top of a hill. Gillean Daffern describes the next section as a "long, drawn-out descent into French Creek Valley," and she's correct. You'll be especially aware of this fact on the seemingly longer return trip!

Right before you reach French Creek, the main trail forks – one going across the creek, the other to the right and slightly uphill. Take the right fork. This lies around GR194267 and may not be completely obvious in times when the snowpack is very deep. Follow this trail as it goes more or less in a straight line through

APPROACHING THE WATER/ICEFALL.

the trees and eventually joins up with French Creek several hundred metres upstream.

Once again you'll probably arrive at a fork (GR193263). The right fork goes uphill and is the continuation of French Creek Trail. Take the left fork that goes easily and quickly to the first water/icefall. Depending on the time of year, the fall may be all ice, all water or likely a combination of the two. You can snowshoe along the right bank of the creek to a point almost right under the fall, but be wary of dangers from above (falling ice, snow or debris). Also be careful you don't step on an unsupportive section of snow and fall into the creek – it's really, really cold – trust me!

Return the same way. The long grind uphill can seem to take forever, but it could be much worse: after completing a 12-hour snowshoe ascent of Mount Jellicoe with Mark and Ferenc Jasco, in March of 2008, this "hill" felt like Mount Everest itself on the way back!

71 SAWMILL TRAILS

(MAP 16, PAGE 485)

The snowshoe trails starting from the Sawmill parking lot have been under development for the past few years but are finally complete. All are terrific beginner routes though lacking in great views. They provide good exercise and the option for many variations, as well as access to more scenic areas, such as "James Walker Lake" (page 318) and the *Kent Ridge outlier* (Snowshoeing in the Canadian Rockies, 2nd Edition*).*

Hardcore shoers can go all the way to the Chester Lake parking lot, via Sawmill Loop, Snowdrift and the upper leg of Frost Heave and then return via the lower leg of Frost Heave and Graupel. That would entail approximately 20 km of snowshoeing, with about 500 m of elevation gain, and would take up the better part of a

A BEAUTIFUL DAY ON THE SAWMILL LOOP. (MATTHEW CLAY)

Chester Sawmill Snowshoe Trails

Canmore 40 km

742

Chester Lake Cross-Country Trail

Chester Lake

2.3

3.4

1.6

1.6

Chester Lake Trail 4

3.4 km one-way from Chester Lake Trailhead Area; 287 m of elevation gain. Shared with skiers for first 0.2 km, then follow the trail signs.

Hogarth Lakes

Mud Lake

0.4

0.2

Chester Lake

0.2

2.1

Hogarth Lakes Loop 3.9

Frost Heave

1.3

1.0

Snowdrift Trail 7

8.3 km with 215m elevation gain.

Mt. Murray Viewpoint

0.6

Hogarth Lakes Loop Trail 5

A 3.9 km loop of flat terrain from Burstall Pass Day Use Area; 30 m of elevation gain.

Burstall Pass

0.6

Snowdrift 3.3

Sawmill Loop Trail 9

5.1 km loop from Sawmill Trailhead, with 155 m elevation gain.

Frost Heave Trail 6

2.4 km with 68 m elevation gain in the final one km.

Graupel 5.6

0.8

Sawmill Loop 2.4

Sawmill Loop 1.9

1.5

Graupel Trail 8

5.6 km with 167m elevation gain.

Sawmill

Highway #40 15 km

Legend

— — Snowshoe Trail
- - - - Cross-country Ski Trail

👤 Trailhead
👥 Viewpoint

0   1   2 Km
1:40,000
All distances shown in kilometres

Chester Lake or Burstall Pass Trailhead ←— 6.2 Kilometres —→ Sawmill Trailhead

THE OFFICIAL SNOWSHOE TRAILS AROUND CHESTER LAKE, HOGARTH LAKES, AND THE SAWMILL AREA, AITH DISTANCES AND ELEVATION GAINS. (MAP COURTESY OF ALBERTA PARKS, KANANASKIS).

day. Another option, if two vehicles are available, is to make a one-way trip via one of those routes and then drive back to the Sawmill parking lot.

72 "JAMES WALKER LAKE"

(MAP 16, PAGE 485)

RATING INTERMEDIATE

ELEVATION GAIN APPROXIMATELY 260 M

ROUND-TRIP DISTANCE 8.5 KM

ROUND-TRIP TIME 3–5 HOURS

MAPS 82 J/14 SPRAY LAKES RESERVOIR, 82 J/11 KANANASKIS LAKES, GEM TREK KANANASKIS LAKES

For those craving a little more challenge and far superior scenery than that offered by the Sawmill trails, this small but picturesque lake is a terrific destination. A well-used summer trail takes you into the heart of one of the stunning hanging valleys of the Kananaskis Range. The lake appears to lack an official name, but given it's the largest body of water that feeds James Walker Creek, the title "James Walker Lake" seems appropriate.

DIRECTIONS

Park at the Sawmill parking lot near the south end of Highway 742. There are several snowshoe trails that leave the lot – take the one behind the outhouse, heading east and uphill. Within minutes you'll reach a signed fork in the trail. Take the left fork, labelled as the "1.5" section. The "1.9" section to the right can also be used, but adds 400 m to the trip. Follow either path to where they intersect. From the intersection, continue in a northwesterly direction for about 350–400 m, looking for an unsigned and narrower trail that branches off to the right and goes uphill

(GR233250). There is an identical-looking trail doing exactly the same thing a few hundred metres before – ignore that one.

You are now on the unofficial "James Walker Lake" trail. Following this trail takes you directly to the lake. The trail is narrow but obvious and more or less goes in long straight lines. Trail-breaking may be quite strenuous if you are the first to do so. Although you are surrounded by trees, good views of the impressive unnamed peak to the north are soon plentiful.

Eventually the straight trail gives way to a more winding path as it heads into the trees. The trail is a little harder to follow, but occasional flagging in the trees helps. In short order a boulder field appears to the left. Here you can stay on the trail, circumventing the field on the right side or go exploring right through this fascinating field of rock (highly recommended). Mount James Walker soon appears at the end of the valley, with the

THE SUPERB SCENERY NEAR THE LAKE. PART OF THE BOULDER FIELD IN THE FOREGROUND, AN UNNAMED PEAK TO THE LEFT, MOUNT JAMES WALKER AT THE DISTANT CENTRE AND MOUNT INFLEXIBLE TO THE RIGHT.

steep walls of Mount Inflexible towering over the right side of the valley.

Continue working your way through the boulder field or around it, eventually ending up at the south end of "James Walker Lake." You can snowshoe around the lake, but views don't really improve. Instead, take in the wonderful views from the south end and then return the same way. In case you were thinking of going farther, the slopes beyond the lake put you in serious avalanche terrain (highly unadvisable unless you are properly equipped).

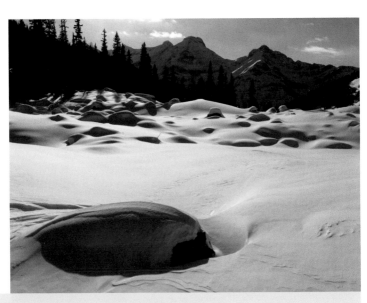

TO THE WEST SIT MOUNT MURRAY (CENTRE) AND UNOFFICIAL "CEGNFS" (RIGHT).

73 WARSPITE LAKE

(MAP 17, PAGE 486)

DIFFICULTY EASY
ELEVATION GAIN 120 M
ROUND TRIP DISTANCE 4 KM
ROUND TRIP TIME 2–4 HOURS
MAPS 82 J/11 KANANASKIS LAKES,
GEM TREK KANANASKIS LAKES

This is a popular trip that is perfect for beginners. The view at Warspite Lake is decent, but going just a little past the lake really opens things up with terrific views of massive Mount Black Prince. Beyond that, you are getting into avalanche terrain, so go no farther.

DIRECTIONS

Park at the Black Prince parking lot, near the south end of Highway 742.

The interpretive trail follows Smith–Dorrien Creek for about 100 m, crosses the creek and then turns back along the creek, before veering off to the right. It is well marked and easy to follow. In winter there is often a small shortcut to the left, near the parking lot, that crosses the creek over a snow bridge. Late in the season this bridge will be either gone or dicey – best to follow the summer trail in that case.

Both trails quickly unite and then a long uphill grind starts, heading to the right (northwest). The slope is not terribly steep and travel will be easy. Expect to see skiers and ski tracks along the way. Stay off the ski tracks.

At the top of the hill the trail seems to swing around to the left (southwest), but the route to the lake takes the less obvious right fork, where a bench sits (probably partially or completely submerged in snow). Stay right and keep following the trail as you lose a chunk of the elevation you just gained. When the terrain levels out, the trail veers slightly to the left, eventually crossing a creek and then heading left again and gently uphill to the lake. There could be a multitude of other ski and snowshoe trails – it's best to just follow the most prominent one.

The actual lake is more like a big puddle and may fail to impress. Of more interest is the intriguing form of Mount Black Prince, looming above the lake. To the left of the lake, an advanced snowshoeing trip continues on to Warspite Cirque. It is definitely worth your while to wander over to the southwest side

THAT CRAZY CALGARY STAMPEDER FAN FROM CRANDELL LAKE TURNS UP AT WARSPITE LAKE – 250 KM NORTH – VERY EERIE!

of the lake and through a small stand of trees. Beyond the trees the scenery opens up again to some beautiful vistas. Much of the steep route to Warspite Cirque is visible and, due to steepness, should make everyone shudder just a little! Travelling farther up the valley will bring you into avalanche terrain. Turn around and return the same way you came in.

THE VIEW FROM BEYOND WARSPITE LAKE, WITH THE ROUTE TO WARSPITE CIRQUE. NOT SURE WHAT THE STAMPEDER FAN IS DOING.

KANANASKIS LAKES TRAIL

Many of the routes along Kananaskis Lakes Trail centre on the amazing Lower and Upper Kananaskis Lakes. Snow depths here can exceed 2 m and may persist well into April and even early May. Like Highway 742, you are almost guaranteed to have good, deep snow to snowshoe on or through from January to mid-April.

The weather can be quite finicky in this area of the Rockies. It is not uncommon for murky, whiteout-like conditions to exist around the lakes, while sunny (or at least sunnier) skies prevail farther north, northeast and east.

ROUTES

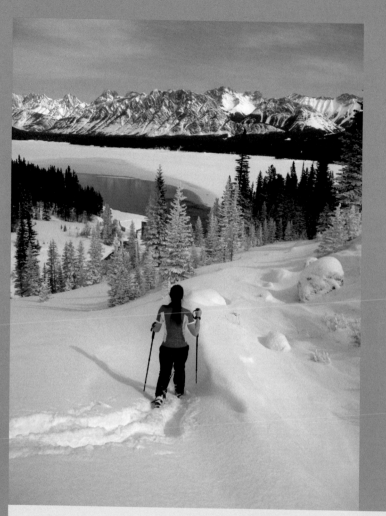

Nina and the view of Lower Kananaskis Lake from near Upper Kananaskis Lake. The magnificent Opal Range always provides a fantastic background.

Peter Lougheed Provincial Park Facility Zone Snowshoe Trails

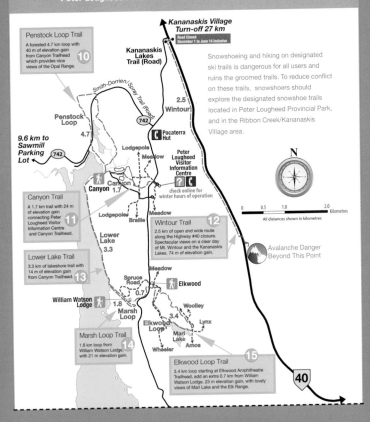

Penstock Loop Trail

A forested 4.7 km loop with 40 m of elevation gain from Canyon Trailhead which provides nice views of the Opal Range. **10**

Kananaskis Village Turn-off 27 km

Road Closed
December 1 to June 14 inclusive

Kananaskis Lakes Trail (Road)

Smith-Dorrien/Spray Trail (Road)

742

Penstock Loop
4.7

9.6 km to Sawmill Parking Lot
742

2.5
Wintour

Pocaterra Hut

Lodgepole

Meadow

Peter Lougheed Visitor Information Centre
check online for winter hours of operation

Snowshoeing and hiking on designated ski trails is dangerous for all users and ruins the groomed trails. To reduce conflict on these trails, snowshoers should explore the designated snowshoe trails located in Peter Lougheed Provincial Park, and in the Ribbon Creek/Kananaskis Village area.

Canyon
Canyon 1.7

Lodgepole
Braille

Canyon Trail

A 1.7 km trail with 24 m of elevation gain connecting Peter Lougheed Visitor Information Centre and Canyon Trailhead. **11**

Meadow

Wintour Trail 12

2.5 km of open and wide route along the Highway #40 closure. Spectacular views on a clear day of Mt. Wintour and the Kananaskis Lakes. 74 m of elevation gain.

Lower Lake
3.3

Lower Lake Trail

3.3 km of lakeshore trail with 14 m of elevation gain from Canyon Trailhead. **13**

Meadow

Spruce Road
0.7

Elkwood

William Watson Lodge 1.8
Marsh Loop

Woolley

Elkwood Loop
3.4

Lynx

Marsh Loop Trail

1.8 km loop from William Watson Lodge, with 21 m elevation gain. **14**

Mari Lake
Amos

Wheeler

15

N

0   0.5   1.0   2.0
Kilometres
All distances shown in kilometres

Avalanche Danger Beyond This Point

Elkwood Loop Trail

3.4 km loop starting at Elkwood Amphitheatre Trailhead, add an extra 0.7 km from William Watson Lodge. 23 m elevation gain, with lovely views of Mari Lake and the Elk Range.

40

OPPOSITE: THE OFFICIAL SNOWSHOE TRAILS AROUND THE
KANANASKIS LAKES – NORTH SECTION…. (MAP COURTESY OF
ALBERTA PARKS, KANANASKIS). BELOW:….SOUTH SECTION
(MAP COURTESY OF ALBERTA PARKS, KANANASKIS).

Lower Kananaskis Lake

Kananaskis Lakes Trail (Road)

Upper Kananaskis Lake

Elk Pass

Boulton Creek

Upper Lake Connector

Fox Creek

Hydroline

Elk Pass

Lookout

Elk Pass 5.8

Alberta

Patterson

Tyrwhitt

Elk Pass

Alberta

Elk Lakes Provincial Park (BC)

Elk Pass Trail 16

This route takes you to the Alberta/BC border via
a 5.8 km long trail; 222 m of elevation gain. You will
have a view of Lower Kananaskis Lake and the
surrounding mountains. Some portions of this trail cross
or share ski trails, so please stay on the edge of the
trails, and yield to oncoming skiers. No dogs allowed.

Legend

--- Snowshoe Trail
- - - Cross-country Ski Trail
🚶 Trailhead
❓ Visitor Information Centre
📞 Phone
▪▪▪ Alberta/BC Boundary

0   0.5   1.0   2.0 Kilometres
All distances shown in kilometres

74 CANYON

(MAP 17, PAGE 486)

> DIFFICULTY EASY
>
> ELEVATION GAIN APPROXIMATELY 50 M
>
> ROUND-TRIP DISTANCE 4.2 KM
>
> ROUND-TRIP TIME 1–2 HOURS
>
> MAPS 82 J/11 KANANASKIS LAKES,
> GEM TREK KANANASKIS LAKES

The Kananaskis Canyon trail basically connects the Peter Lougheed Visitor Information Centre with the canyon parking lot. Either location can be used as a starting point. Described below is the route from the canyon parking lot. Consider combining this route with an interesting detour through Kananaskis Canyon, as described on page 329, and/or a pleasant stroll on Lower Kananaskis Lake I (page 332).

DIRECTIONS

Drive 3.9 km along Kananaskis Lakes Trail and turn onto the Canyon road. Follow it to the parking lot.

From the parking lot the first snowshoe sign can be found near the northeast end, close to the lake. This is also the start of the Penstock Loop. The canyon trail stays close to the road and then drops down into Canyon Campground. Soon it takes a sharp right into the forest. Follow the signs up to the Kananaskis Lakes Trail road. Unless you intend to stop in at the visitor centre, there's no point in crossing the road and continuing on. Simply turn around and head back the way you came.

75 KANANASKIS CANYON

(MAP 17, PAGE 486)

> DIFFICULTY INTERMEDIATE
> ELEVATION GAIN APPROXIMATELY 50 M
> ROUND-TRIP DISTANCE APPROXIMATELY 2 KM
> ROUND-TRIP TIME 0.75–1.25 HOURS
> MAPS 82 J/11 KANANASKIS LAKES,
> GEM TREK KANANASKIS LAKES

This delightful canyon provides interesting and varied scenery and is nice and short to boot! The trip earns an intermediate rating because of the snow-covered stairs that must be ascended and a short but steep descent into the other side of the canyon.

DIRECTIONS

Drive 3.9 km along Kananaskis Lakes Trail and turn onto the Canyon road. Follow it to the parking lot.

The start of the trip is the same as that for the Canyon trail. From the parking lot the first snowshoe sign can be found near the northeast end, close to the lake. This is also the start of the Penstock Loop. The Canyon trail stays close to the road and then drops down into Canyon Campground. Soon after, the Canyon trail takes a sharp right turn into the forest. Ignore the right turn and keep going straight and then slightly to the left to the tan-coloured Kananaskis Canyon trail sign.

This is the start of the interpretive summer trail around the canyon. It goes in a counter-clockwise direction. However, for winter trips a clockwise direction is preferable, even though it means going against the "One Way" sign. Going against the grain allows you to ascend the stairs, instead of the more dangerous task of descending them.

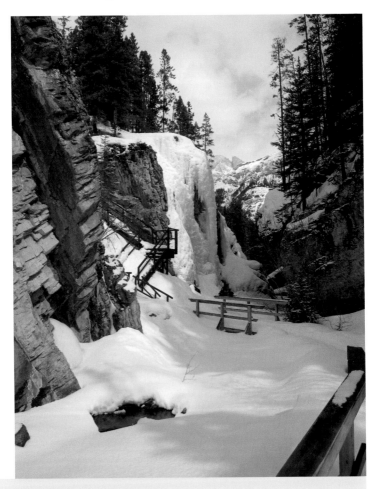

IN THE FASCINATING CANYON, LOOKING TOWARD
THE ICE CLIMBS AT THE END.

The trail immediately drops down to the canyon, crosses the creek and then follows the creek. A couple of ice climbs are quickly reached, and if you are lucky you can take a break to watch ice climbers scaling the frozen waterfalls.

Ascending the stairs can be very easy, very tricky or somewhere in between, depending on the snow and ice conditions. The amount of snow and ice will dictate whether you go up with your snowshoes on or off. Atop the stairs, follow the fence as it starts to descend

AN ICE CLIMBER MAKING HIS WAY UP THE FROZEN WATER.

to the other side of the canyon, making a sharp and steep turn to the right when near the bottom. The vertical rock and open pools of water make this side of the canyon interesting. Stay on the trail, crossing to the other side of the creek on a bridge. Unless you are up for a very frigid dip in nearly 0° water, do not test the strength of the ice anywhere in the canyon – it is notoriously weak.

Once on the other side, the trail follows the creek for a very short distance and then takes a sharp turn to the right and ascends the opposite bank of the canyon. Quickly you will find yourself back at the trailhead. Return to your vehicle the same way you came in.

76 LOWER KANANASKIS LAKE I

(MAP 17, PAGE 486)

DIFFICULTY EASY	
ELEVATION GAIN APPROXIMATELY 30 M	
ROUND-TRIP DISTANCE 5.6 KM	
ROUND-TRIP TIME 1.5–2.5 HOURS	
MAPS 82 J/11 KANANASKIS LAKES, GEM TREK KANANASKIS LAKES	

The Lower Lake snowshoe trail is just the summer trail, but with snow. Expansive views are available from beginning to end.

DIRECTIONS

Drive 3.9 km along Kananaskis Lakes Trail and turn onto the Canyon road. Follow it to the parking lot.

There are three ways to snowshoe this route: along the designated trail, on the embankment above the lake, or directly on the lake. Provided there is good snow coverage, I recommend using the embankment on the way in and following the designated trail on the way back or vice versa. Your decision regarding which route to start with may depend on the weather. The embankment route has better views and therefore favours good weather. Both routes are described below.

LOWER LAKE TRAIL ROUTE

This route starts at the trailhead sign and is clearly marked with an orange snowshoe sign. The popularity of the trail means that it will probably be packed down and very easy to follow. The trail goes through the trees, staying relatively close to the lakeshore for the first half and then moving very close to the shore for the second half. Views of the lake and its surroundings are obviously better on the second half of the trip.

The trail ends at an obvious peninsula with a small brown building at the end. This is also the north end of the Marsh Loop. Time, energy and motivation permitting, you may want to complete the 1.3-km Marsh Loop and then return via Lower Lake Trail or the embankment.

EMBANKMENT ROUTE

This route is perhaps even easier to follow than the designated trail. From the parking lot snowshoe a few metres north onto the bank of Lower Lake. Head west and then curve around to the south, staying above the lake. Views toward the Opal Range to the northeast are fantastic right off the bat, as are views toward Mount Warspite due west. Rounding the corner, Invincible and

THE REWARDS OF THE EMBANKMENT ROUTE ARE INSTANT VIEWS OF THE OPAL RANGE ...

ABOVE: ...AND THE BATTLE OF JUTLAND GROUP. BELOW: A LATE-SEASON TRIP REVEALS LARGE FRACTURES AND FISSURES IN THE ICE ON THE EMBANKMENT. A WEEK EARLIER THESE CRACKS WERE ALL FILLED IN WITH A WEAK LAYER OF SNOW. TAKE CARE.

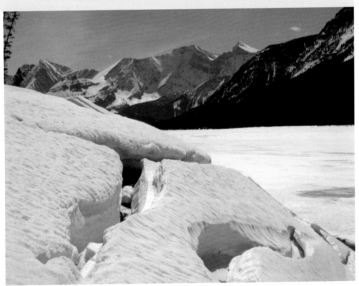

Indefatigable soon appear and finally Sarrail, Foch and Fox in the distant south.

Take extreme care if at any time you decide to descend to the lake. Deep snow can hide large cracks and holes in the broken slabs of thick ice that often line the lakeshore.

Continue following the lake south for several kilometres. Your goal is to snowshoe to the small brown building at the end of a peninsula and then follow the peninsula east to the designated trail (snowshoe sign to the left). The snowshoe sign to the right is for the north end of the 1.3-km Marsh Loop, and you may want to complete that short trip while in the area (page 350).

For return, either retrace your steps along the embankment or, for a little variety, follow the designated trail back to the parking lot. The gentle ups and downs of the trail make this a very pleasant route to take.

ELK PASS

(MAP 17, PAGE 486)

RATING INTERMEDIATE
PASS HEIGHT 1950 M
NET ELEVATION GAIN 222 M
ROUND-TRIP DISTANCE 11.6-12.4 KM
ROUND-TRIP TIME 3–5 HOURS
MAPS 82 J/11 KANANASKIS LAKES, GEM TREK
KANANASKIS LAKES

The Elk Pass snowshoe trail is a good day of exercise, but not much else. Views are limited throughout and at the pass there is hardly a view at all. However, the trail can be used as an approach to Kananaskis Lookout or Fox Lake. You can also make a pleasant loop route by going to Elk Pass via the snowshoe trail and then returning via Fox Creek. This area is used often by skiers so please respect their space and tracks.

DIRECTIONS

Drive approximately 12 km on Kananaskis Trail and park at the Elk Pass parking lot. The snowshoe trail starts at the southeast end of the parking lot. It very quickly empties out onto the wide Hydroline ski trail. From here the official snowshoe trail is well signed and easy to follow. A detailed description is not required, however a few pointers may help.

The trail ascends to the top of the first hill, going into the trees a couple of times along the way. First on the right side of the Hydroline and then on the left. Continue up until you arrive at a point where the trail overlooks a deep canyon, with a continuation of the Hydroline far on the other side. The snowshoe trail

THE DEWIT FAMILY, KAYCIE, HANNEKE AND NIKO, ASCEND THE WIDE HYDROLINE. NOTE THAT THE FAMILY IS MAKING A SEPARATE SNOWSHOE TRAIL ALONGSIDE THE SKI TRAIL — KUDOS TO THEM! MOUNT INDEFATIGABLE BASKS IN THE SUN BEHIND THEM. (VERN DEWIT)

now joins up with the ski trail and descends to the bottom of the valley. Stay to the side of the path and watch for skiers. At the bottom, the trail turns left and then takes an immediate right into the trees, where it parallels Fox Creek, before popping out back onto the ski trail.

Turn left and ascend a long gentle slope back up to the Hydroline. At the top you may want to quickly veer off to the left to take in a pretty decent view of Kananaskis Lakes and Mount Indefatigable.

The remainder of the trip involves a somewhat mundane plod to Elk Pass along the Hydroline. Don't expect any mind-blowing views on the way or at the pass. About 1 km along you have the option to give Kananaskis Lookout a try. See page 339 for that trip.

Otherwise, continue up to the high point of Elk Pass, around GR367055. An "End of the Trail" sign marks the end of the ascent.

For return you can retrace your steps back or complete a loop route via Elk Pass Trail. This second option is recommended, but note that this means you will be on a ski trail for a large section. Stay to the side and yield to all skiers throughout. The route is again obvious.

Hop onto Elk Pass Trail and descend easily to the valley below. Consider a side trip to Fox Lake at this point (see page 341). Eventually the trail joins up with Fox Creek and parallels it for a while. This is probably the most pleasant part of the trip, with terrific scenery along and in the creek.

About 4.4 km from the high point at Elk Pass, Elk Pass Trail joins up with Hydroline Trail. The reminder of the trip is the same as what you ascended.

78 KANANASKIS LOOKOUT

(MAP 17, PAGE 486)

RATING	INTERMEDIATE
LOOKOUT HEIGHT	2118 M
NET ELEVATION GAIN	400 M
ROUND-TRIP DISTANCE	14 KM
ROUND-TRIP TIME	4–6 HOURS
MAPS	82 J/11 KANANASKIS LAKES, GEM TREK KANANASKIS LAKES

As long as you walk around the area a little, there are some excellent views to be experienced at Kananaskis Lookout. The Elk Pass snowshoe trail provides a good approach. However, once you leave the snowshoe trail, you are on a groomed, double-track ski trail. This trip should therefore only be attempted by snowshoers very late in the season (April and later) when the wide trail has been thoroughly packed down and there is plenty of room for a separate snowshoe trail. There will also be far fewer skiers at that time of the year because of poor skiing conditions. DO NOT under any circumstances snowshoe on the ski tracks.

DIRECTIONS

This trail is very obvious and easy to follow. It descends to Boulton Creek, turns northeast and then grinds its way up approximately 240 m of elevation to the lookout. There are a few steep hills but nothing that your snowshoes won't handle with ease. Again, a reminder to stay off the ski tracks. At a good clip you can make it up to the lookout in about 45 minutes from the turnoff (2 hours from the parking lot).

The best view at the lookout lies to the west and the best place to see this view is from the west side of the lookout. Just watch where you go. The lookout is a private residence. Be respectful of that fact.

Return the same way. Upon rejoining the Elk Pass snowshoe trail, you have the option to go back the way you came or complete a loop as described in the Elk Pass and Fox Lake trips. This makes for a long but rewarding day. Fit, motivated parties can visit the lookout, Elk Pass and Fox Lake in about 7 hours round-trip (21 km round-trip, 600 m total elevation gain).

JACK TANNETT CAPTURES THE MAGICAL WINTER VIEW TOWARD KANANASKIS LAKES. (JACK TANNETT)

79 FOX LAKE

RATING INTERMEDIATE
LAKE HEIGHT 1950 M
NET ELEVATION GAIN 300 M (VIA ELK PASS)
ROUND-TRIP DISTANCE 14.4 KM (VIA ELK PASS)
ROUND-TRIP TIME 4–7 HOURS
MAPS 82 J/11 KANANASKIS LAKES, GEM TREK
KANANASKIS LAKES

As with many winter visits to lakes, the highlight of this trip is not the actual lake. Fox Lake in winter is usually a white, frozen flatland and far more interesting in the summer. The winter reward is the journey there and the view of Mount Fox above the lake. The recommended route is a loop using the Elk Pass snowshoe trail on ascent and Fox Creek for return.

DIRECTIONS

Follow the directions to Elk Pass. From the pass hop onto Elk Pass Trail and descend to the valley below. This is an easy and pleasant descent on skis or snowshoes.

As you near the bottom of the hill look for a "More Difficult," blue ski sign. Here, you will take a sharp left turn onto the summer trail that leads to a major junction. Snowshoe southeast for about 300 m, soon arriving at the large clearing. Even here the view of Mount Fox is quite eye-catching.

On the west side of the clearing you should see a large sign. Make your way over to it. The trail to Fox Lake is well signed (hopefully the sign is not completely buried in snow) and it heads west.

AT THE CLEARING AND LOOKING WEST TOWARD THE LARGE SIGN
AND STUNNING MOUNT FOX. LS=LARGE SIGN. F=MOUNT FOX.

Follow the trail for 200 m to another sign, where you will take a 90° turn left, onto another trail. This trail goes through the trees and then empties out into more open terrain. Going straight at this intersection leads to Frozen Lake, but it's a steep grind to get there and certainly not recommended as a winter trip. Visit Frozen Lake in the summer – the view is spectacular!

Route-finding may get a little tricky here, depending on whether a trail to the lake has already been broken or not. The goal is to find the creek that drains Fox Lake and follow it on its right bank to the lake (Elkan Creek). Head to the right and up. Eventually you will run into the creek. If not, start trending left as you slowly gain elevation. If that doesn't work, set your GPS to

GR354045 to guide you to the lake. If you don't have any form of technology to assist you, it may be time to pray for directions!

Once you have located the creek, simply follow it for several hundred metres to Fox Lake. Take in the view of Mount Fox and then start returning the same way. When you get back to the blue ski sign turn left back onto Elk Pass Trail. You can now follow this trail, paralleling Fox Creek, all the way back to the Elk Pass snowshoe trail. Rejoin the snowshoe trail and return to the parking lot. Climbing back up the big hill is not as strenuous as you are probably dreading, and then it's a smooth sail downhill all the way back.

ANDRA MACKNIGHT CAPTURES THE SERENE BEAUTY OF FOX LAKE, THE SNOW-COVERED TREES AT THE BACK OF THE LAKE AND THE MAGNIFICENT FORM OF MOUNT FOX BEHIND THE LAKE. (ANDRA MACKNIGHT)

80 PENSTOCK LOOP

(MAP 17, PAGE 486)

DIFFICULTY	EASY
ELEVATION GAIN	40 M
ROUND-TRIP DISTANCE	4.7 KM
ROUND-TRIP TIME	1.5–2.5 HOURS
MAPS	82 J/11 KANANASKIS LAKES, GEM TREK KANANASKIS LAKES

"A forested 4.5 km loop from Canyon Day Use which takes in some interesting historical features, such as the Pocaterra Dam penstock and the Kent Creek sluiceway, and provides nice views of the Opal Range." Thus reads the billing on the Kananaskis Country Snowshoe Trails pamphlet. This loop has a bit of everything, including two road crossings, so be alert. Note that changes were made to this area in spring of 2012 and the described route may change in the future. Check at the Peter Lougheed Visitor Centre before going out.

DIRECTIONS

Drive 3.9 km along Kananaskis Lakes Trail and turn onto the Canyon road. Follow it to the parking lot.

From the parking lot the first snowshoe sign can be found near the northeast end, close to the lake. This is also the start of the canyon trail. The loop can be completed in either direction. Clockwise is described below. Snowshoe east for a short distance and then turn north, crossing the dam. Follow the wide path to the north end of Lower Kananaskis Lake. From there, carefully (and quickly) cross Highway 742, looking for an orange snowshoe sign on the other side.

WHEN YOU COME FROM A COUNTRY WITH LITTLE TO NO SNOW, ADAPTING TO SNOWSHOES MAY BE CHALLENGING AT FIRST. UNCLE BILL FROM ENGLAND KEEPS THE TROOPS ENTERTAINED BY DEMONSTRATING SOLID FORM IN FALLING!

It is now simply a matter of following the obvious path and signs, first alongside the Kent Creek sluiceway, then into a heavily forested area. The path soon turns east and then south before crossing the highway again. Good views of the Opal Range appear occasionally.

The loop ends at the huge leaky pipe that each year turns into a sculpture of fascinating ice formations.

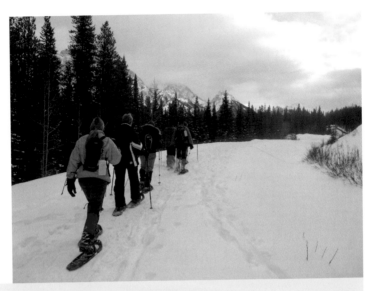

ABOVE: AN ORDERLY LINE OF SNOWSHOERS ENJOY
THE EASY TRAIL. BELOW: COOL ICE FORMATIONS
CAUSED BY THE LEAKY PIPE. (MARKO STAVRIC)

81 ELKWOOD LOOP

(MAP 17, PAGE 486)

DIFFICULTY EASY
ELEVATION GAIN 23 M
ROUND-TRIP DISTANCE 3.4 KM
ROUND-TRIP TIME 45–90 MINUTES
MAPS 82 J/11 KANANASKIS LAKES,
GEM TREK KANANASKIS LAKES

The Elkwood Loop takes you through pleasant forest to scenic Marl Lake, where good views of Mount Indefatigable await. The loop can be completed in either direction, but clockwise seems to be the preferred choice and is described below. For a fuller day, the route can easily be combined with the Marsh Loop via the William Watson Connector.

DIRECTIONS

Drive 5.8 km along Kananaskis Lakes Trail and pull into the Elkwood Amphitheatre parking lot.

Locate the first orange snowshoe sign and snowshoe a short connector to an important three-way junction. Turn left (Elkwood Loop) and follow the snowshoe signs through the campground and sections of forested terrain to the start of Marl Lake Interpretive Trail, about 15 minutes from the parking lot.

The interpretive trail is easy to follow and, provided they are not buried under snow, the interpretive signs are interesting and offer good points to stop and enjoy the scenery. Several open areas give views of small sections of the Opal Range to the east.

When you reach Marl Lake the views open up even more, with a good look at Mount Indefatigable. Those who have ventured up into the Aster Lake area will recognize Warrior Mountain to the distant left of Indefatigable.

At this point you have the option to extend the trip by snowshoeing around the perimeter of the lake. It will add about 1.5 km and 25–40 minutes to the overall trip, but the additional views will reward those who make the effort. This is an extension you'll want to do in late winter or early spring, when snow coverage and ice conditions are usually safe.

Whether you do the extension or not, you'll end up at the northwest end of the lake, where the trail continues for a short distance before turning right, into the trees, up a steep and very short hill. You then emerge back in the campground. Follow the snowshoe signs back to the Elkwood three-way junction. From there you can return to your car or extend your day using the William Watson Connector, as described below.

William Watson Connector

From the three-way junction it's about 700 m to William Watson Lodge and the start of the Marsh Loop. Simply follow the signs, quickly crossing the main road and then snowshoeing through light forest to the lodge. If the trail is packed down, you may want to do this connector on foot, carrying your snowshoes. Otherwise, it will entail a couple of short sections of walking on concrete – never a good idea for the health of your snowshoes! The signed trailhead for the Marsh Loop is to the right (north) of the main lodge.

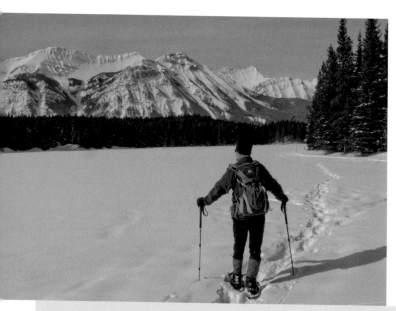

THE VIEW OF MOUNT INDEFATIGABLE FROM
MARL LAKE. (GILLEAN DAFFERN)

82 MARSH LOOP

(MAP 17, PAGE 486)

DIFFICULTY EASY
ELEVATION GAIN APPROXIMATELY 25 M
ROUND-TRIP DISTANCE 1.8 KM
ROUND-TRIP TIME 0.5–1 HOUR
MAPS 82 J/11 KANANASKIS LAKES,
GEM TREK KANANASKIS LAKES

Like many of the snowshoe trails in the area, this loop can easily be combined with other routes in order to make the most of your day. Lower Kananaskis Lake Trail (page 332) and Elkwood Loop (page 347) are both connected to the Marsh Loop.

DIRECTIONS

Drive 5.9 km along Kananaskis Lakes Trail and pull into the William Watson Lodge parking lot.

The trailhead is to the right (north) of the main lodge. Descend to a three-way junction and turn left. The obvious trail descends gently, almost reaching the road before it takes a hairpin turn, heading northwest. Before you negotiate the hairpin turn, take a look to the east and southeast for some potentially good views of mountains in the Opal, Misty and Highwood ranges. At times, it may even be worth crawling quickly across the road to enjoy the view, as I did on a late-April trip (anything for a good photo op!).

It eventually takes you close to the shores of Lower Kananaskis Lake. Along the way, enjoy good views of the southern end of the British Military Group – most notably Mounts Indefatigable and Invincible, both named after battleships that were part

FROM LEFT TO RIGHT: MOUNT FOX, THE TURRET, MOUNT FOCH AND MOUNT SARRAIL ARE ALWAYS MAGNIFICENT TO LOOK AT ON A CLEAR WINTER OR SPRING DAY. PHOTO TAKEN FROM THE PENINSULA.

of the Battle of Jutland in the First World War. Another sharp turn marks the start of the ascent back to William Watson Lodge.

Before heading back to the lodge, be sure to follow the peninsula at the north end of the trail to a small brown building at the end. The views and terrain here are very interesting.

Should you feel like extending the trip, once you reach the northernmost point of the Marsh Loop, you can join the Lower Lake Trail, heading north along the shoreline (unsigned, but obvious), or take the designated snowshoe trail through the trees. That trail is 2.8 km long and spits you out at the Canyon parking lot. Either return the same way you came in or have a second car waiting for you at Canyon.

THE MARSH LOOP LIVES UP TO ITS NAME LATE IN THE SEASON. THE MARSHY VIEW TO THE EAST AND SOUTHEAST FROM THE POINT OF THE LOOP WHERE THE TRAIL COMES CLOSE TO THE ROAD.

83 LOWER KANANASKIS LAKE II

(MAP 17, PAGE 486)

DIFFICULTY INTERMEDIATE
ELEVATION GAIN MINIMAL
ROUND-TRIP DISTANCE VARIABLE
ROUND-TRIP TIME VARIABLE
MAPS 82 J/11 KANANASKIS LAKES,
GEM TREK KANANASKIS LAKES

For those wanting to avoid the potential crowds along Lower Kananaskis Lake I trail (page 332), see a slightly different section of Lower Kananaskis Lake and/or engage in some potentially serious trail-breaking, this area is a great alternative to Lower Kananaskis Lake I. The intermediate rating of this trip reflects the fact that there are no official trails in this area and there exists the potential for route-finding and trail-breaking.

DIRECTIONS

Drive 9.7 km along Kananaskis Lakes Trail and turn onto the Lower Lake road. Follow it to the parking lot.

The lake is only a few hundred metres from the parking lot. This is a great opportunity to gain experience breaking new trail, without too much commitment. It's easy to turn around at any time.

Once near or on the lake, snowshoeing in pretty much any direction will grant you great views of something! Due west lies

Mount Indefatigable. Mount Lyautey is the huge massif to the southwest. Farther south sit the familiar forms of Mounts Sarrail, Foch and Fox. The diminutive but very distinctive mountain between Foch and Fox is called The Turret. As you travel farther west on the lake, views of the magnificent Opal Range to the east start to open up.

NINA HEADS OUT TOWARD THE LAKE. THE STRIKING PEAKS AT THE LEFT ARE OUTLIERS OF MOUNT LYAUTEY, AND MOUNT INDEFATIGABLE SITS TO THE RIGHT.

You don't need to go too far west before the
Opal Range is revealed to the east.

84 UPPER KANANASKIS LAKE I

(MAP 17, PAGE 486)

DIFFICULTY	INTERMEDIATE
ELEVATION GAIN	MINIMAL
ROUND-TRIP DISTANCE	VARIABLE
ROUND-TRIP TIME	VARIABLE
MAPS	82 J/11 KANANASKIS LAKES, GEM TREK KANANASKIS LAKES

If you are looking for great views of Mount Indefatigable, this is the place to see some. The best way to do this is by snowshoeing on the lake, around the south shore. If the lake is not sufficiently frozen, use Rawson Lake Trail. The intermediate rating of this

trip reflects the fact that there is potential for route-finding and trail-breaking, unless you stick to the official trails going around the lake.

DIRECTIONS

Drive 12.4 km along Kananaskis Lakes Trail and turn onto the Upper Lake road. Follow it to the parking lot at the southeast end of Upper Kananaskis Lake.

Either snowshoe immediately down to the shore of the lake as your starting point or follow the obvious trail that goes around the southeast corner of the lake (same as for Rawson Lake, page 358). When the lake is fully frozen you can explore this area in any direction you like. Going straight into the middle of the lake will be fantastic for views. Following the shoreline in either direction is also a great way to experience this awe-inspiring environment.

LOOKING ACROSS THE LAKE FROM THE PARKING LOT. ACRES AND ACRES OF BEAUTIFUL VIEWS AND TERRAIN TO ENJOY. (GREG STRINGHAM)

85 RAWSON LAKE

(MAP 17, PAGE 486)

> DIFFICULTY INTERMEDIATE
> ELEVATION GAIN 300 M
> ROUND-TRIP DISTANCE 8 KM
> ROUND-TRIP TIME 3–5 HOURS
> MAPS 82 J/11 KANANASKIS LAKES,
> GEM TREK KANANASKIS LAKES

This small lake sits below the awe-inspiring northeast face of Mount Sarrail. A well-used trail goes all the way there. The extension to the ridge north of Rawson Lake grants a great view of the considerably larger Kananaskis Lakes, but it is beyond the scope of this book because of avalanche danger.

DIRECTIONS

Drive 12.4 km along Kananaskis Lakes Trail and turn onto the Upper Lake road. Follow it to the parking lot at the southeast end of Upper Kananaskis Lake.

From there, start along the easy-to-follow trail that swings around the southeast end of Upper Kananaskis Lake and then parallels the south side. About 1 km along you'll cross a bridge that spans Sarrail Creek. Shortly after, a trail sign instructs you to leave the main trail and turn left (southwest) onto Rawson Lake Trail. Follow this trail for 2 km as it winds its way up treed slopes to Rawson Lake. Take some time to enjoy the tranquil beauty of this area. Provided the lake is sufficiently frozen, you can snowshoe across it; however, there are avalanche concerns on the opposite side. The best strategy is to follow the perimeter of the lake for short distances in either direction to get some different perspectives. Return the same way you came in.

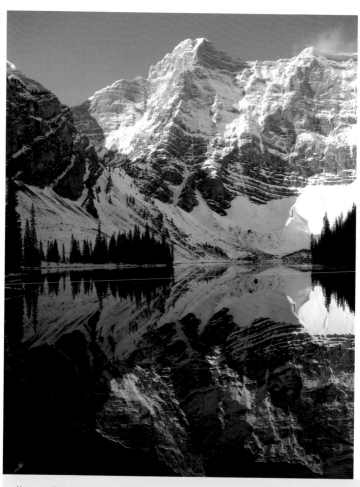

MOUNT SARRAIL REFLECTED IN THE PLACID WATERS OF RAWSON LAKE. PROBABLY NOT A GOOD TIME TO ATTEMPT TO SNOWSHOE ACROSS THE LAKE!

86 UPPER KANANASKIS LAKE II

(MAP 17, PAGE 486)

DIFFICULTY	INTERMEDIATE
ELEVATION GAIN	MINIMAL
ROUND-TRIP DISTANCE	VARIABLE
ROUND-TRIP TIME	VARIABLE
MAPS	82 J/11 KANANASKIS LAKES, GEM TREK KANANASKIS LAKES

The second of two starting points on Upper Lake offers terrific views of massive Mount Lyautey and the Sarrail/Foch/Fox trio. When it is sufficiently frozen, you can snowshoe directly on the lake. If conditions on the lake are suspect, a very popular trail goes around the north side of the lake. For those of you who are goal oriented, the treed island, sometimes called Hawke Island, in the middle of the lake is a good objective. The intermediate rating of this trip reflects the fact that there is potential for route-finding and trail-breaking, unless you stick to the official trails going around the lake.

DIRECTIONS

Drive 14.7 km along Kananaskis Lakes Trail and turn left onto the North Interlakes road, reaching the parking lot shortly after.

Upper Lake is metres away from the parking lot. Do not jump onto the lake immediately. The release of water at the dam makes this area of the lake very unstable. Instead, snowshoe northwest, across the initial section of the dam, and then make your way onto the lake when it is feasible (and safe). Once on the lake, it's up to you where and how far you go.

The other option is to stay on the south side of the dam and follow the shore.

ABOVE: UPPER KANANASKIS LAKE. THE NORTHWEST OUTLIERS OF MOUNT LYAUTEY DOMINATE THE BACKGROUND. NOTE THE LAKE AREA AT THE FRONT IS SUSCEPTIBLE TO WEAK ICE AND SHOULD BE AVOIDED. (GARY HEBERT) BELOW: MARK KOOB AND SON SNOWSHOEING AROUND THE UPPER KANANASKIS LAKE. (TANYA KOOB)

87 MOUNT INDEFATIGABLE VIEWPOINT

(MAP 17, PAGE 486)

RATING	ADVANCED
MAXIMUM HEIGHT	1976–2106 M
ELEVATION GAIN	270–300 M
ROUND-TRIP DISTANCE	5.4–6 KM
ROUND-TRIP TIME	2–4 HOURS
MAPS	82 J/11 KANANASKIS LAKES, GEM TREK KANANASKIS LAKES

The trail to this magnificent viewpoint was decommissioned in 2005, to protect grizzly bear habitat. Nevertheless, the route described here does not venture into areas where you are likely to run into grizzlies, especially during the winter months when they are hopefully in a peaceful and very long slumber! Do the trip in the dead of winter to minimize any possibility of actually waking the sleeping bear. Route-finding challenges and steep terrain put this trip in the category of Advanced for Experienced Beginners.

DIRECTIONS

Drive to the end of the Kananaskis Lakes Trail and park at the Interlakes parking lot. The objective is clearly visible from here. You may want to carry your snowshoes to the trailhead. Cross the dam and continue on the wide trail for a short distance until you see the big Parks Canada sign off to the right, describing why the trail was decommissioned. Put on your snowshoes here.

DAVID AND LINDSAY ROUSSEAU, OWNERS OF OLLIA MACARONS & TEA
(THE PISTACHIO AND LEMON ARE EXQUISITE!) IN CALGARY, JOIN
NICOLE LISAFELD ON UPPER KANANASKIS LAKE. THE OBJECTIVE IS
BEHIND. MI=MOUNT INDEFATIGABLE. WE=WENDY ELEKES VIEWPOINT.

The trail is still very obvious and easy to follow. It winds through the trees for a while, before turning to the right and crossing a creek. On the other side of the creek, the trail starts to gain elevation more rapidly, soon ascending the west side of the ridge where the viewpoint lies. You will appreciate heel lifts from here on in.

Closing in on the ridge, you will soon see it directly in front of you, and flagging in the trees to the left. The trail follows the flagging, but the direct route up to the ridge is more scenic, more challenging and more fun, once you get on the ridge.

Both routes eventually lead up to a wonderful viewpoint at

GR309113, 1976 m, often called the Wendy Elekes viewpoint. The view of Kananaskis Lakes backdropped by mounts Sarrail, Foch and Fox is fantastic. Many may decide to make this the high point of the day. If so, return the same way.

Continuing up the trail to a higher viewpoint has its merits, but the view doesn't change significantly. The route is obvious. Follow the ridge up in a northerly direction. You'll soon be acutely aware of the nasty drop-off on the right side of the mountain. Stay away from the edge. There are a couple of places to call it a day: 1. At GR308116, 2070 m, the trails levels off a little and grants a terrific, open view of the aforementioned mountains and much of the Opal Range to the east; 2. A little higher, two very closely spaced trees by a boulder at GR308117, 2106 m, provides much

NICOLE, LINDSAY AND DAVID TACKLE THE MORE CHALLENGING RIDGE ROUTE TO THE WENDY ELEKES VIEWPOINT.

THE VIEW TO THE SOUTH FROM THE POPULAR WENDY ELEKES VIEWPOINT.

the same view but at higher elevation. Travel beyond this second spot is not recommended. The view doesn't get any better and the trail gets very close to the edge of the ridge and that nasty drop-off. Return the same way.

BANFF

Banff is Canada's classic mountain town. Visitors flock from every corner of the planet throughout the year to see Banff and the national park. Though not as snowy as its equally popular neighbour to the northwest, Lake Louise, Banff gets enough snow to keep the average snowshoer in business for the length of the season. As well, the weather tends to be a little more stable than it is at Lake Louise, due to Banff's more easterly location.

On average, Banff receives its largest deposits of snow in December and January. However, usually the best snowshoeing conditions occur in February and March, when the snowpack has settled and consolidated.

For the most part, finding accommodations in Banff is pretty easy, the townsite being home to a great number of hotels. However, don't expect that to be inexpensive, and book in advance, especially for long weekends.

A national park pass is required for all trips in Banff.

ROUTES

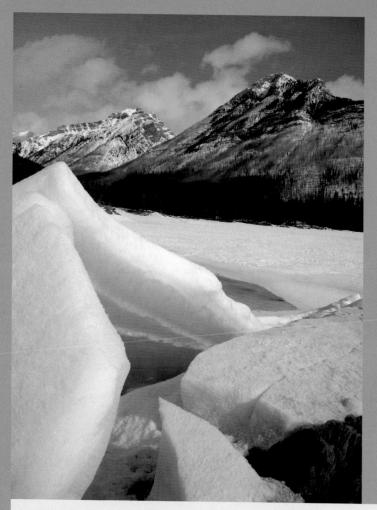

DRAMATIC UPLIFTS OF ICE ALONG THE
LAKE MINNEWANKA SHORELINE.

88 CASCADE PONDS

(MAP 18, PAGE 487)

DIFFICULTY EASY

ELEVATION GAIN NONE

ROUND-TRIP DISTANCE APPROXIMATELY 1–2 KM

ROUND-TRIP TIME 0.5–1 HOUR

MAPS 82 O/04 BANFF,
GEM TREK BANFF AND MOUNT ASSINIBOINE

If you are looking for a very short and easy trip with a killer view of Cascade Mountain, the ponds are the ticket: great for an introduction to walking on snowshoes and as a family outing. The only downside to this trip is the constant hum of traffic from the Trans-Canada Highway. After seeing the ponds, it's only a short drive to Johnson Lake, Two Jack Lake or Lake Minnewanka for additional trips.

DIRECTIONS

From the Trans-Canada Highway, take the Lake Minnewanka turnoff near Banff. Take an immediate right at the Cascade Ponds sign, drive about 200 m down a small hill and take another right onto the road that circles around the west and south sides of the ponds. Park at either of the two parking areas, although the first one seems more suitable.

A specific route description is hardly necessary here. Simply snowshoe around the outer edges of the ponds, exploring as you desire. Two bridges make life a little easier. Leaving the beaten path is a good way to get an easy introduction to trail-breaking. Use discretion if you decide to snowshoe directly on the ponds.

Looking toward the formidable form of Cascade Mountain,

ABOVE: CASCADE MOUNTAIN LOOMS OVER THE PONDS
AND A SNOWMAN WHO'S LOST HIS HEAD! BELOW: MOUNT
RUNDLE AND ONE OF THE PONDS' BRIDGES.

you may see ice climbers slowly making their way up the very popular Cascade Falls. Other familiar views include Mount Rundle to the south and the unnamed peaks around Lake Minnewanka to the north.

89 JOHNSON LAKE

(MAP 18, PAGE 487)

DIFFICULTY EASY; INTERMEDIATE IF TRAIL IS
ICY

ELEVATION GAIN MINIMAL

ROUND-TRIP DISTANCE 2.8 KM

ROUND-TRIP TIME 0.75–1 HOUR

MAPS 82 O/03 CANMORE,
GEM TREK BANFF AND MOUNT ASSINIBOINE

For terrific views of Mount Rundle and Cascade Mountain, Johnson Lake is a first-rate choice. The trail is relatively well travelled and snowshoes may or may not be necessary. However, there are basically two loops around the lake. If you want to make sure your snowshoes see some wear, follow the less-travelled outer loop. Take snowshoes along in case you want to take the outer loop or if they are required for the inner loop.

DIRECTIONS

From the Trans-Canada Highway, take the Lake Minnewanka turnoff near Banff. Drive 4.7 km and turn right at the Johnson Lake turnoff. Note the winter detour along the way, about 1 km after leaving Highway 1. The parking lot is 2.2 km down Johnson Lake Road.

The loop around the lake can be completed in either direction. A clockwise direction is described below. Specific directions are not necessary, as the trail is well established and easy to follow throughout. However, take note of the following.

The inner loop follows the lakeshore very closely and is the more scenic of the two routes. Travel on top of the frozen lake

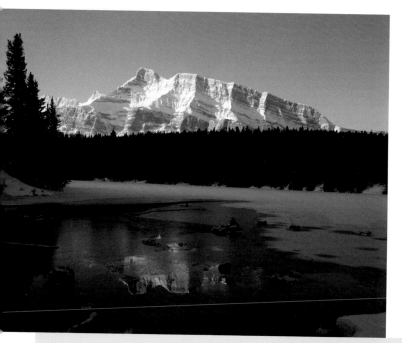

THE NORTHEAST FACE OF MOUNT RUNDLE IS REFLECTED IN
A SMALL POOL OF OPEN WATER ON JOHNSON LAKE. BARELY
VISIBLE IN THE CENTRE OF THE FACE IS THE WORLD-
FAMOUS WATERFALL ICE CLIMB CALLED SEA OF VAPOURS.

is not recommended, due to dangerous areas of open water. This
is an environmentally sensitive area, and you should stay on the
trail at all times. The trail can get very icy and is narrow in a few
places. Care should be taken when the trail is running alongside
and slightly above the lake – a slip down the right side would be
unpleasant at best!

Nearing the end of the lake, the familiar form of Cascade
Mountain appears. Travel around the south and then west sides

of the lake is enjoyable and grants the occasional view of the formidable trio at the north end of the Fairholme Range: Inglismaldie, Girouard and Peechee. Note that there is the option, at the southwest end of the lake, to move onto the outer loop. The trip ends after crossing a bridge over the lake outlet.

THE TRIO, FROM LEFT TO RIGHT, OF
INGLISMALDIE, GIROUARD AND PEECHEE.

90 TWO JACK LAKE

(MAP 18, PAGE 487)

DIFFICULTY EASY

ELEVATION GAIN NONE

ROUND-TRIP DISTANCE 2–3.4 KM

ROUND-TRIP TIME 45–90 MINUTES

MAPS 82 0/03 CANMORE, 82 0/04 BANFF,
GEM TREK BANFF AND MOUNT ASSINIBOINE

Like its southerly neighbour, Johnson Lake, Two Jack Lake sports excellent views of Mount Rundle and Cascade Mountain. There is no official trail around the lake, but snowshoeing along the west shore can be a wonderful experience. January and February, when the lake is fully frozen, are the best months for this trip.

DIRECTIONS

From the Trans-Canada Highway, take the Lake Minnewanka turnoff near Banff. Drive 6.8 km and turn right, into the Two Jack Lake picnic area. Note the winter detour along the way, about 1 km after leaving Highway 1, and the two Two Jack signs before the Two Jack Lake picnic sign.

From the parking area, descend to the lake and start snowshoeing southwest along the lakeshore, taking in splendid views of Rundle and Inglismaldie right away. More than likely the lake will be sufficiently frozen to allow snowshoeing directly on the ice. However, it is recommended that you err on the side of caution and stay on or very close to the shore.

It's up to you how far along the shore you travel, but at least snowshoe around the first major bend, where a terrific view of Cascade awaits. As well, the farther south you go, the better the views to the north. Several unnamed peaks on the north shore of Lake Minnewanka can look very impressive under clear skies.

Past the campground on your right (west), the lake starts to narrow into a canal. At this point you may start to encounter stretches of open water, and travel will have to continue on land. This is also a good place to turn around and head back.

Once back near the parking area, you may want to continue going northeast along the shoreline for a few hundred metres more. Again, open water may eventually end your progress, so don't go too far. Another option is to hop in your vehicle and head to nearby Johnson Lake or Lake Minnewanka for more entertainment.

LOOKING NORTH ACROSS TWO JACK LAKE FROM NEAR ITS SOUTH END.

91 LAKE MINNEWANKA AND STEWART CANYON

(MAP 18, PAGE 487)

DIFFICULTY EASY FOR LAKE MINNEWANKA;
INTERMEDIATE FOR STEWART CANYON

ELEVATION GAIN MINIMAL FOR THE LAKE;
APPROXIMATELY 100 M FOR STEWART CANYON

ROUND-TRIP DISTANCE 2–6 KM

ROUND-TRIP TIME 0.75–2.5 HOURS

MAPS 82 O/03 CANMORE,
82 O/06 LAKE MINNEWANKA,
GEM TREK BANFF AND MOUNT ASSINIBOINE

You can't go wrong visiting this outstanding lake on a clear day. The scenery on the lake is terrific and the views around the lake are wonderful. Although there is a good trail around the west side of the lake, the best way to enjoy the scenery is by staying very close to the shore. This means some travel on the lake, so be sure it is sufficiently frozen by going in January or February. Extending the trip to include a trek up Stewart Canyon is a good way to get some additional exercise, but the scenery is not as good as that on the lake. Note that Stewart Canyon is an intermediate trip because of short sections where you must travel close to a drop-off.

DIRECTIONS

From the Trans-Canada Highway, take the Lake Minnewanka turnoff near Banff. Drive 9.4 km to the Lake Minnewanka parking lot. Note the winter detour along the way, about 1 km after leaving Highway 1.

From the parking lot, make your way down to the lake and start snowshoeing north along the lakeshore. If the huge uplifts of cracked ice along the shore don't keep you entertained, the immediate views of Inglismaldie and the unnamed peak on the north side of the lake should.

Those who have seen this lake in the summer know full well that in many places the lake bottom simply drops off at the shore, without a gradual slope. Just another reminder to be sure of the strength of the ice as you make your way around the lake. If at

THE UNIQUE CHEMISTRY AND PHYSICS OF ICE — ONE OF THE FEW SUBSTANCES THAT EXPANDS WHEN TURNING FROM LIQUID TO SOLID. NOTE THE LARGE SHELTER TO THE LEFT: A GOOD OBJECTIVE FOR THE TRIP.

any point travel along the lakeshore seems risky, leave the shore and find the trail to the west.

Go as far as you like before turning around. Some of the most interesting scenery is about 700 m to 1 km along the shore. A good objective that is not too strenuous is to go around the lakeshore until you see a large shelter with a trailhead kiosk behind it. Leaving the lake, you can then take the easy trail back to the parking lot in a very short amount of time. If you want a little more exercise, go to the aforementioned Lake Minnewanka kiosk by the shelter. Snowshoe or hike 800 m farther along the trail to the cool bridge spanning the Cascade River and a pleasant view up Stewart Canyon. Return to the parking lot via the wide trail or continue up Stewart Canyon for some more exercise.

EXTENSION TO STEWART CANYON

You'll probably do this extension more for the exercise than the scenery. The terrain is interesting but views are limited. Also, through a few sections, the trek up the canyon does follow along the edge of a very steep drop-off into the canyon below. Those not used to such situations may find travel a little unnerving for brief periods.

Directions

From the Lake Minnewanka kiosk by the shelter, snowshoe or hike 800 m farther along the trail to the bridge spanning the Cascade River. Cross the bridge and turn left, continuing on the trail that now parallels the Cascade River but high above it. Approximately 150 m later you'll arrive at a major, signed junction. Take the left trail (Stewart Canyon) and continue up the canyon. The trail gets fairly close to the edge of the canyon and may feel a little exposed when there's snow. Expect the trail to be broken, but if it isn't you may have to routefind your way up. As long as you are relatively close to the canyon, finding the way up shouldn't be too difficult.

The trail ends after it descends and then crosses a creek that comes down from the right. At the "Poorly Defined Trail Ahead" sign it is best to make your way over to the creek to check out the scenery and then return the way you came in. It is definitely possible to continue up the valley if you still have some energy. There is no real objective or specific destination. Just keep going the same way up the valley until you've had enough and then turn around.

92 STONEY SQUAW MOUNTAIN

(MAP 18, PAGE 487)

DIFFICULTY EASY	
ELEVATION GAIN 190 M	
ROUND-TRIP DISTANCE 4.4 KM	
ROUND-TRIP TIME 1.5–2.5 HOURS	
MAPS 82 O/04 BANFF, GEM TREK BANFF AND MOUNT ASSINIBOINE	

This is about as easy as a route up an official peak gets. Views are limited, so don't expect to be blown away! Undoubtedly, your drive time to and from the peak will be double or even triple the time you spend ascending and descending it. To make the most of your day, you can combine this ascent with another nearby peak/trip, such as Tunnel Mountain (page 392) or Lake Minnewanka (page 377). Note that the elevation gain is significant for a trip rated easy.

DIRECTIONS

At the second (most westerly) turnoff to Banff, follow the signs to Mount Norquay. Drive up the hairpin switchbacks, enjoying the fact that you are gaining a large chunk of the elevation in your car! Turn in to the Norquay parking area and park immediately at the trailhead sign to the right.

This is a popular trail and so more than likely it will be packed down. If you decide to go on foot, take your snowshoes just in case.

The trail enters the trees immediately and stays there throughout. It meanders through the forest, changing direction frequently, but in general it heads southeast. Just before the summit it circles around the southeast side of the mountain and then proceeds up to the summit. Unfortunately, much of the summit view is blocked by trees, so don't go up expecting an earth-shattering panorama.

Either return the same way you came in or make a pleasant loop route by continuing on the trail as it goes down the ridge toward the northwest. You'll lose elevation quite quickly before the trail starts to trend more to the left. A long section of flatter terrain that traverses the side of the mountain follows. After that you'll have to regain a little elevation. The trail suddenly pops out of the trees onto a wider trail. Turn left and follow this trail easily back to the Norquay ski resort and your vehicle.

MARKO STAVRIC MANAGES TO ELOQUENTLY CAPTURE A GOOD VIEW FROM THE HEAVILY TREED SUMMIT OF STONEY SQUAW. CASCADE MOUNTAIN IS TO THE LEFT. (MARKO STAVRIC)

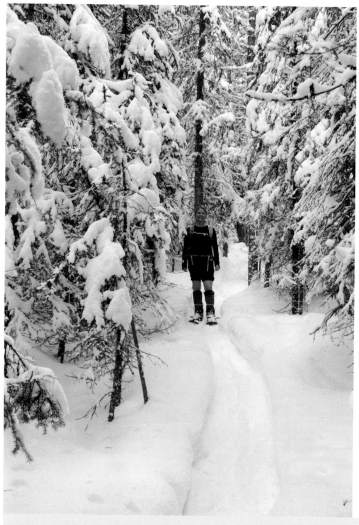

SNOWSHOEING DOES NOT NECESSARILY EQUATE WITH COLD
WEATHER. AMELIE TAKES ADVANTAGE OF A WARM APRIL DAY
AND COMPLETES THE TRIP IN SHORTS. (MARKO STAVRIC)

93 CASCADE AMPHITHEATRE

(MAP 18, PAGE 487)

BANFF

RATING	ADVANCED
AMPHITHEATRE HEIGHT	2110 M
TOTAL ELEVATION GAIN	690 M
ROUND-TRIP DISTANCE	14 KM
ROUND-TRIP TIME	4–6 HOURS
MAPS	82 O/4 BANFF, GEM TREK BANFF AND MOUNT ASSINIBOINE

This trip is similar in some ways to Taylor Lake (page 400): great destination – not so thrilling journey! The significant total elevation gain is in part due to a necessary 130-m loss near the beginning of the trip, and of course the requisite gain at the end. The popularity of the route means that trail-breaking may be minimal, allowing you to complete the trip in surprisingly little time.

DIRECTIONS

From Highway 1 near Banff, follow the signs to the Norquay ski resort. Walk or snowshoe 900 m through the ski area to the Spirit chairlift. This is where the Cascade Amphitheatre trailhead lies. The trail stays near the ski resort, eventually arriving at the Mystic chairlift in 700 m. It then continues basically in the same direction (NNW). A hiking sign is quickly reached, directing you to stay to the left. The trail undulates a little before embarking on a gradual, 130-vertical-metre descent to Forty Mile Creek. The last little bit is not exactly gradual and descends steeply, curving to the right and arriving at a bridge over the creek.

Cross the creek and turn right, paralleling the creek for about 50 m. The trail then turns left and in no time you are going up, toward the turnoff to the amphitheatre. Travelling north with a couple of short switchbacks to the south, it's 1.4 km to the turn-off, on a perfectly graded trail. If Goldilocks were snowshoeing this trail, she would say the angle is "juuust right!" – gentle enough to ascend at a decent and steady pace and steep enough to offer a rapid and almost effortless descent.

Keep an eye out for the signed turnoff to the right, around GR970765, 1755 m. Now comes 3.6 km of switchbacks up to the destination. Again, travel is relatively easy and the trail is quite obvious, even if it hasn't been broken.

Around GR979767, 2104 m, the terrain starts to level off and route-finding may become more challenging if a broken trail

IN THE AMPHITHEATRE, LOOKING AT THE SCRAMBLER'S ROUTE UP CASCADE MOUNTAIN.

doesn't exist. Keep travelling in a southeasterly direction and in short order you will arrive at the amphitheatre and a large cairn in the form of an inukshuk at GR983768, 2109 m.

You are almost completely surrounded by the intricate and massive form of Cascade Mountain at this point. The ridge to the southeast in front of you (described in *Snowshoeing in the Canadian Rockies, 2nd Edition*), is part of the scrambler's route to the summit of Cascade. Enjoy the scenery and then return the same way. Travelling farther into the amphitheatre is not recommended due to avalanche hazard.

The descent is a fast and easy one until you arrive back at Forty Mile Creek and have to gain 130 m of elevation back to the parking lot. Goldilocks would NOT be saying it's "juuust right"!

> DIFFICULTY EASY
>
> ELEVATION GAIN MINIMAL
>
> ROUND-TRIP DISTANCE VARIABLE TO 9 KM MAXIMUM
>
> ROUND-TRIP TIME VARIABLE
>
> MAPS 82 O/O4 BANFF, GEM TREK BANFF AND MOUNT ASSINIBOINE

The Vermilion Lakes area offers multiple vantage points from which to take in splendid views of one of Banff's two classic mountains, Mount Rundle (the other being Cascade Mountain). Anyone looking for that postcard picture of Rundle will want to visit the lakes. Make the trip later in the day to ensure that the full brunt of the sun is trained on the mountain.

The shallow, marshy lakes usually freeze by mid-December, but chinook weather can leave open pools of water at any time of the year, so use caution. Also, this area is home to much wildlife and is very environmentally sensitive. If there is an insufficient amount of snow to use snowshoes, it is better to just walk the road, enjoying the scenery from there.

DIRECTIONS

From the Trans-Canada Highway, take the Mount Norquay / Banff turnoff and turn left toward Banff. After crossing the highway on a bridge, turn right onto Vermilion Lakes Drive.

There are several ways to experience this unique area:

1. Park right at the beginning of Vermilion Lakes Drive. Hike

the road for about 600 m and when feasible snowshoe onto the first lake. Snowshoe west, paralleling the road to the second and third lakes, exploring the area as conditions dictate. Again, a reminder to be respectful of the environment and avoid trampling down vegetation if it is exposed. It's about 4 km to the third lake. Go as far as you want and then return via the same route, or hike back along the road.

2. Drive 4.5 km to the end of Vermilion Lakes Drive. Obey the speed limit and drive with extreme caution, as hikers often walk this road. From the parking area, snowshoe east from the third lake to the first or as far as you like.

3. If the area is not busy (i.e., on a weekday), stop at various points on the road and snowshoe in that area. There are places to pull over at the 1-, 2- and 4-km marks that grant good access to the lakes. The 1-km mark is recommended because there is space there for several cars to park. (Be considerate of others and use trip options 1 or 2 if it's a busy day. Having numerous cars pulled over on the sides of the road is dangerous for other drivers.)

VIEWS AND PHOTOS OF MOUNT RUNDLE

Many people enjoy the view of Mount Rundle from the third lake because it includes a decent section of the north end of Sulphur Mountain, named Sanson Peak. Having said that, on a clear day, even a mediocre view is nowhere to be found in this area.

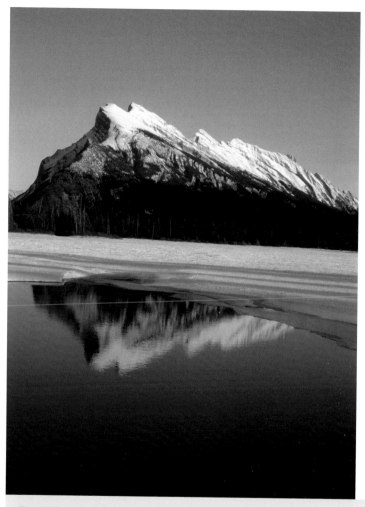

MOUNT RUNDLE REFLECTED IN AN OPEN POOL NEAR THE ROAD.

95 TUNNEL MOUNTAIN DRIVE

(MAP 18, PAGE 487)

DIFFICULTY EASY

ELEVATION GAIN APPROXIMATELY 80 M

ROUND-TRIP DISTANCE 3.4 KM

ROUND-TRIP TIME 0.75–1 HOUR

MAPS 82 O/04 BANFF,
GEM TREK BANFF AND MOUNT ASSINIBOINE

This is one of the easier trips in the Banff area and in this book. Recommended as a pleasant family outing, it can be combined with Sundance Trail and/or Hoodoo Viewpoint. Of course, you must drive from one trailhead to the other. The crux will be negotiating the Banff townsite roads to find the trailhead!

DIRECTIONS

From the Trans-Canada Highway, heading west, take the first turnoff to Banff and drive along Banff Avenue into the townsite. Take a left turn onto Moose Street. Moose Street ends and turns right, becoming Grizzly Street. Veer left onto St. Julien Road and then left again onto St. Julien Way. A final left turn onto Tunnel Mountain Road leads quickly to the road closure. Park off to the side and not in front of the closed gate.

A route description is unnecessary for this one. The trail is 1.7 km along Tunnel Mountain Drive to the closure at the other end. Along the way you will gain about 40 m of elevation to the high point just beyond the Tunnel Mountain trailhead, and then you will lose most of it down the other side. There is a good view of Cascade Mountain as you turn one corner.

At the end of the road, be sure to make your way into the open field on your right, where you'll be treated to good views of the northeast face of Tunnel Mountain, the north side of Mount Rundle and the Fairholme Range to the east. Of course, if you start the whole trip from the other end, on Tunnel Mountain Drive, you'll get that view about 30 seconds from your car! Return the same way you came in.

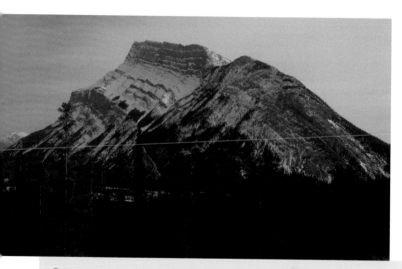

THE NORTH SIDE OF MOUNT RUNDLE, AS SEEN FROM
THE OPEN AREA AT THE END OF THE ROUTE.

96 TUNNEL MOUNTAIN

(MAP 18, PAGE 487)

DIFFICULTY ADVANCED
ELEVATION GAIN 245 M
ROUND-TRIP DISTANCE 4.6 KM
ROUND-TRIP TIME 1.5–2.5 HOURS
MAPS 82 O/04 BANFF,
GEM TREK BANFF AND MOUNT ASSINIBOINE

This is an interesting trip that can be combined with the Stoney Squaw Mountain route (page 381). Of course, you have to drive between destinations. Tunnel Mountain is Stoney Squaw Mountain's twin. They have a very similar elevation and orientation, and both sport impressively steep northeast faces. Tunnel Mountain's east side is home to several traditional climbing routes. The excellent trail to the summit is used year-round. If the trail is unbroken, snowshoes may be necessary; otherwise go on foot. Given the heavy traffic on the trail, icy sections may develop. In this case, spikes or snowshoes will help for better traction.

DIRECTIONS

From the Trans-Canada Highway, heading west, take the first turnoff to Banff and drive along Banff Avenue into the townsite. Take a left onto Moose Street. Moose Street ends and turns right, becoming Grizzly Street. Veer left onto St. Julien Road and then left again onto St. Julien Way. A final left turn onto Tunnel Mountain Road leads quickly to the road closure. Park off to the side and not in front of the closed gate.

Snowshoe up the road for several hundred metres to the big trailhead sign on the right side of the road. Be sure to read the information about Tunnel Mountain and the trail. The instruction to "stay on the trail and avoid shortcuts" is one everybody should follow religiously, even in winter when damage to the environment is less pronounced.

Specific directions are unnecessary because the trail is easy to follow. The path winds its way up the mountain in a series of large, gently graded switchbacks. For the final section, the trail turns north along the very steep northeast face. Don't go too near the edge. Also be aware that climbers do ascend this face. As a sign clearly points out, do not throw anything down that face. Metal railings provide some security, and you'll want to check out the views by the railings.

THE DRAMATIC VIEW OF MOUNT RUNDLE'S NORTHWEST SIDE. (ROB ASHPOLE)

The summit is treed, but if you wander around a little, respectable views lie in most directions. Views of the northwest arm of Mount Rundle and the Fairholme Range to the east, and looking down on the Banff townsite in its entirety, will likely be the most interesting. A short descent to a lower plateau around the north side of the mountain opens up the view to the west and north a little more. Return the same way you came up. Do not attempt any shortcuts down the west side of the peak.

MOUNT RUNDLE AND THE BOW RIVER. THE HOODOOS CAN JUST BE SEEN NEAR THE LOWER CENTRE.

97 HOODOO VIEWPOINT

(MAP 18, PAGE 487)

DIFFICULTY EASY
ELEVATION GAIN APPROXIMATELY 50 M
ROUND-TRIP DISTANCE APPROXIMATELY 1 KM
ROUND-TRIP TIME 20–30 MINUTES
MAPS 82 0/03 CANMORE, 82 0/04 BANFF,
GEM TREK BANFF AND MOUNT ASSINIBOINE

Unless you do this very short trip right after a major snowfall, snowshoes will probably be unnecessary, although they may help with traction on the icy sections. Microspikes are a great alternative for this trip. If you are in the area (i.e., you have just completed the Tunnel Mountain Drive trip [page 390] or Sundance Trail and Canyon [page 396]), the Hoodoo Viewpoint provides a terrific vista of the surrounding area. Wait for a clear day.

DIRECTIONS

The trailhead can be reached from either direction on Tunnel Mountain Road. Easiest is to turn onto Tunnel Mountain Road from the north end of Banff Avenue and drive 3.3 km, turning left into the parking area on the south side of the road.

Hike or snowshoe easily to the high point, stopping to read the interesting interpretive signs, take in the excellent view and return the same way.

98 SUNDANCE TRAIL

(MAP 18, PAGE 487)

DIFFICULTY EASY

ELEVATION GAIN 70 M

ROUND-TRIP DISTANCE 7.2

ROUND-TRIP TIME 2–3 HOURS

MAPS 82 0/04 BANFF,
GEM TREK BANFF AND MOUNT ASSINIBOINE

Good views of the Bow Valley and the scenic environs of the Bow River characterize this route. Most of the interesting scenery is seen near the beginning of the trip, so take the time to enjoy it. An excellent extension of the trip to Sundance Canyon exists, but this is definitely an advanced trip, only for experienced snowshoers.

DIRECTIONS

Drive through Banff on Banff Avenue and turn right, onto Cave Avenue after crossing the Bow River. Follow the signs to the Cave and Basin National Historic Site. The trail starts on the west side of the building. Follow the trail in a west direction. It quickly veers northwest and soon converges with the Bow River, and an enjoyable trek alongside the waterway follows. This part of the trip is one of the more scenic sections. Hopefully, clear skies will prevail, revealing good views of Mounts Cascade, Norquay and Edith across the river and the bulky profile of the Massive Range to the west.

The trail is very easy to follow and well signed. It eventually veers away from the river and soon curves left at a major junction.

The Sundance picnic area is reached shortly after. Unfortunately, views here are non-existent, given the trees and slopes all around.

This marks the end of Sundance Trail. However, it is worthwhile to continue south to see at least the entrance to Sundance Canyon. Snowshoe several hundred metres farther up the trail to the entrance, cross a small bridge and you'll be at the bottom of the beautiful canyon. For most beginners this is the end of the line. Continuing to complete the canyon loop is an advanced trip that is steep, tricky in places and has some avalanche concerns.

Everything is the same on the return route, although you can detour onto the Marsh Loop (page 350) to add a little more distance and a lot more scenery to the trip (highly recommended).

Extension to Sundance Canyon

This fascinating canyon is definitely an advanced snowshoeing trip for beginners and is recommended only for those who are comfortable on steep terrain and familiar with avalanche assessment. Although an avalanche in the canyon is unlikely, there are a couple of short sections you'll want to move through quickly, just in case. Also, if the trail has not been broken already, it is strongly advised that beginner snowshoers do not enter the canyon – you may encounter route-finding difficulties higher up. The loop is 2.1 km and adds about 60 m of elevation to the total trip. Allow 45–90 minutes to complete the loop.

Directions

One of the avalanche concerns occurs right near the beginning. The trail ascends the left side of the canyon, below steep slopes that could slide under specific conditions. Again, this is unlikely, but you should move through this section quickly and then ascend a staircase that more than likely will be under a foot of snow. Cross to the other side of the canyon on a bridge and continue up steep terrain to the top. The rock and snow scenery throughout is fascinating.

Atop the canyon, the trail recrosses the stream and continues up the valley on the left side of the waterway. Several hundred metres later you'll cross to the right side and again resume travel up the valley. Another 300–400 m beyond the bridge, the trail veers to the right, ascending for a short distance and then resuming a course parallel to the stream.

Eventually the trail takes a hairpin turn to the right and starts heading back toward the canyon entrance. However, the route is a circuitous one. Expect to veer off to the left (west), about 500 m after the hairpin turn and then embark on a series of switchbacks down to where you started from. There are many wooden fences along the way to guide you and prevent you from falling in places where you don't want to fall! Back at the canyon entrance, return to your vehicle the way you came in, perhaps making the recommended detour onto the Marsh Loop, as previously suggested.

LOOKING UP SUNDANCE CANYON. THE TRAIL STARTS AT THE
LEFT AND THEN CROSSES TO THE RIGHT VIA THE BRIDGE.

99 TAYLOR LAKE

(MAP 20, PAGE 487)

RATING ADVANCED
LAKE HEIGHT 2078 M
ELEVATION GAIN 585 M
ROUND-TRIP DISTANCE 13 KM
ROUND-TRIP TIME 4–6 HOURS
MAPS 82 N/8 LAKE LOUISE, GEM TREK LAKE
LOUISE AND YOHO

A long grind up to a picturesque lake. The actual snowshoeing is at an intermediate level, but the sheer length of this trip and significant elevation gain required push it into the advanced category. The trail is heavily used throughout the year, so trail-breaking may not be a concern. Microspikes or just hiking boots can usually get you most of the way, but as usual it is recommended that snowshoes are worn, in order to minimize damage to the trail.

DIRECTIONS

Driving west on Highway 1, turn left into the Taylor parking lot, about 7.6 km west of the Highway 93 turnoff. The trail is very obvious almost all of the way up, so a detailed route description is not required. If you end up trail-breaking through deep powder in thick forest, you are desperately off route!

Go through the gate, turn right and snowshoe for about 200 m to a trail sign. Turn left and away you go. Taylor Creek is soon crossed on a bridge and then the trail starts gaining elevation. Hopefully you brought a few friends to chat with along the way. It feels like a million kilometres to the next bridge!

Shortly after crossing a subsidiary creek on another bridge, the trail forks at an unsigned and easily missed intersection (GR638834, 2074 m) – look for flagging in the trees. Straight (right) goes to Panorama Meadows and left goes to Taylor Lake. Turn left and follow the trail and a sign to the lake outlet at GR636833.

The lake is backdropped by the impressively steep walls of Mount Bell and the less steep but still cool slopes of Panorama Ridge. Snowshoeing around or across the lake doesn't provide significantly better views – best to just hangout at the outlet and enjoy the surroundings.

If you are looking for more exercise or different scenery, consider extending the day to Panorama Meadows. Otherwise, return the same way. Even though the descent is mercifully easy when compared with the ascent, it still feels like a million kilometres!

TAYLOR LAKE, WITH MOUNT BELL (LEFT) AND PANORAMA RIDGE (RIGHT).

THE MEADOW IS A GREAT PLACE TO SEE PANORAMA
RIDGE'S FORMIDABLE EAST SIDE. (SOISTHEMAN)

PANORAMA MEADOWS

*This extension of the Taylor Lake trip gets you to an open meadow
on the southeast side of convoluted Panorama Ridge. It adds 3 km
return of horizontal distance and 100 m of vertical gain to an already lengthy day. On a clear day you will get an excellent view of
the steep east face of Panorama Ridge. The view from the meadow
is pleasant but hardly sensational! Good for the exercise.*

Directions

Return to the intersection at GR638834 and turn left (northwest),
paralleling the subsidiary creek. The trail may vary from year to
year, depending on snow conditions, but in general follows the
creek on its left side, goes through the trees near the creek and
then traverses right into the creek, before reaching the meadow.
Around GR633838, leave the creek, cutting to the left and then
resume travel northwest into the meadow.

For beginners, this is the end of the line (GR632838, 2168 m). Advanced snowshoers can ascend "Panorama Hill" at the right side of
the valley (see *Snowshoeing in the Canadian Rockies, 2nd Edition*). Enjoy the great view of Panorama Ridge and then return the same way.

100 INK POTS

DIFFICULTY INTERMEDIATE
TOTAL ELEVATION GAIN 420 M
ROUND-TRIP DISTANCE 12–14 KM
ROUND-TRIP TIME 3–5 HOURS
MAPS 82 O/05 CASTLE MOUNTAIN,
82 O/04 BANFF, GEM TREK BANFF

This is a great trip that takes you into the beautiful Johnston Creek valley. Travel is easy throughout, but the 420 m of elevation gain make this an intermediate route, perhaps even an advanced route for those snowshoers not used to large elevation gains. The trip can be completed as a loop route with the very popular Johnston Canyon. Choose a clear day to best enjoy the wonderful scenery at the Ink Pots.

DIRECTIONS

The trailhead (Moose Meadows hiking trail, not Moose Meadows Exhibition) sits about 4.6 km east of Castle Junction, or 2 km west of the Johnston Canyon parking lot on the north side of Highway 1A.

From the trailhead kiosk, a trail sign is immediately visible, directing you to follow the trail up and to the right. The next 3.2 km take you through light forest. Trail signs are sporadic but the path should be fairly obvious. More than likely the trail will already be broken, and it will be just a matter of following those who have gone before. Also, this trail can be popular with skiers. The wide path has plenty of space for separate tracks, so try to stay off any ski tracks that have been made.

At the important junction, 3.2 km up, turn left. The trail gains elevation on the far east shoulder of Helena Ridge before plummeting down into the valley to the north. You'll lose about 90 m of elevation on the way down to the Ink Pots. The scenery finally starts to open up as you approach the Ink Pots, the aesthetic form of Mount Ishbel dominating the view.

The Ink Pots themselves may be a little disappointing in winter, as their greenish-blue hues are not as vibrant. Of course, some or all of the seven or eight pools may be completely covered by snow and ice. However, the pristine valley around them should more than make up for the "shortcomings" of the wintery pots. Although the only visible named peaks are Mount Ishbel and Block Mountain, the valley is home to many striking outliers and ridges.

The "Stay On the Designated Trail" signs are primarily geared toward summer visitors, but this environmentally sensitive area deserves the same consideration even when snow protects (to a degree) the vegetation. If you decide to venture farther north for some extra exercise, stay on Johnston Creek Trail. The trail crosses the creek on a bridge and then heads north. There really isn't too much point going any farther unless you plan to winter camp at the campground, 1.7 km north. It's probably better to hang out around the Ink Pots and take in the scenery.

For the return trip, grind your way back up the shoulder of Helena Ridge (another 90 m of elevation gain) and then descend to the aforementioned junction. Here you have two options. Easiest and fastest is to return the way you came in via Moose Meadows Trail. The longer but more interesting route is via Johnston Canyon. Be warned, however, that you will be sharing this trail with a multitude of hikers, thereby preventing a Mach 2 descent! Keep your snowshoes on for this route, as the trail gets very icy. Once back to Highway 1A, a 2-km hike along the road takes you back to Moose Meadows.

THE INK POTS AND MOUNT ISHBEL MAKE A
GREAT COMBINATION. (SHAWN BENBOW)

HIGHWAY 93 SOUTH

Highway 93 South is the gateway to British Columbia's Kootenay National Park. There are only a handful of easy snowshoe routes along the north end of Highway 93 South, but those that are available to the beginner shoer are terrific! Marble Canyon is hands down the most scenic and interesting trip in the entire book that is under one hour in duration.

The park receives significant amounts of snow throughout the season and once it falls, it stays. However, relatively low starting elevations for the trips described here mean that the snow on the routes will be the first to melt. January, February and early March are usually the best months to visit the area.

Of special interest along and around the north section of the highway are the scars of a major forest fire that ripped through the park in 2003. Though innumerable dead and blackened trees still stand, the new growth is now emerging in green splendour. Of course snow hides most of the new trees in winter. Best to visit the park in summer if you want to see them.

ROUTES

Vermilion Peak makes a great backdrop for Marble Canyon.

101 BOOM LAKE

(MAP 20, PAGE 487)

RATING	INTERMEDIATE
LAKE HEIGHT	1893 M
ELEVATION GAIN	175 M
ROUND-TRIP DISTANCE	10.8 KM
ROUND-TRIP TIME	2.5–4.5 HOURS
MAPS	82 N/8 LAKE LOUISE, GEM TREK KOOTENAY NATIONAL PARK

If the huge elevation gain required for Taylor Lake (page 400) doesn't appeal to you, there's Boom Lake – similar terrific view with less than a third of the uphill grind. Do the trip in the morning or early afternoon to increase the chances of the sun illuminating the beautiful view at the lake. The trail is popular with skiers. Stay well to the right side of the trail to avoid collisions.

DIRECTIONS

Drive 7 km south on Highway 93 and turn right, into the Boom Lake parking lot. Instructions are hardly required, as the trail is obvious throughout. Also, Boom Lake Trail is one of those rare trails that is easily wide enough to support a snowshoe track and one or two ski tracks. Snowshoe on the far right side of the trail and use the same track on the return trip. This will allow skiers to create an uptrack in the centre and a downtrack on the left or vice versa.

The trail crosses Boom Creek right away, goes a short distance and eventually switchbacks to the left. A steady but gentle elevation gain ensues. At the 2.3-km mark a trail sign is reached. Right goes to O'Brien Lake. Go straight. The next 3.1 km are more undulating, but still very easy and obvious. Near the end, the trail descends down and to the left to the lake. It drops you out at the lakeshore (GR639795), about 600 m west of the lake outlet.

When the sun is shining on the lake and surrounding mountains you are in for a treat. Boom Mountain, outliers of Chimney Peak, Quadra Mountain and Bident Mountain all tower majestically over the lake. You can snowshoe in either direction along the lake, but there are some avalanche slopes coming down off Mount Bell to the north. Stay away from those ones. If the lake is frozen, going over to the south side will grant you better views of Bell and Bident. Return the same way.

102 STANLEY GLACIER VALLEY

(MAP 21, PAGE 488)

RATING	ADVANCED
MAXIMUM HEIGHT	1800 M
ELEVATION GAIN	200 M
ROUND-TRIP DISTANCE	4.6 KM
ROUND-TRIP TIME	1.5–3 HOURS
MAPS	82 N/1 MOUNT GOODSIR, GEM TREK KOOTENAY NATIONAL PARK

This valley is famous for world-class ice climbs (Nemesis and French Reality) and also the receding Stanley Glacier. Unfortunately, the upper valley is prone to avalanches and therefore off limits to those without avalanche training and gear. However, the beginner snowshoer can go far enough into the valley to get a good workout and some great views. The sun doesn't get into this valley much, so late-season, late-day trips are recommended.

DIRECTIONS

Drive 13 km south on Highway 93 and turn left, into the Stanley Glacier parking lot. Snowshoe down to the Vermilion River and cross it on a bridge. The trail now takes a series of switchbacks through an area of burnt forest, up to the valley above. When it levels off you are treated to a great view of the valley ahead, as well as all the mountains to the west, south and north. Mount Whymper is especially eye-catching.

Start going up the valley. The trail soon curves to the left and goes down a little before crossing Stanley Creek on a log bridge.

THE VIEW INTO THE STANLEY GLACIER VALLEY.
BELOW: EVEN IN THE TREES, THE SCENERY
CAN BE BREATHTAKING. (SOISTHEMAN)

You can continue up the valley for another 200 m or so before getting into avalanche terrain. Unfortunately trees hide much of the view here, but going farther may put you at risk. Turn around and return the same way. If this trip wasn't enough for the day, check out the Paint Pots, Marble Canyon and/or Boom Lake.

103 MARBLE CANYON

(MAP 21, PAGE 488)

RATING EASY
ELEVATION GAIN 50 M
ROUND-TRIP DISTANCE 1.6 KM
ROUND-TRIP TIME 0.5–1 HOURS
MAPS 82 N/1 MOUNT GOODSIR,
GEM TREK KOOTENAY NATIONAL PARK

Marble Canyon is awesome! It's short, easy and throughout has fantastic views of the canyon and surrounding mountains. There are a couple of steeper sections that are perfect for snowshoes. I witnessed several people on foot struggling up the first slope. If the trip is too short, you can extend the day by snowshoeing on a good trail down to the Paint Pots (page 415) or take a little stroll up Tokumm Valley.

DIRECTIONS

Drive 17 km south on Highway 93 and turn right, into the Marble Canyon parking lot. Two trails leave the parking lot: one for Marble Canyon and the other for Tokumm Valley. Take the Marble Canyon trail that lies to the left. No route instructions are required from here. Follow the obvious path. Multiple bridges and pathways cross and line the canyon and each one is worth checking out. The slope after the first bridge is the steepest and if icy will require snowshoes or another form of foot traction. Also note the connector trail to the Paint Pots, going through a gate at the end of the first bridge.

The views down into the canyon are amazing. However, also be aware that as the snow piles up on the bridges, the rails get

ABOVE: Winter splendour in Marble Canyon.
BELOW: Great views of the Vermilion River
and Stanley Peak along the shoreline.

lower and lower, relatively speaking. At times, it might be easy to fall over a railing on one of the bridges. I would keep kids away from the edges.

Once you get to the end, either return the same way, or for some extra exercise go north to find the Tokumm Valley trail. Then follow it in a northwesterly direction until you've had enough.

A better way to extend your day is by descending down to the Paint Pots trail, although the trip from the Paint Pots to Marble Canyon and then back down again may be preferable.

PAINT POTS CONNECTOR

Note that there is a warning from Parks Canada about danger from falling trees on this trail. The burnt trees from the 2003 forest fire are susceptible to fall without warning. Be aware of this if you are going to use this trail.

The trail starts right after the first bridge. It curves up and around the canyon below and then starts gently downhill, eventually paralleling the Vermilion River, but high above it. When the trail gets close to the river you can either stay on the trail or, if the adventurer in you is awake, go right down to the river and follow it downstream. Depending on the snow and ice conditions along the river, this route may require route-finding around deadfall and some trickier terrain. However, the scenic rewards are well worth it. The trail is never too far away if you decide to get back on it.

The connector trail is 2.7 km in length. If you did take the scenic route, you'll want to return to the trail about 500 m before the end. Eventually you'll end up at the bridge that crosses the Vermilion River and then goes to the Paint Pots parking lot. Either check out the Paint Pots area (see page 415) or return the way you came. Hiking back up to the Marble Canyon parking lot using the highway is not recommended, because of the potentially high volume of fast-moving traffic.

104 PAINT POTS

(MAP 21, PAGE 488)

RATING	EASY
ELEVATION GAIN	MINIMAL
ROUND-TRIP DISTANCE	2 KM
ROUND-TRIP TIME	0.5–1 HOURS
MAPS	82 N/1 MOUNT GOODSIR,
GEM TREK KOOTENAY NATIONAL PARK	

In 1970 the late and great B.B. King lamented that "The Thrill Is Gone" (song written by Hawkins and Darnell). Unfortunately, such can be said of the Paint Pots in winter! The thrill of the Paint Pots is the striking orange colour of the iron-enriched soil. Covering the land in snow all but kills that thrill (see photo). However, the winter version still has many scenic thrills of its own, is short and easy, and there are several options to extend the day, including a rewarding trip up to Marble Canyon.

DIRECTIONS

Drive 20 km on Highway 93 South and turn right, into the Paint Pots parking lot. Follow the trail down to the Vermilion River and cross the river on a bridge. Turn left at the sign near the other side of the bridge and follow the trail to a big wooden sign that marks the beginning of the ochre fields (probably not visible because of the snow).

Snowshoe west through open meadows, going to the next sign. The trail eventually joins up with Ochre Creek, paralleling the creek on its right side. You may see some of the distinct colouring here. Follow the trail up, past the "Cone" and up to another open area, with "Ochre Spring Peak" in the background (ascent described in *Snowshoeing in the Canadian Rockies, 2nd Edition*). This is more or less the end of the line for the Paint Pots trail. If you do want to continue, find the sign for Ochre Creek on the other side of the open area. You can follow this trail for as long as you would like, but the base of the ascent slope for "Ochre Spring Peak" around GR571698, approximately 2.5 km from the end of the Paint Pots trail, is a logical place to stop.

A much better option is to return to the bridge and then follow the Paint Pots connector trail to Marble Canyon.

MARBLE CANYON CONNECTOR

Note that there is a warning from Parks Canada about danger from falling trees on this trail. The burnt trees from the 2003 forest fire are susceptible to fall without warning. Be aware of this if you are going to use this trail.

Return to the trail sign by the bridge and start going northeast toward Marble Canyon, as directed by the sign. The trail is easy to follow, paralleling the Vermilion River, sometimes right alongside it and sometimes at a distance. There is some awesome scenery to be experienced if you occasionally leave the trail and snowshoe right along the shoreline.

From the sign it's a 2.7-km jaunt up to Marble Canyon. As you get closer to that mark, it is important that you return to the trail. Staying along the river will soon lead to canyon-like terrain that cannot be negotiated. The trail eventually moves away from the Vermilion River and soon joins up with Tokumm Creek and Marble Canyon. If you have made it that far, a 20–30 minute trek around the fascinating canyon is mandatory (see page 412).

Return the way you came. Hiking back down to the Paint Pots parking lot using the highway is not recommended, because of the potentially high volume of fast-moving traffic.

THE PAINT POTS WITH AND WITHOUT SNOW. OCHRE SPRING PEAK IN THE BACKGROUND. SURPRISINGLY, I USED MY SNOWSHOES TO ASCEND 600 VERTICAL METRES OF THAT MOUNTAIN ON THE DAY WHEN THE LEFT HALF OF THE STITCHED PHOTO WAS TAKEN. BELOW: LEAVING THE TRAIL FOR SOME EXPLORATION SOMETIMES YIELDS VERY INTERESTING WINTER SCENERY.

LAKE LOUISE

If you have never heard of Lake Louise, you are either new to this province or new to this planet! To call the lake "the jewel of the Canadian Rockies" is certainly an accurate description. The unequalled appearance of Lake Louise in calendars, books, magazines and on postcards is but a small testament to the power this body of water (or ice, in this case) holds over the viewer. I cannot begin to count how many times I've been to the lake over the years, and I still get that "deer in the headlights" look every time I see it!

Four of the five snowshoe routes described in this section centre on the lake. Only Highline moves away from the lake, but even that route starts at the lakeshore.

A national park pass is required for all trips in the Lake Louise area.

ROUTES

THE CLASSIC LAKESHORE VIEW TOWARD MOUNT
VICTORIA AND VICTORIA GLACIER. NOTE THE SKATING
RINK IF YOU WANT TO BRING YOUR SKATES.

105 LOUISE CREEK

(MAP 22, PAGE 488)

DIFFICULTY INTERMEDIATE

ELEVATION GAIN 195 M

ROUND-TRIP DISTANCE 5.6 KM

ROUND-TRIP TIME 2–3 HOURS

MAPS 82 N/08 LAKE LOUISE,
GEM TREK LAKE LOUISE AND YOHO

The prize at the end of this trail is the all too familiar but never tiresome view of spectacular Lake Louise. Of course, you can drive almost all the way to the lake, but what fun would that be? Better to get some exercise, enjoy the interesting scenery around Louise Creek and then pat yourself on the back when you reach the top and its terrific view.

DIRECTIONS

Drive to Lake Louise and park in the Samson Mall parking lot, at the northwest corner of the first four-way stop.

Don't put your snowshoes on yet because you must cross two roads before reaching the trailhead. Regain Lake Louise Drive (the road you drove in on) on foot and hike west over the Bow River. Almost right after the river, cross Lake Louise Drive at the pedestrian crossing and walk down and slightly right to the well-signed trailhead. From that point on, follow the signs to Lake Louise via Louise Creek Trail.

The popularity of this trail means it is unlikely that route-finding and/or trail-breaking will be a concern. While many people go on foot, I find it to be far more enjoyable to wear snowshoes and take advantage of the improved traction. This is especially

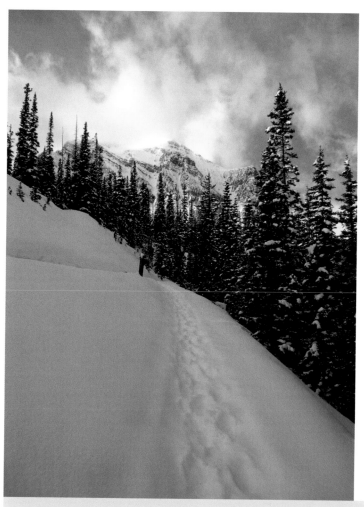

SHORTLY AFTER CROSSING (ON TOP OF THE ROAD) LAKE
LOUISE DRIVE, THE SNOWSHOE TRAIL JOINS UP WITH
THE SKI TRAIL COMING IN FROM THE LEFT.

true on descent, when you can plunge-step down with far more reckless abandon than those on foot can!

After crossing a second bridge, the terrain does get steeper and heel lifts may be helpful. Perhaps one of the more interesting features of the trip is the tunnel that goes under Lake Louise Drive. Unfortunately, the hard, snowless ground in the tunnel is snowshoe unfriendly, but most will choose to leave their snowshoes on anyway and go quickly and lightly to the other side. Unusually heavy snow years may actually block the entrance and exits to the tunnel, in which case you will have to cross the road above.

Beyond the tunnel the trail keeps going straight and drops a little before regaining its path alongside Louise Creek. After you cross to the north side of the creek, a long uphill grind ensues, eventually ending at another crossing of Lake Louise Drive. Cross the road (carefully) and resume travel by the creek, this time heading west. Soon the snowshoe trail joins up with a ski trail. There is lots of room for both. A few hundred metres later you will end up at the east end of the parking lot. Don't stop here. Of course you must visit the lakeshore for a look and/or an additional trip (The Shoreline [page 430], Mirror Lake and Lake Agnes [page 432] or Fairview Lookout [page 423]). Depending on how much snow there is in the parking lot, you may want to take your snowshoes off to get across it and over to the lake. Return the same way you came in.

106 FAIRVIEW LOOKOUT

(MAP 22, PAGE 488)

DIFFICULTY	INTERMEDIATE
ELEVATION GAIN	125 M
ROUND-TRIP DISTANCE	2 KM
ROUND-TRIP TIME	45–90 MINUTES
MAPS	82 N/08 LAKE LOUISE, GEM TREK LAKE LOUISE AND YOHO

MOUNT FAIRVIEW AS SEEN FROM LAKE LOUISE. THE LOOKOUT PLATFORM IS AMONG THE TREES. CAN YOU SPOT IT?

This short but steep trail ends up about 125 vertical metres above the lake. The view is still respectable but forest growth around the observation platform has blocked much of the panorama. This route is best completed before or after another trip in the area.

DIRECTIONS

Drive to Lake Louise and take the 4-km road to the chateau. The east end of the lake is only a few hundred metres from the public parking lot. Walk to the lake, put on your snowshoes and go left at the big Lake Louise sign near the lakeshore. The trailhead for Fairview Lookout is well signed, but there are a multitude of trails heading in various directions. Follow the signs and trail uphill, eventually reaching a major, signed intersection. Turn right (southwest) at the intersection and gain steeper terrain, where you may find heel lifts helpful.

You'll gain all of the elevation here before the terrain levels out and trends slightly to the right. Time to put the heel lifts down! The trip ends with the trail descending to the lookout platform. Except for one tree that conveniently stands in exactly the wrong place, the view of the lake and Chateau Lake Louise is pretty decent. On a clear day you will also see the enormous form of Mount Hector to the north and Mount Richardson to the northeast. Unfortunately, trees block the views in all other directions.

After taking in the view, return the same way you came in. Do not attempt the loop route. It will put you in avalanche terrain.

You will find the descent to be remarkably fast.

If you plan on doing the Highline Trail at some point, you may want to consider tacking it on now. Return to the major intersection and turn right. Follow the trail for about 50 m to a horse trail sign and turn left onto the new trail. See the Highline Trail trip for the remainder of the directions (page 426).

ABOVE: THE SUMMIT OF MOUNT HECTOR POKES THROUGH THE CLOUDS. THE SKILLED PHOTOGRAPHER ZOOMED IN TO HIDE THE FACT THAT AN ENORMOUS TREE IS BLOCKING THE VIEW. BELOW: SO MUCH FOR SKILLS! THE PROMINENT PEAK TOWARD THE LEFT IS MOUNT RICHARDSON.

107 HIGHLINE

(MAP 22, PAGE 488)

DIFFICULTY INTERMEDIATE
ELEVATION GAIN APPROXIMATELY 200 M
ROUND-TRIP DISTANCE 9 KM
ROUND-TRIP TIME 2.5–3.5 HOURS
MAPS 82 N/08 LAKE LOUISE,
GEM TREK LAKE LOUISE AND YOHO

You'll probably want to do this route in conjunction with Fairview Lookout (page 423) and/or Lake Louise Shoreline (page 430). The Highline is a long romp through forest on the east side of Mount Fairview and is great for some decent exercise. However, it is completely lacking in views. The best (only) scenery you will see is at the lake, before you even get onto the trail. If you are adventurous, you may wish to make a loop via Moraine Lake Road.

DIRECTIONS

Drive to Lake Louise and take the 4-km road to the chateau. The east end of the lake is only a few hundred metres from the public parking lot.

Walk to the lake, put on your snowshoes and go left at the big Lake Louise sign near the lakeshore. For 500 m or so you will be following the signs to Fairview Lookout. When the turnoff to Fairview Lookout appears, continue on the main trail for another 50 m, looking for a horse trail sign. This is the start of the Highline Trail. Turn left onto the Highline and away you go for approximately 3.4 km to the end.

The first half of the trail stays more or less at the same elevation. About 10 minutes in you will come across an old avalanche runout. Judging by the tree growth in March 2012, this area has not had a significant avalanche event in many years. However, don't let your guard down. Best not to linger here, even though it provides the only views (mediocre ones at that!) on the Highline Trail.

After hurrying through the avalanche zone, continue south along the trail. Eventually the trail starts to meander a little more up the hillside, changing directions and gaining elevation. Hopefully, it has been broken and it will just be a matter of following the tracks. If at any point route-finding becomes an issue, or you feel you are not on the trail, turn around immediately. This is unlikely, however, as the path through the trees is fairly obvious throughout most of the trip.

The Highline Trail ends 3.4 km after the turnoff at a trail sign and a bigger sign regarding hiking restrictions related to bear activity – not to worry, I'm sure they are all still sleeping! At this point you can return the same way you came in – the safest and most conservative option – or you can make a loop via Moraine Lake Road.

Return via Paradise Creek Trailhead, Moraine Lake Road and Lake Louise Drive

This is also is a fairly straightforward option and does offer some views if you backtrack a few hundred metres up Moraine Lake Road. Follow the "trailhead" signs to the Paradise Creek trailhead, 1.2 m away. Note that this is a popular trail with skiers, and if a ski trail has been broken you should break a snowshoe trail parallel to the ski trail. Once you reach Moraine Lake Road, turn right and snowshoe a few hundred metres up the road to at least get a partial view of the icy north face of Mount Temple and the combination of Sheol Mountain and Haddo Peak. Turn around and go about 1.5 km along Moraine Lake Road to Lake Louise Drive. This is a groomed ski trail, and obviously you'll want to stay away from the ski tracks. Reaching Lake Louise Drive, turn left and snowshoe alongside the road back to the Lake Louise parking lot.

Return via Paradise Creek, Moraine Lake Road and Lake Louise Drive

This option is the most scenic and the most challenging. If leaving the beaten path and breaking a new trail alongside (and sometimes right across) a creek doesn't sound like fun, stick with one of the other options. Start by snowshoeing 300 m southeast, along Moraine Lake Highline Trail. At the next signed intersection, snowshoe a short distance south to reach Paradise Creek. Turn left (east) and follow the creek out to Moraine Lake Road. This may not be as easy as it seems. Deep snow can put you several metres above the creek. Falling into the creek or having a snow bridge across the creek collapse while you are on top is of concern. Be conservative in your route choices.

Be sure to turn around periodically to see the views of Sheol and Haddo behind you. When you reach Moraine Lake Road, turn left (north). Again there are some partial views of the northeast side of Mount Temple. Snowshoe about 1.5 km along Moraine Lake Road to Lake Louise Drive. This is a groomed ski trail and you'll want to stay away from the ski tracks. Reaching Lake Louise Drive, turn left and snowshoe alongside the road back to the Lake Louise parking lot.

Sheol Mountain and Haddo Peak poke out above the trees, as seen from Moraine Lake Road. You will only see this view if you choose to do one of the alternative return routes. (Bernie Nemeth)

(MAP 22, PAGE 488)

DIFFICULTY EASY	
ELEVATION GAIN MINIMAL	
ROUND-TRIP DISTANCE 4 KM	
ROUND-TRIP TIME 1–2 HOURS	
MAPS 82 N/08 LAKE LOUISE, GEM TREK LAKE LOUISE AND YOHO	

Don't expect to be alone on this route! The obvious trail goes west, around the north side of the lake. Of course, if the lake is sufficiently frozen, it is also possible to snowshoe directly across it as you head toward its west end. Backdropped by magnificent Mount Victoria and its glacier, the scenery and views are impressive throughout.

DIRECTIONS

Drive to Lake Louise and take the 4-km road to the chateau. The east end of the lake is only a few hundred metres from the public parking lot. Pick either shoreline to follow (the north being more popular and well packed down), or snowshoe directly across. While the terrific view of Mount Victoria is ever present, the equally impressive Mount Lefroy soon makes an appearance.

At the west end of the lake sits a world-famous climbing area, appropriately named "Back of the Lake." Also be sure to check out the 110-m ice climb, Louise Falls, before returning to the chateau via the lake surface or the shoreline. For the most variety it might make sense to return via the route you didn't use on the way in (again, as long as the lake is frozen solid).

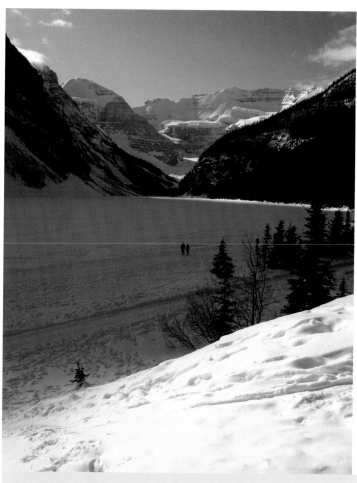

LOOKING DOWN THE LAKE, WITH MOUNT LEFROY BECOMING MORE PROMINENT AT THE LEFT. PHOTO TAKEN FROM JUST ABOVE THE SHORELINE TRAIL.

109 MIRROR LAKE AND LAKE AGNES

(MAP 22, PAGE 488)

DIFFICULTY INTERMEDIATE TO MIRROR LAKE; ADVANCED TO LAKE AGNES

ELEVATION GAIN 295 M TO MIRROR LAKE; ADD 90 M TO LAKE AGNES

ROUND-TRIP DISTANCE 5.4 KM RETURN FOR MIRROR LAKE; ADD 1.8 KM RETURN FOR LAKE AGNES

ROUND-TRIP TIME 2.5–4 HOURS

MAPS 82 N/08 LAKE LOUISE,
GEM TREK LAKE LOUISE AND YOHO

Although it's a fair climb to reach Mirror Lake, the gentle grade makes travel quite easy. The scenery is respectable, but continuing on to Lake Agnes rewards you with spectacular views of the lake and surrounding mountains. Unfortunately, you must travel through a short section of avalanche terrain to get to Agnes. Avalanches that run over the trail are rare, but it's best to check with the park wardens before you go. You'll want to pick a clear day and go in the morning to get the best sun on the lakes.

DIRECTIONS

Drive to Lake Louise and take the 4-km road to the chateau. From the public parking lot, find your way to the shore and start snowshoeing (or hiking) along the upper trail around the right (north) side of the lake. The signed trailhead is a short distance up. Make sure you are on the Lake Agnes snowshoe/hiking trail and not on one of the telemarking trails.

The trail is usually well-packed down, so wearing snowshoes will improve your traction. Route-finding is never an issue, as the trail is obvious. It ascends the steep, forested face in two long switchbacks at a relatively gentle grade. After the second

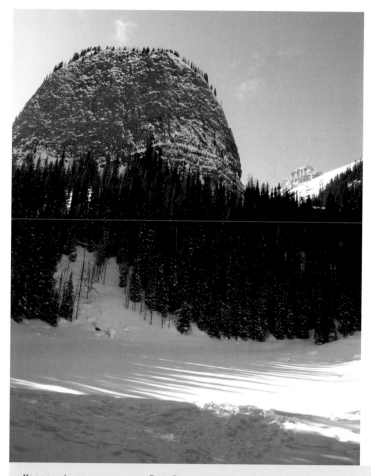

MIRROR LAKE, WITH THE BIG BEEHIVE TOWERING ABOVE IT.

switchback, the route goes deeper into the forest before spitting you out at Mirror Lake. The scenery at Mirror Lake is decent but it pales in comparison to that at Lake Agnes, which is now less than a kilometre away.

EXTENSION TO LAKE AGNES

Again, there is some avalanche potential going to Lake Agnes. The trail is never steep but if the slopes above the trail slide, the trail (with you on it!) may get buried. Remember to check in with park wardens before taking this trip extension.

Directions

Continue north up the trail and then swing around to the west for the final push to the lake and teahouse. Hurry through this section and advance one person at a time, just in case. The only snowshoeing challenge might come right at the end when you have to ascend the snow-covered stairs. Be careful here. A slip could be very painful.

Unfortunately, a hot cup of tea will not be waiting for you at the famous Lake Agnes Teahouse. The teahouse closes for the winter. However, what may be waiting (weather permitting) is a stunning view of the snow-covered lake, backdropped by the wonderful forms of Mounts Niblock and Whyte and the strikingly jagged rock formations of Devil's Thumb. Hopefully, all will be bathed in beautiful sunlight.

Sitting at an elevation of 2134 m, the lake remains frozen through most of the winter. Snowshoeing across it is generally quite safe. Otherwise, snowshoe around the perimeter on either side to see more of the beautiful surroundings. Do not venture too far along the side of the lake. Although unlikely, avalanches from the slopes above are possible.

Also, though the temptation may be great, avoid attempting the trail to the Big Beehive, 185 m above. This could put you on serious avalanche terrain. On return, the same is true for the traverse to the Little Beehive. Unless you are experienced on steep terrain and can assess avalanche conditions, stay clear of these detours.

Return the same way you came up. Wearing snowshoes for the descent will enable you to fly down the trail in no time.

ABOVE: LAKE AGNES. THE STRIKING PEAK AT THE LEFT IS CALLED DEVIL'S THUMB. MOUNT WHYTE SITS AT THE CENTRE, AND MOUNT NIBLOCK IS THE SMALL BUT OBVIOUS BLOCK AT THE FAR RIGHT. WHYTE AND NIBLOCK ARE TERRIFIC SUMMER SCRAMBLES, DESCRIBED IN ALAN KANE'S SCRAMBLES IN THE CANADIAN ROCKIES. RIGHT: THE SUMMIT BLOCK OF MOUNT NIBLOCK, AS SEEN FROM A SHORT DISTANCE ALONG THE SOUTH SHORE OF LAKE AGNES.

YOHO

Yoho National Park lies on the eastern edge of British Columbia and starts about 10 km west of Lake Louise, on the Trans-Canada Highway. The park is the smallest in area of the four contiguous national parks (Banff, Kootenay and Jasper completing the list) but still has great potential for good snowshoeing routes. Sherbrooke Lake and Emerald Lake, both in Yoho, are two of the more scenic trips in the Rockies.

Due to the park's proximity to the Continental Divide, the eastern side of Yoho receives enormous volumes of snow throughout the winter and is a good destination when areas on the east side of the Rockies are melting out. However, the southwest section of the park is approximately 400 m below the eastern side. The snow in the southwest will melt much earlier than that in the east. Keep this in mind for Wapta Falls (page 451) and Chancellor Peak Road (page 449).

A national park pass is required for all trips in Yoho.

ROUTES

AWESOME WEATHER AND SCENERY AT EMERALD LAKE.

(MAP 23, PAGE 488)

DIFFICULTY EASY

ELEVATION GAIN APPROXIMATELY 100 M

ROUND-TRIP DISTANCE 5.4 KM

ROUND-TRIP TIME 1.5–2.5 HOURS

MAPS 82 N/08 LAKE LOUISE,
GEM TREK LAKE LOUISE AND YOHO

This small lake, nestled under the steep walls of rock of Narao Peak, is easily reached via a road and hiking trail. Those walls prevent the sun from ever seeing the south side of the lake, giving it a somewhat inhospitable feeling. The park suggests a 9.5-km loop route via Lake O'Hara, but only the 5.4-km one-way route is described here.

DIRECTIONS

Drive west on the Trans-Canada Highway, past Lake Louise toward Field. Turn left at the Lake O'Hara turnoff, about 2.7 km west of the "Welcome to British Columbia" sign. Drive a couple hundred metres down the road, cross the railway tracks and park where the road suddenly turns right.

The first 1.4 km of the route is actually along a road that becomes a ski trail in winter. Thus it is very wide and there is tons of room for everyone. Be sure to steer clear of all ski tracks. About 1 km along, Sink Lake appears to your left. Backdropped by Mount Bosworth, the lake makes for a very satisfying scene.

Snowshoe 400 m past Sink Lake and you'll see a big sign for Ross Lake. Note that this is a road sign, not a trail sign, so the turnoff is about 100 m farther along. Turn right onto Ross Lake

ABOVE: THE VIEW OF MOUNT BOSWORTH, AS SEEN FROM THE SOUTHEAST SIDE OF ROSS LAKE. BELOW: THE VIEW OF THE MOUNT HECTOR MASSIF, AS SEEN FROM THE SOUTHWEST SIDE OF THE LAKE.

trail. The trail is very popular with skiers but not so much with snowshoers. Therefore if a separate snowshoe trail has not already been broken, it's time to step up to the plate and do your civic duty! Not to worry, it's only about 1.3 km and never gets too steep. Except for a couple of very short sections, there is room for both a ski trail and a snowshoe trail. The trail twists and turns a little but generally heads due south to the picturesque lake.

Basically the only view you get upon reaching your destination is that of the huge walls around the lake, although they are impressive in their own right. To get additional views, snowshoe around both sides of the lake, advancing one at a time. It is possible to simply complete one loop around the lake, but the south end sits below obvious avalanche terrain. I do not recommend you go below those slopes. Instead, circle around the east side until the trees above to your left start to thin. Here you'll enjoy a terrific view of Mount Bosworth. To see the enormous Mount Hector massif, do the same thing around the west side of the lake.

When satiated, return the same way you came in. There is the option to complete a loop by following the trail 3.6 km west to Lake O'Hara Road and then back to your vehicle. Having not completed this loop, I cannot describe it here. If you attempt the route, expect a good 100 m of additional elevation gain and lots of strenuous uphill trail-breaking. Most parties will choose instead to relax and enjoy the environs of Ross Lake.

111 SHERBROOKE LAKE

(MAP 23, PAGE 488)

DIFFICULTY ADVANCED

ELEVATION GAIN APPROXIMATELY 200 M

ROUND-TRIP DISTANCE 6.2 KM

ROUND-TRIP TIME 2.5–3.5 HOURS

MAPS 82 N/08 LAKE LOUISE,
GEM TREK LAKE LOUISE AND YOHO

This is yet another "wait for a clear day" snowshoe trip. The views at the south end of this huge lake are fantastic. Snowshoes with good crampons are a must for the relentless grade and sometimes icy nature of the trail. This trail is frequently used by skiers as a descent route from Waputik Icefield. Be aware that they may be coming down the trail at significant speed, and get out of their way if that happens.

DIRECTIONS

Drive west on the Trans-Canada Highway, past Lake Louise toward Field. Continue about 1.8 km past the Lake O'Hara turnoff and turn right at the Great Divide Lodge. The trailhead is at the northwest end of the parking lot.

Put on your snowshoes and get ready for a solid 200 m of elevation gain in about 1.4 horizontal kilometres. The grade is never obscenely steep but it is quite relentless and should elevate your heart rate. The trail basically takes a long sweeping line along and up the southwest side of Paget Peak. Depending on who broke the trail, it may or may not follow the summer trail for the first

1.4 km. If the trail hasn't been broken (very unlikely), route-finding could be a challenge, so you may want to bail and try Ross Lake instead.

Most of the elevation is gained in the first 1.4 km, at which point you will hopefully arrive at a sign for Sherbrooke Lake and Paget Lookout. Take the left fork to Sherbrooke Lake. Travel north on more level terrain for 1.6 km to the south end of the lake. Again, the specific location of the trail may differ from year to year and with it the amount of extra elevation gain. Expect

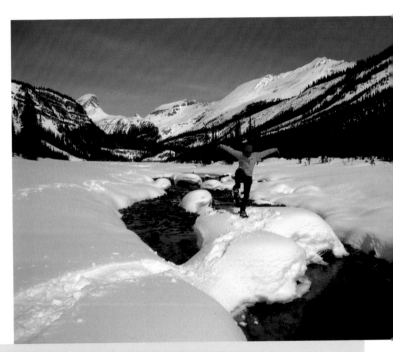

WHO KNEW THE KARATE KID WOULD BE HANGING OUT AT
SHERBROOKE LAKE? AND HE'S WEARING SNOWSHOES!
MOUNTS NILES AND DALY RISE BEHIND THE LAKE.

ABOVE: To the south lie the familiar forms of Victoria, Huber and Cathedral. BELOW: The steep east face and corniced ridge of Mount Ogden. When the cornices collapse they can trigger huge avalanches down the face.

at least one more section of strenuous uphill travel and then a gentle descent to the lake.

If you have heeded my advice about "waiting for a clear day" and the weather has cooperated, the scenery at the lake should not disappoint in the least. The massive and impressively steep peak towering over the west side of the lake is Mount Ogden, with the less impressive Paget Peak on the east side. The very distinctive and shapely peak at the north end is Mount Niles, and Mount Daly sits to the right of Niles; both are scrambles described in Alan Kane's *Scrambles in the Canadian Rockies*. Note the little pyramid between Niles and Daly. And if that wasn't enough, turn around and you are treated to wonderful views of Mount Victoria and Cathedral Mountain.

Explore the south end of the lake as conditions allow. At certain times of the year, when some but not all of the snow has melted, the snow scenery can be spectacular. Crossing the outlet of the lake also allows you to see more of the terrific views, but do so with care.

The south end of the lake is the end of the line for beginner snowshoers. Going farther puts you into avalanche terrain. Although it is highly unlikely that an avalanche could reach you if you were to snowshoe north up the middle of the lake, on the day I was there small avalanches on both sides of the lake could be heard at unnervingly regular intervals. Return the same way you came in.

112 EMERALD LAKE

DIFFICULTY EASY

ELEVATION GAIN MINIMAL

ROUND-TRIP DISTANCE 5.3 KM

ROUND-TRIP TIME 1.5–2.5 HOURS

MAPS 82 N/07 GOLDEN,
GEM TREK LAKE LOUISE AND YOHO

Missing the beautiful bright-green waters of Emerald Lake by snowshoeing around or across it in winter is a small price to pay for the fantastic scenery around this pristine lake. Waiting for a clear day is a must here – you will be disappointed otherwise. If you are unsure of the safety of the lake ice, ask the staff at the lodge. Otherwise, use the summer trail. The ice should be sufficiently strong for your purposes during January, February and March.

DIRECTIONS

Drive to Field, BC, on the Trans-Canada Highway and turn right (north) onto Emerald Lake Road, a few kilometres west of Field. It's about 9.2 km to the Emerald Lake parking lot (don't park in the overnight guest parking).

Hike or snowshoe down to the lake. The direction of travel may depend on the time of day. Very early morning trips favour a clockwise direction because of the sun's position in the sky. Mid-morning and later are better done counter-clockwise. Counter-clockwise is described below.

Although there is a summer hiking trail around the entire lake, the winter snowshoe/ski route usually stays right on the lake, near the shore and sometimes well away from it. Be aware that the ski and snowshoe routes can be one and the same. There is tons of space for everyone, so, as usual, stay off any ski tracks. For early-season trips and when the ice on the lake is unstable, find the summer hiking route. Travelling this route may require a very healthy dose of trail-breaking.

From beginning to end the surrounding views are magnificent. Although you are staring at the same mountains throughout, the different angles and new scenery appearing now and then should be plenty to keep you entertained. Starting from the southeast and going counter-clockwise, you will be enjoying the striking forms of Mount Burgess, Wapta Mountain, Michael Peak, the magnificently glaciated President and Vice President, and Emerald Peak, looming ominously over the northwest end of the lake.

Even if the scenery from the east side of the lake does start to get monotonous, working your way around to the northeast end

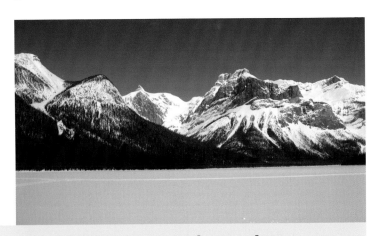

THE AWE-INSPIRING PEAKS OF THE PRESIDENT RANGE
ARE A CONSTANT COMPANION THROUGHOUT THE TRIP.

SOME POOR SOUL LEARNING THAT WEARING SNOWSHOES DOES NOT GUARANTEE GOOD BALANCE!

is definitely worth the effort. Depending on your specific route, you will eventually run into a wide stretch of braided streams feeding the lake. Trying to negotiate these waterways can be very dangerous. It's best to avoid them by either going around them to the south, travelling directly on the lake, or working your way north to the obvious bridge. The bridge is highly recommended, as it is safe and scenic.

Once over the bridge, continue working your way around the lake. The snow scenery at this end can be very interesting because of snow cover on the undulating terrain. As you start back toward the southwest end of the lake, stay near the shoreline for the first half, but soon you'll want to start moving away from the shore. This is because you are nearing the domain of the in-famous Emerald Slide Path. Although perhaps the most innocu-ous-looking of the mountains around the lake, Emerald Peak is anything but. The avalanche path on the southeast face of the peak is so well known that it actually gets its own name! Clearly visible, this enormous path collects huge amounts of snow and it slides regularly, often with devastating results. Skiers often "skin up" the path to enjoy an exhilarating and speedy ride down, but only when the avalanche risk is very low. Staying away from the runout zone of the slide path is imperative and that is why the ski and snowshoe trail will veer left, across the lake and toward the lodge. Use that path to enjoy an easy and scenic return to the start.

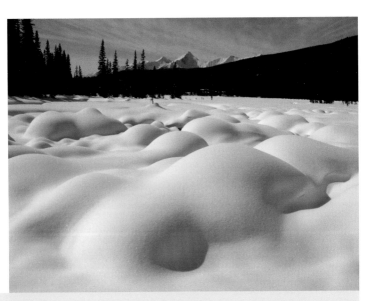

TERRIFIC SNOW SCENERY AT THE NORTH END OF EMERALD LAKE.

113 CHANCELLOR PEAK ROAD

(MAP 24, PAGE 489)

DIFFICULTY	EASY
ELEVATION GAIN	MINIMAL
ROUND-TRIP DISTANCE	4 KM
ROUND-TRIP TIME	1–2 HOURS
MAPS	82 N/02 MCMURDO

If you are in the area and craving an hour or two of light exercise with decent views, this is a good choice. However, no one is going to drive 2.5–4 hours from one of the major cities to complete this short and sometimes mundane trip. Your best bet is to combine it with another trip in Yoho, such as Wapta Falls (page 451) or Emerald Lake (page 445).

DIRECTIONS

On the Trans-Canada Highway heading west, drive 23.4 km past Field, BC, to the signed trailhead on the north side of the road (Chancellor Peak Campground). Park and hit the snow-covered road to snowshoe 2 km north to the campground. A more interesting variation is to leave the road and snowshoe north in the flats to your right (east). Eventually you'll come to the Kicking Horse River. Be careful around the river, as it can run fast and deep. Hopefully you've taken a real fancy to Mount Vaux and Chancellor Peak because they will be your constant and only companions throughout. The scenery doesn't change too much from one end to the other.

At the campground, you can do a lap or two around it, but

ABOVE: THE ALMOST 3310-M FORM OF MIGHTY MOUNT VAUX.
BELOW: CHANCELLOR PEAK LIES TO THE SOUTH OF MOUNT VAUX.

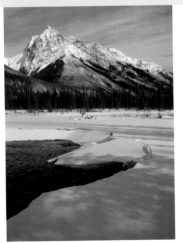

don't expect too much in the way of views. Return via the road or the flats.

114 WAPTA FALLS

(MAP 24, PAGE 489)

DIFFICULTY	INTERMEDIATE TO ADVANCED
ELEVATION GAIN	APPROXIMATELY 200 M
ROUND-TRIP DISTANCE	8.6 KM
ROUND-TRIP TIME	2.5–3.5 HOURS
MAPS	82 N/02 MCMURDO

Wapta Falls occurs on one of Canada's best-known whitewater rafting waterways – the Kicking Horse River. Getting there can be a somewhat tedious affair, but the falls themselves are spectacular. They are located near the west end of Yoho National Park, about 2.5–3 hours of driving time from Calgary. Make the trip worthwhile: consider waiting for a clear day and completing the Emerald Lake Loop before or after the Wapta Falls trip.

DIRECTIONS

On the Trans-Canada Highway heading west, drive 24.2 km past Field, BC, to the trailhead on the south side of the road. There is a trailhead sign when approaching from the west, but a sign is mysteriously missing (as of March 2012) when approaching from the east (Field). Be careful not to miss the turnoff. It's 900 m south of the Chancellor Peak Campground turnoff.

Don't be misled at the trailhead kiosk when you read the elevation loss to be 30 m. This is the net loss to the falls only and does not reflect the ups and downs, some of them significant, of the whole trip. Expect about 200 m of total elevation gain and a little more loss.

Snowshoe the gravel road for 2 km to the summer trailhead sign indicating it's another 2.4 km to the falls. Continue going south, following the more or less straight path through the trees. This path is often used by skiers. It is narrow, but with care snowshoers can walk on either side of the path, avoiding any ski tracks. There are short sections where you will have no choice but to walk in the centre.

About 1 km along, the trail gets into thicker forest and descends a little. It then follows a relatively gentle but long ascent on the side of a hill. This takes you to the high point of an embankment, high above the falls. Be sure to take a look down. A metal fence prevents a fatal slip. This section of the trail can be very icy. You may be very thankful for the traction-improving crampons on your snowshoes.

Take in this interesting perspective before you complete the trip down to the base of the falls. The descent is made in two

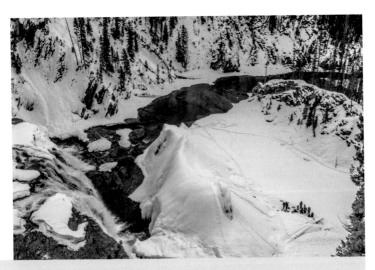

LOOKING DOWN ON THE FALLS AND THE EXTRAORDINARY COLOURS. A LARGE GROUP DECIDE TO TAKE IN THE EXQUISITE BEAUTY OF THE AREA. (SHAWN BENBOW)

long switchbacks. The first moves well away from the Kicking Horse River, and then a hairpin turn leads back to the river. You will emerge from the trees and immediately see the falls to your left. From afar they may not look that impressive, but hopefully a closer look will reveal some stunning water/snow/ice scenery.

Before you run over there and inadvertently plunge to an unexpected and icy death, note the following:

1. Between you and the falls are several large pools of water. More than likely they will be frozen and snow-covered, so you can walk right across them. However, if this is not the case, stick to the left, alongside the cliff face.

2. A large hill of rock sits in front of the falls. It is steep on the side not facing the falls and even steeper on the other side. Snow and water work together to form interesting formations of ice near the falls. In fact, a significant snow/icebridge was created from the hill to the falls when I visited the area in March of 2012. As beauteous and incredible as these features are, they can also be unstable and extremely dangerous. Explore the area with caution and don't go anywhere that might seem risky.

JENNIFER BENBOW AT THE FALLS. IT DOESN'T GET ANY BETTER THAN THIS! (SHAWN BENBOW)

ABOVE: *Beautiful but very dangerous conditions near the falls. Be careful! Below: Mount Vaux, as seen from the alternative return route by the stream.*

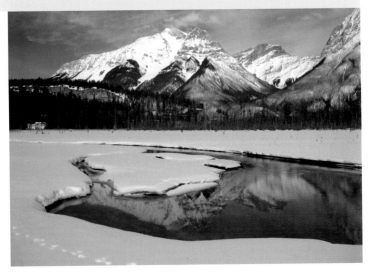

When you have finished admiring nature's awesome creation, return the same way you came in.

ALTERNATIVE RETURN ROUTE

For a little variation and some pleasant scenery on the return trip, once you get back to the summer trailhead, snowshoe about 500 m farther (northwest) and then cut right (northeast) into the forest, quickly arriving in an open area with a stream (perhaps snow-covered). Continue north alongside the stream, enjoying excellent views of Chancellor Peak and statuesque Mount Vaux farther north. You can snowshoe all the way to the road and then back to your vehicle or cut back to the west when you are close to the road.

HIGHWAY 93 NORTH

Highway 93 North, also called the Icefields Parkway, is as breathtaking an area as you can find on this planet – especially when snow has covered the landscape. The highway weaves its way between innumerable, strikingly beautiful peaks and several expansive icefields, the most notable of which is the world-famous Columbia Icefield. Near the south end of the road sits the Wapta Icefield. This sheet of ice and the peaks around it are very accessible to skiers and intermediate to advanced snowshoers.

While routes for the beginner snowshoer along the highway are limited because of access issues and avalanche danger, there are at least six terrific objectives, described here. All the routes are relatively short with the option to be extended into a longer trip.

As well, because of their limited time requirements, it is possible to do multiple routes in one day. Personally, I would wait for a bluebird day and then complete two or three of the routes in the same day. You will experience some of the best and varied scenery in the Rockies, with minimal effort. Drive all the way north to Mistaya Canyon and then you can go south and pick off any of the routes that are appealing to you. Of course any number of combinations are possible, but here are a few suggestions for multiple trips:

- Mistaya Canyon followed by any of the other routes
- Waterfowl Lakes, Peyto Lake Viewpoint

CROWFOOT MOUNTAIN IS THE BACKDROP OF BOW LAKE.
OBVIOUSLY THE BRIDGE SEES LIMITED TRAFFIC IN WINTER!

- Silverhorn Creek, Bow Lake
- Bow Lake, Mosquito Creek
- Mistaya Canyon, Bow Lake, Mosquito Creek
- Mistaya Canyon, Peyto Lake Viewpoint, Mosquito Creek

Note that this highway is minimally maintained during the winter and can get very icy. Have backup plans just in case. Anything in Lake Louise or Yoho is always a good choice.

ROUTES

115 MOSQUITO CREEK

(MAP 25, PAGE 490)

> RATING EASY
> ELEVATION GAIN MINIMAL
> ROUND-TRIP DISTANCE 1.6–4 KM
> ROUND-TRIP TIME 1–2 HOURS
> MAPS 82 N/9 HECTOR LAKE, GEM TREK BOW LAKE
> AND SASKATCHEWAN CROSSING

Many people are familiar with the route UP Mosquito Creek toward the campground, Mosquito Mountain and eventually Molar Pass, but the route going downstream is less known and it shouldn't be. The scenery where the creek and the Bow River meet is fantastic and within minutes of the road. This is a great beginner trip, with the freedom to make it as long or as short as you want. After going downstream, you can return to the highway and head upstream to a scenic icefall. Regardless of the direction, be prepared to break a separate snowshoe trail and avoid all ski tracks where possible.

DIRECTIONS

Drive about 24 km north on Highway 93 North to the Mosquito Campground sign, and park at one of the pullouts on either side of the bridge, on the west side of the road. From either pullout, snowshoe down to the creek and start following it in a westerly direction, through the campground. It does not matter too much which side of the creek you are on, as views of the surrounding area start to improve regardless. Chances are, there will be numerous solid snow and ice bridges spanning the creek, so that crossing from one side to the other will be easy at any time.

If you haven't already noticed, you are surrounded by some

pretty impressive mountains: Noseeum and Andromache to the east and southeast, Dolomite Peak to the north and Bow Peak immediately west. Pyramid-shaped Little Hector soon makes an appearance.

Less than a kilometre along, Mosquito Creek joins up with the beginnings of the Bow River, around GR459201. This is where you are likely to encounter some of the best scenery of the trip, and the whole area is worth some exploration time.

The trip can be extended by following the Bow River in a southerly direction for as long as you like. There is more cool scenery for several hundred metres downstream. Return the same way when you've had enough.

MOSQUITO CREEK EAST

Upon return, there is the option to continue going up the creek. This is not the regular Mosquito Creek trip that parallels the creek, but high above it and to the north. Also note that this extension may require you to travel right in the snow-covered creek or cross it using snowbridges. Exercise extreme caution

WHERE CREEK MEETS RIVER. MOUNT ANDROMACHE
AND LITTLE HECTOR IN THE BACKGROUND.

and conservative decision making. A slip into the creek could be very serious.

As you approach the bridge over the highway, instead of ascending back up to the highway, go right under the bridge and follow the creek along its north bank. Again, remember to travel with extreme care, as the creek contains deep pools of icy water that may be hidden under a layer of snow.

A small but interesting frozen waterfall is reached in short order. This will probably be the end of the line for most. Travel past the icefall gets pretty tricky but is possible with the right snow and ice conditions. Continuing will definitely require you to cross the creek on a snowbridge, with very unpleasant consequences if the bridge fails. Travel will end when you reach an impressively deep pool of water, surrounded by steep canyon walls and more frozen waterfalls. Return the same way.

THE FIRST FROZEN WATERFALL. GETTING PAST THE FALL MAY LOOK EASY, BUT ON MY TRIP THE ICE UNDERFOOT WAS BRITTLE AND DIDN'T INSPIRE CONFIDENCE. BE VERY CAREFUL!

116 BOW LAKE

(MAP 25, PAGE 490)

DIFFICULTY EASY

ELEVATION GAIN 0–80 M MAXIMUM

ROUND-TRIP DISTANCE VARIABLE TO 8 KM
MAXIMUM

ROUND-TRIP TIME VARIABLE

MAPS 82 N/09 HECTOR LAKE, GEM TREK BOW
LAKE AND SASKATCHEWAN CROSSING

As soon as a clear day dawns, you should make your way to Bow Lake. The area around the lake is absolutely magnificent and should be experienced when the skies are clear and the sun is shining. You can explore the area around the colourful Num-Ti-Jah Lodge, snowshoe north along the flanks of "Mount Jimmy Junior" or cross the lake and head toward Bow Falls (or do all three!). This is a must-see area for all outdoor enthusiasts.

DIRECTIONS

Drive approximately 36 km north on Highway 93 and turn left into the Num-Ti-Jah Lodge parking lot. Once there, you have a number of options.

Explore

Depending on snow conditions, the area around the lodge can provide many visual rewards. Wind-blown snow formations, a couple of bridges sticking out of the snow, the historic lodge itself and a creek are but a few of the interesting features. Of course, this is all surrounded by the breathtaking forms of mountains around Bow Lake and on the spectacular Wapta Icefield. Loosely

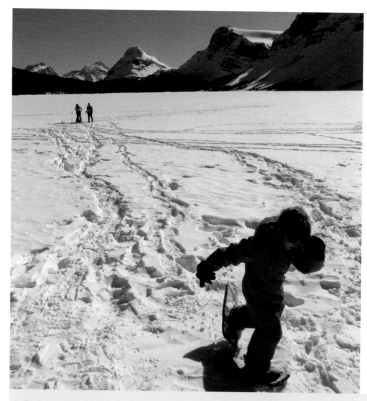

FAMILY SNOWSHOEING ON BOW LAKE. ROGAN NUGARA LEADS THE WAY.

following the northern perimeter of the lake is a great way to see more of the icefield. However, do not go too far beyond the northwest corner of the lake. Avalanche terrain will soon appear to your right if you do push on.

Go north
Snowshoe west past the lodge and turn north. There is a trail here, though it may be impossible to find under all the snow. Go

as far as you want in a NNW direction, through light forest and then out into the more open areas, east of the lower slopes of unofficially named "Mount Jimmy Junior." Do not venture west into the vicinity of those slopes, because they can be very avalanche prone. Stay within a few hundred metres of the road. When satiated, either return the way you came in or snowshoe to the road and hike back to the parking area.

Go across

Crossing the north end of the lake is generally a safe and easy affair. The route is extremely popular with ski and snowshoe mountaineers, so several well-packed trails will invariably go in that direction. Obviously you'll want to pick the snowshoe trail or make your own if one doesn't exist. Arriving at the gravel flats

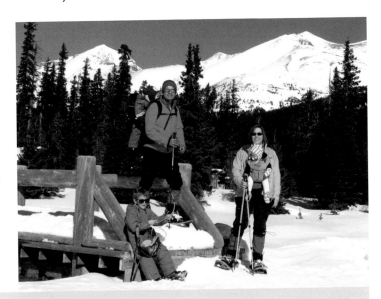

AT LEAST THE BRIDGE CAN SERVE AS A GOOD SPOT FOR A PHOTO! MARK, KERI AND THE KIDS, WITH OBSERVATION PEAK BEHIND.

at the west end of the lake, you can continue on alongside the stream for about 500 m. Beyond this lies a narrow canyon that must be bypassed on the left side. This terrain can be steep and avalanche prone, and it is not for the novice snowshoer. Stop, enjoy the scenery and then return the same way you came.

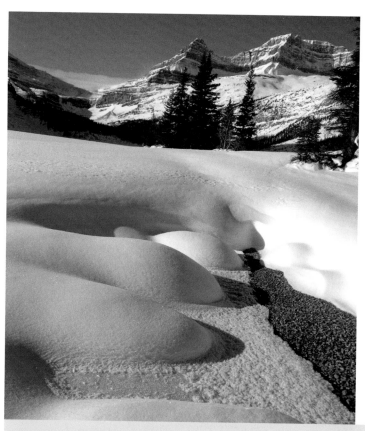

SCENERY ON THE NORTH SHORE OF THE LAKE NEAR THE PARKING LOT. PORTAL PEAK (CENTRE) AND MOUNT THOMPSON ARE BUT TWO OF THE MANY IMPRESSIVE PEAKS AROUND THE LAKE.

117 PEYTO LAKE VIEWPOINT

(MAP 25, PAGE 490)

DIFFICULTY EASY

ELEVATION GAIN 25–50 M

ROUND-TRIP DISTANCE 1.2–2 KM

ROUND-TRIP TIME 0.5–2 HOURS

MAPS 82 N/09 HECTOR LAKE, 82 N/10 BLAE-
BERRY RIVER, GEM TREK BOW LAKE AND
SASKATCHEWAN CROSSING

When your starting elevation from the car is close to 2100 m, good to spectacular views are guaranteed within minutes. Such is the case with Peyto Lake Viewpoint. The amazing view of Peyto Lake, far below, is about a 10–15 minute snowshoe from the parking lot. You can then do an extension to the glades south of the viewpoint. As at Bow Lake, if you are in the area and enjoying good weather, this is a must-do trip.

DIRECTIONS

Drive approximately 40 km north on Highway 93 and turn left into the Bow Summit / Peyto Lake parking lot. Follow the road to the parking area, which can be very busy, especially on weekends. This area is deservedly popular with skiers wanting to get in some turns, and it is sometimes the location for mountaineering courses such as AST 1 or 2.

There are two loops to complete. The direction of travel may depend on whether a trail has been broken or not. I recommend using the summer interpretive trail to go directly to the viewpoint and then head south to complete the other loop. There is a series of interpretive plaques mounted on blue supports along here that you could follow, but the plaques are far between, the second is not visible from the first and so forth. Therefore, if no previous track exists, finding these signs may require some searching. If this is the case, it may be better to do the route in a clockwise direction.

COUNTER-CLOCKWISE

Go to the north end of the parking lot and look for a trail. If there isn't one, make your own, heading northwest and then west. Try to follow the interpretive signs as much as possible. The viewpoint is about 600 m from the parking lot. If at any time you get lost or disoriented, turn around and follow your tracks back to the parking lot, then use the clockwise route.

CLOCKWISE

The trail starts by the kiosk, arriving quickly at the unplowed road. The road goes up and to the right for a while before swinging around to the left (south). A sign pointing at lofty Observation Peak (a terrific scramble in the summer) is quickly reached. At the sign, cut back to the right (northwest) and go slightly downhill to the viewpoint, about 100 m away.

THE VIEWPOINT

As expected, the highlight of the panorama is the distinctive outline of Peyto Lake, nestled under Caldron Peak's impressive east face. To the southwest lies the tongue of Peyto Glacier, one of several gateways to Wapta Icefield. Peyto Peak lies to the left of Caldron. The striking peak due south of the viewpoint is an outlier of "Mount Jimmy Simpson." A close look may reveal multiple paths of S turns made by skiers enjoying the terrain.

THE CLASSIC VIEW FROM PEYTO LAKE VIEWPOINT.

SECOND LOOP

From the viewpoint, snowshoe southeast back to the Observation Peak sign, about 100 m away. Continue going south through open terrain. Again, there may be tracks to follow or you may be forging your own path. There are two important things to remember here: don't snowshoe on ski tracks and don't follow them southwest toward the steeper and more dangerous slopes of the Jimmy Simpson outlier. Instead, stay south on gentle terrain, eventually making a counter-clockwise loop back to the unplowed road or to the parking lot.

118 SILVERHORN CREEK

(MAP 26, PAGE 490)

RATING EASY TO ADVANCED (MISTAYA LAKE)	
ELEVATION GAIN MINIMAL	
ROUND-TRIP DISTANCE VARIABLE TO 6.5 KM (MISTAYA LAKE)	
ROUND-TRIP TIME 1–3 HOURS	
MAPS 82 N/15 MISTAYA LAKE, GEM TREK BOW LAKE AND SASKATCHEWAN RIVER CROSSING	

Silverhorn Creek is very similar to Mosquito Creek – easy, with great views from the start and the option to make the trip as short or as long as you like. Of course the trail-breaking may be taxing, but it's a small price to pay for the instant scenic rewards. Those craving a real workout can go all the way to Mistaya Lake.

DIRECTIONS

Drive about 11 km north of the Bow Summit turnoff and park in the small pullout for Silverhorn Campground. The road to the campground is blocked, but there is usually enough room for a couple of vehicles. Silverhorn Creek is often completely snow-covered at this point and lies south of the parking area.

The route is obvious – follow Silverhorn Creek in a westerly and then northwesterly direction, past the campground and beyond. On a clear day the surrounding mountain scenery is magnificent right from the start. Mount Patterson to the south, Weed and Noyes to the east, Breaker and Aries to the west and all the striking but unnamed peaks around Mount Murchison to the north are a few of the highlights.

The challenge of the route can be trying to determine when it is safe to travel right in the creek (easiest but potentially dangerous if the ice breaks) or alongside the creek (often very strenuous because of deep snow).

Travel as far downstream as you like and then return the same way.

MISTAYA LAKE

The ultimate extension of the Silverhorn Creek trip is to journey all the way to Mistaya Lake. Expect plenty of trail-breaking and a little route-finding. Follow Silverhorn Creek for about 3 km in a northwesterly direction to where the creek intersects the early stages of the Mistaya River at GR271406. Now follow the Mistaya River as it curves around to the southwest, soon reaching the north end of Mistaya Lake. The 4-km long, glacially fed lake is fairly narrow at this end but quite wide at its south end.

THE VIEW TO THE WEST FROM THE PARKING AREA AND FIRST PART OF THE ROUTE TO THE CAMPGROUND. MP=MOUNT PATTERSON. SC=SILVERHORN CREEK. BM=BREAKER MOUNTAIN. AP=ARIES PEAK.

You can return the same way or make a small loop by staying on the lake for a while. Snowshoe south and southeast along the lakeshore or directly on the lake for about a kilometre. When the lakeshore curves to the south, turn east into the trees and make your way back to Silverhorn Creek, around GR279399. You will have to perform about 500 m of strenuous trail-breaking to get back on your original track. Turn right (southeast) and return to your vehicle.

119 WATERFOWL LAKES

(MAP 26, PAGE 490)

> RATING EASY FOR WATERFOWL LAKES, ADVANCED TO CHEPHREN LAKE
>
> ELEVATION GAIN MINIMAL FOR WATERFOWL LAKES, 120 M TO CHEPHREN LAKE
>
> ROUND-TRIP DISTANCE 0.5–4 KM FOR WATERFOWL LAKES, 3.4–5.4 KM FOR CHEPHREN LAKE
>
> ROUND-TRIP TIME 0.5–3 HOURS
>
> MAPS 82 N/15 MISTAYA LAKE, GEM TREK BOW LAKE AND SASKATCHEWAN RIVER CROSSING

You don't even need to get out of your vehicle to be blown away by the view from the east side of Waterfowl Lakes! Snowshoeing alongside the lakeshore on a clear day can be an awe-inspiring and beautifully serene experience at once. The extension to Chephren Lake presents a more challenging objective that is equally stunning.

DIRECTIONS

North of Waterfowl Lakes Campground, there are two pullouts for Waterfowl Lakes. The northernmost pullout is recommended as a starting point and is situated 2.2 km north of the Waterfowl Campground's unplowed turnoff (1.3 km north of the first pullout).

The lake is only a couple of minutes from the pullout. Descend to the lakeshore and take in the outstanding views of Mount Chephren and Howse Peak to the west. If clouds cover the mountains you will be very disappointed; if the skies are clear you will be blown away! There are two fairly extreme climbing routes (Wild Thing and East Face) that go right up the east face of Chephren. When I sprout wings I may try one of them.

Options are numerous at this point:

1. Snowshoe southeast, directly on the lake or on the bank of the lake, for a kilometre or so and then return the same way. Views toward Epaulette Mountain, Kaufmann Peaks and Mount Sarbach, to the north of Chephren, improve as you go farther south.
2. Snowshoe the entire perimeter of the lake, crossing over the lake at the northwest end on return.
3. Snowshoe southeast for a short distance and then go across the lake to the west side. Any trip across the lake grants you excellent views of mounts Noyes and Weed to the southeast.
4. Snowshoe northwest, cross the lake and go toward Chephren Lake.

ONE OF THE MOST IMPRESSIVE VIEWS THE ICEFIELDS PARKWAY HAS TO OFFER. FROM LEFT TO RIGHT, HOWSE PEAK, MIGHTY MOUNT CHEPHREN, EPAULETTE MOUNTAIN, KAUFMANN PEAKS AND MOUNT SARBACH.

5. For an easy but slightly longer trip, I would recommend snowshoeing the entire perimeter of the lake, or a portion of it. You can always just do half of the lake.

If you are looking to really take advantage of the day, combine the last two options and go all the way to Chephren Lake, as described below.

CHEPHREN LAKE

Although unnecessary, first go southeast down the lake for a little while. This exposes you to full views of the lake and surrounding mountains. Next, cross to the west side of the lake, provided the surface is sufficiently frozen. Turn northwest and follow the

THE RIVER DIPS SOUTHWEST. AROUND THE CORNER IS WHERE YOU LEAVE THE RIVER TO BUSHWHACK TO THE CREEK THAT DRAINS CHEPHREN LAKE.

lakeshore to the wide lake outlet at the northwest end of the lake, very soon to become the Mistaya River.

The river goes west and then dips to the southwest before turning to the northwest. Here, you get an open view of the river running northwest. Although there is a creek that joins Chephren Lake to the Mistaya River a short distance downstream, this creek is hard to find and brutally hard to follow. The best route once you get to this open area (GR241446) is to cut left (southwest) into the trees and make your way up and through the trees, eventually intersecting the aforementioned creek. Expect trail-breaking for this entire section to be very gruelling. Once you find the creek, follow it in a southerly direction up to Chephren Lake.

Again, views toward Mount Chephren and Howse Peak are outstanding. You can snowshoe south along the east shoreline (the west is not recommended, because of potential avalanches) for any distance you feel like and then return the same way. The lake is deceivingly long. Snowshoeing all the way to the south side will perhaps be a little too ambitious, although the view of Chephren will be awesome.

120 MISTAYA CANYON

(MAP 27, PAGE 490)

RATING EASY TO MODERATE
ELEVATION GAIN 35 M
ROUND-TRIP DISTANCE 0.6–2.4 KM
ROUND-TRIP TIME 0.5–2 HOURS
MAPS 82 N/15 MISTAYA LAKE, GEM TREK BOW
LAKE AND SASKATCHEWAN RIVER CROSSING

This deep, water-eroded gorge is awe-inspiring to say the least and a mere 300 m from the road. After an extended stint ogling the canyon, following the Mistaya River upstream for a little less than a kilometre can be equally rewarding and fun.

DIRECTIONS

Park at the Mistaya Canyon pullout, about 14 km north of the Waterfowl Lakes turnoff (3.3 km south of the bridge over the North Saskatchewan River). The trail starts a few metres north of the pullout and is easy to find and easy to follow. You will lose 35 m of elevation and arrive at the bridge over the canyon and Mistaya River in less than 10 minutes. Enjoy the spectacular, water-eroded canyon from the safety of the bridge. To the southeast, distant but massive Mount Sarbach overlooks the river.

Return the same way if that was your only objective. Hopefully the beauty of the area will inspire you to explore further. Cross the bridge and turn left. Note the cautionary signs. Any slip into the canyon would be fatal, and snow and ice make the terrain even more dangerous.

Parallel the river for 20–40 metres until you can find a safe path down to the river. The terrain can be challenging in certain conditions so pick an easy line. Once on the bank on the river, follow it upstream for as far as you would like. Travel is usually possible on either side, as snow and ice bridges frequently form over the water. Once again, however, extreme caution is advised. Stay on the riverbank and off the ice for the safest route.

Take your time and enjoy the scenery – the small as well as the big. Some of the most interesting and beautiful ice formations I've ever seen were encountered here (see photo).

About 900 m upstream, a steep slope comes down from the left (east) to meet the river (GR187539). This is a logical place to call it a day if you already haven't. Travel beyond this point

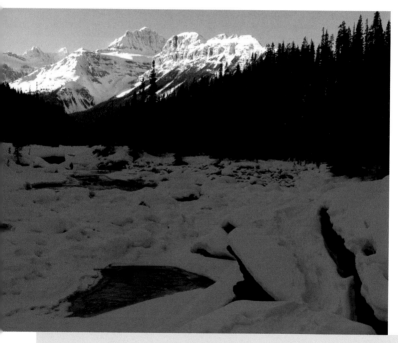

MOUNT SARBACH AND THE MISTAYA RIVER. NOTE
THE TRICKY TERRAIN AT THE RIGHT.

becomes less interesting, and there is actually some minor avalanche potential from that slope. Return the same way, perhaps on the opposite side of the river.

FASCINATING ICE FORMATIONS ON THE RIVER. I HAD TO CRAWL INTO A SMALL GAP IN THE ICE TO GET THIS PHOTO, BUT IT WAS SO WORTH IT (MAYBE NOT SO MUCH IF THE ICE UNDERNEATH ME HAD BROKEN AND I HAD ENDED UP IN THE CHILLY RIVER).

Map 1
WATERTON: BEAR'S HUMP,
HORSESHOE BASIN TRAIL

Map 2
WATERTON: CRANDELL LAKE,
AKAMINA PASS, CAMERON LAKE

Map 3

HIGHWAY 774: MOUNT BACKUS, CARBONDALE HILL

Map 4

CROWSNEST PASS: BYRON
HILL, "POKER PEAK"

Map 5

CROWSNEST PASS:
SASKATOON MOUNTAIN,
WEDGE MOUNTAIN,
"THE SADDLE"

Map 7

HIGHWAY 541; BULL CREEK HILLS, GRASS PASS, HELL'S RIDGE (NORTH END), HIGHWAY 40 SOUTH (BEYOND THE LOCKED GATE)

Map 6

CROWSNEST PASS; ISLAND RIDGE

Map 8

HIGHWAY 549; SINNOT HILL, MESA BUTTE

Map 9

ELBOW VALLEY EAST

Map 10

ELBOW VALLEY WEST

Map 11
Highway 68

Map 12
Highway 68: KIFIT

Map 13
HIGHWAY 40

Map 14
THE HIGHWOOD

Map 15
HIGHWAY 742 NORTH

Map 16

HIGHWAY 742 SOUTH

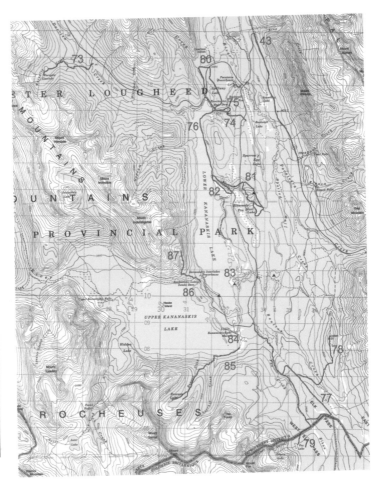

MAPS

Map 17

KANANASKIS LAKES TRAIL

Map 18
Banff

Map 19
Banff: Ink Pots

Map 20
Castle Junction: Taylor Lake, Boom Lake

Map 22
LAKE LOUISE

Map 21
HIGHWAY 93 SOUTH

Map 23
YOHO: ROSS
LAKE,
SHERBROOKE
LAKE,
EMERALD LAKE

Map 24

YOHO: CHANCELLOR
PEAK ROAD,
WAPTA FALLS

Map 25
HIGHWAY 93
NORTH: MOSQUITO
CREEK, BOW
LAKE, PEYTO
LAKE VIEWPOINT

Map 26
HIGHWAY
93 NORTH:
SILVERHORN
CREEK,
WATERFOWL
LAKES

Map 27
HIGHWAY 93 NORTH:
MISTAYA CANYON

APPENDIX A: TRIPS ORGANIZED BY LEVEL OF DIFFICULTY

EASY

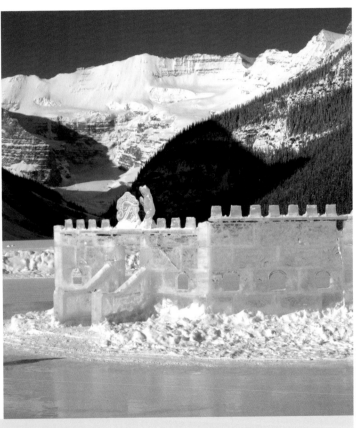

THE ICE CASTLE ON LAKE LOUISE IS ALWAYS A TREAT TO SEE.

INTERMEDIATE

MARK INSPECTS A CORNICE AT THE OUTLET OF SPRAY LAKE (BEYOND BULLER POND). NOT A PLACE TO LINGER!

Advanced

APPENDIX B: TRIP COMBINATIONS

Many beginner snowshoeing routes are relatively short, in both time and distance. You may wish to combine two or more trips to fill out your day. Below are some suggestions for trips that can be easily combined. The list describes routes in which you can do one trip after the other without driving between starting points or even taking your snowshoes off.

1. Bull Creek Hills (page 134) and Grass Pass (page 137)
2. Snowshoe Hare Loop (page 158) and Snowy Owl (page 160)
3. Paddy's Flat Interpretive Trail (page 168) and Riverview Trail (page 170)
4. Riverview Trail (page 170) and Sulphur Springs Trail (page 174)
5. Evan-Thomas Creek (page 227) and Wedge Pond (page 230)
6. 742-E (Buller Pond) (page 264) and Beyond Buller Pond (page 266)
7. Chester Lake (page 300) and Lower Chester Loop and Mount Murray Viewpoint (page 304)
8. Hogarth Lakes (page 307) and Burstall Lakes (page 309)
9. Canyon (page 328) and Kananaskis Canyon (page 329)
10. Kananaskis Canyon (page 329) and Lower Kananaskis Lake I (page 332)
11. Kananaskis Canyon (page 329) and Penstock Loop (page 344)
12. Lower Kananaskis Lake I (page 332) and Marsh Loop (page 350)
13. Elkwood Loop (page 347) and Marsh Loop (page 350)
14. Upper Kananaskis Lake I (page 356) and Rawson Lake (page 358)

15. Tunnel Mountain Drive (page 390) and Tunnel Mountain (page 392)
16. Marble Canyon (page 412) and Paint Pots (page 415)
17. Louise Creek (page 420) and Fairview Lookout (page 423)
18. Fairview Lookout (page 423) and Highline (page 426)
19. Fairview Lookout (page 423) and Lake Louise and Shoreline (page 430)
20. Lake Louise and Shoreline (page 430) and Mirror Lake and Lake Agnes (page 432)

If you don't mind doing a trip and then driving to the next start point, the list of possible combinations is endless (Crandell Lake followed by Cameron Lake, or Boom Lake followed by Marble Canyon, for example). Given that many starting points are within a short drive of one another, you are limited only by time and your imagination.

Of course, you can complete trips distant from one another on the same day. For example, assuming you started from Calgary, after experiencing the amazing environs of Emerald Lake in Yoho, it is very easy to stop at Cascade Ponds in Banff on the way home. In fact, I completed Emerald Lake, Wapta Falls, Chancellor Peak Road and Cascade Ponds all on the same day in March of 2012 (and still made it back to Calgary to enjoy one of my favourite episodes of *Seinfeld* at 8:30 p.m.!).

APPENDIX C: FAMILY TRIPS

This list offers trip recommendations for families taking children under three years of age (i.e., they are not using snowshoes). Labelled in brackets are the trips that are best for Chariot Carrier users. For those with children who do wear snowshoes, consult easy trips in Appendix A. Obviously you'll want to pick the shortest routes in that list for very young children.

4. Cameron Lake, page 84 (Chariot)
18. Highway 40 South, page 146 (Chariot)
25. Paddy's Flat Interpretive Trail, page 168
28. Beaver Lodge Interpretive Trail, page 177
31. Highway 66, page 188 (Chariot)
39. Troll Falls, page 222
42. Wedge Pond, page 230
43. Wintour Road, page 232 (Chariot)
44. Elbow Lake, page 236
46. Canmore Park, page 247 (Chariot)
62. Watridge Lake, page 286 (Chariot)
67. Lower Chester Loop and Mount Murray Viewpoint, page 304
68. Hogarth Lakes, page 307 (Chariot)
69. Burstall Lakes, page 309 (Chariot)
71. Sawmill Trails, page 316
73. Warspite Lake, page 321
81. Elkwood Loop, page 347
82. Marsh Loop, page 350
88. Cascade Ponds, page 369
89. Johnson Lake, page 372
92. Stoney Squaw Mountain, page 381
94. Vermilion Lakes, page 387
95. Tunnel Mountain Drive, page 390 (Chariot)

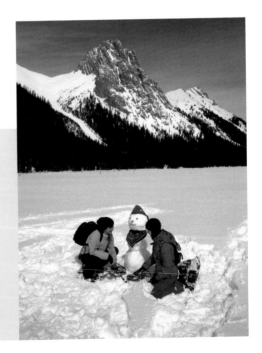

NICOLE AND
MICHELLE PROVIDE
A DENIZEN OF
BURSTALL LAKES
WITH A MORE
EFFECTIVE MODE
OF LOCOMOTION
— SNOWSHOES!
COMMONWEALTH PEAK
SITS PROUDLY IN
THE BACKGROUND.

APPENDIX D: ADVANCED TRIPS FOR EXPERIENCED SNOWSHOERS

As outlined in the preface, these trips are designed to introduce the experienced, beginner snowshoer to elements of intermediate/advanced snowshoeing, such as steep terrain, longer distances and route-finding challenges. If the Moderate and Difficult rated trips in *Snowshoeing in the Canadian Rockies, 2nd Edition*, are in your future, then the trips listed below will give you a little taste of what to expect. Please note, however, that avalanche training will be a pre-requisite for those trips in the advanced book. The trips listed below DO NOT require avalanche training.

Appendix E: New to this Edition

For those who have the first edition, here is a list of trips new to this edition:

Appendix F: Favourites

This is a list of my favourite trips from the book. Needless to say, this list is completely subjective and anyone's individual experience and perception may differ greatly from mine. My primary motivation for going to the mountains is for the spectacular scenery and views. Therefore I tend to favour routes that highlight those elements of the mountain environment. I am less concerned with the nature and/or aesthetic qualities of the route itself. We all have our own reasons for going to the mountains and no single person's reasons or opinions are better than the next person's.

(In addition, I completed all of these favourites on perfect or near-perfect weather days – it was sunny with few or no clouds – which further contributes to a bias!)

Also note that the conditions and snow scenery will invariably change from year to year and may be very different at various times of the season. For example, the exposed ice that my brother and I saw at the south end of Spray Lake is one of the reasons that trip makes it onto the list. However, we just happened to be on the lake after a major wind event where the surface of the ice was visible. Those specific conditions may be the exception to the rule. More than likely the surface would be completely snow-covered.

Take this list for what it is: one individual's viewpoint.

4. Cameron Lake (page 84): I simply can't get enough of that awe-inspiring view of Mount Custer.
9. "Poker Peak" (page 107): Difficult access, but great ascent, amazing ridgewalk and phenomenal summit views.
54. Beyond Buller Pond (page 266): Excellent views of the surrounding mountains and terrific snow scenery around the inlet.

58. 742-H (page 276): Wide-open snowshoeing, surrounded by striking peaks. I could go up and down this valley all day!

62. Watridge Lake extension to Spray River and Spray Lake (page 289: Replaces the South End of Spray Lake. Similar to that trip, but with a ton more cool scenery and interesting terrain. The view of Cone Mountain from the bridge is wicked!

100. Ink Pots (page 403): This valley is a real treasure of pristine mountain scenery. Mount Ishbel is awesome!

103. Marble Canyon (page 412): A totally cool canyon surrounded by totally cool mountains and all of it less than 10 minutes from the parking lot. Plus, you have options to do other nearby trips such as the Paint Pots.

111. Sherbrooke Lake (page 441): A good physical workout leads to phenomenal views at the south end of the lake. My late-season (mid-April) trip, yielded some seriously cool snow scenery around the lake outlet.

112. Emerald Lake (page 445): Feels remote, even with the lodge on the lakeshore. The mountains around the lake are absolutely beautiful.

116. Bow Lake (page 462): Some of the best mountain scenery you will ever experience and it's less than five minutes away from your vehicle.

120. Mistaya Canyon (page 476): A stunning, water-eroded canyon and the option to follow the beautiful Mistaya River.

Appendix G: Information Centres

When looking for advice and information regarding trail conditions, trip suggestions, weather forecasts, accommodations etc., you can visit or call one of numerous information centres in the Rockies.

Highway 40 South

The Barrier Lake Information Centre is located 8 km south on Highway 40 and is open Monday to Thursday 9 a.m.–4 p.m. and Friday to Sunday 9 a.m.–5 p.m. Call 403-673-3985 for inquiries.

Kananaskis Lakes Trail

The Peter Lougheed Visitor Centre is located at 3.6 km along Kananaskis Trail and is open year-round. Call 403-591-6322 for inquiries.

Banff

The Banff Information Centre is located at 224 Banff Avenue in the Town of Banff. The centre's hours of operation vary throughout the year. Call 403-762-1550 for inquiries.

Lake Louise

The Lake Louise Visitor Information Centre is located in the Village of Lake Louise, next to Samson Mall. The centre's hours of operation vary throughout the year. Call 403-522-3833 for inquiries.

Yoho

The Yoho National Park Visitor Centre is located at 5764 Trans-Canada Highway, Field, BC. Call 250-343-6783 for inquiries.

Bibliography

Daffern, Gillean. *Gillean Daffern's Kananaskis Country Trail Guide*. 4th edition, Volume 1. Calgary: Rocky Mountain Books, 2010.

———. *Gillean Daffern's Kananaskis Country Trail Guide*. 4th edition, Volume 2. Calgary: Rocky Mountain Books, 2011.

———. *Gillean Daffern's Kananaskis Country Trail Guide*. 4th edition, Volume 3. Calgary: Rocky Mountain Books, 2013.

———. *Gillean Daffern's Kananaskis Country Trail Guide*. 4th edition, Volume 4. Calgary: Rocky Mountain Books, 2012.

———. *Gillean Daffern's Kananaskis Country Trail Guide*. 4th edition, Volume 5. Calgary: Rocky Mountain Books, 2015.

Kane, Alan. *Scrambles in the Canadian Rockies*. 3rd edition. Calgary: Rocky Mountain Books, 2016.

Potter, Mike. *Ridgewalks in the Canadian Rockies*. 2nd edition. Airdrie, Alta.: Luminous Compositions, 2009.

Scott, Chic, and Darren Farley. *Ski Trails in the Canadian Rockies*. 5th edition. Calgary: Rocky Mountain Books, 2016.

Index

INDEX

INDEX

THE AUTHOR

Andrew Nugara was born in Rugby, England, and moved to Canada in 1979. He earned bachelor degrees in Music Performance and Education from the University of Calgary and presently teaches high-school physics and music in Calgary, Alberta. Since 2001 Andrew has completed more than 900 trips in the Rocky Mountains, including approximately 700 summits.

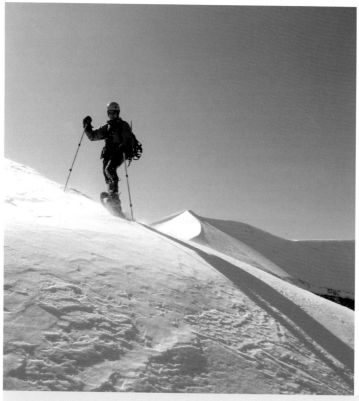

THE AUTHOR ON FORUM PEAK IN WATERTON.